Communications
in Computer and Information Science   1232

More information about this series at http://www.springer.com/series/7899

Boris Villazón-Terrazas ·
Fernando Ortiz-Rodríguez ·
Sanju M. Tiwari · Shishir K. Shandilya (Eds.)

Knowledge Graphs and Semantic Web

Second Iberoamerican Conference and
First Indo-American Conference, KGSWC 2020
Mérida, Mexico, November 26–27, 2020
Proceedings

 Springer

Editors
Boris Villazón-Terrazas (iD)
Tinámica
Madrid, Spain

Fernando Ortiz-Rodríguez (iD)
Tamaulipas Autonomous University
Ciudad Victoria, Mexico

Sanju M. Tiwari (iD)
Tamaulipas Autonomous University
Ciudad Victoria, Mexico

Shishir K. Shandilya (iD)
VIT Bhopal University
Bhopal, India

ISSN 1865-0929   ISSN 1865-0937 (electronic)
Communications in Computer and Information Science
ISBN 978-3-030-65383-5   ISBN 978-3-030-65384-2 (eBook)
https://doi.org/10.1007/978-3-030-65384-2

This Springer imprint is published by the registered company Springer Nature Switzerland AG
The registered company address is: Gewerbestrasse 11, 6330 Cham, Switzerland

Preface

The importance of disseminating Artificial Intelligence (AI) practices on R&D are crucial for the future and economic development of developing countries. In this book, we particularly try to attract top-class research and practices in several fields of AI, such as knowledge representation and reasoning, natural language processing/text mining, machine/deep learning, semantic web, and knowledge graphs.

The Iberoamerican Knowledge Graphs and Semantic Web Conference (KGSWC) and the Indo-American Knowledge Graph and Semantic Web are an international scientific gathering, devoted to knowledge representation, natural language processing/text mining, and machine/deep learning research. The goals of the conference are (a) to provide a forum for the AI community, bringing together researchers and practitioners in the industry to share ideas about R&D projects and (b) to increase the adoption of the AI technologies in these regions.

This volume contains the main proceedings of the second Iberoamerican KGSWC, jointly with the first Indo-American Knowledge Graphs and Semantic Web Conference, which was held in Mérida, Yucatán, Mexico, in November 2020. We received a tremendous response to our calls for papers from a truly international community of both researchers and practitioners.

Every paper was thoroughly evaluated following practices appropriate for this conference and its evaluation measure. The breadth and scope of the papers finally selected for inclusion in this volume speak to the quality of the conference and to the contributions made by researchers whose work is presented in these proceedings. As such, we were all honored and proud that we were invited to serve the community in the stewardship of this year's edition of KGSWC.

This year, KGSWC was a collection of four events. We would like to warmly thank all the people who contributed toward making this edition possible, workshop chairs, Program Committee members, hackathon chiars, local organizers, researchers, industry participants, and sponsors. Special thanks to the winter school organizers and tutors.

November 2020

Boris Villazón-Terrazas
Fernando Ortiz-Rodríguez
Sanju M. Tiwari
Shishir K. Shandilya

Organization

Workshops

Ivan Lopez-Arevalo	Cinvestav, Mexico
José Melchor Medina Quintero	Universidad Autónoma de Tamaulipas, Mexico
Demian Abrego Almazán	Universidad Autónoma de Tamaulipas, Mexico

Winter School

Nelson Piedra	Universidad Técnica Particular de Loja, Ecuador

Program Chair

Ghislain Auguste Atemezing	Mondeca, France

Program Committee Iberoamerican Conference

Aidan Hogan	DCC, Universidad de Chile, Chile
Alberto Fernandez	University Rey Juan Carlos, Spain
Alejandro Rodríguez	Universidad Politécnica de Madrid, Spain
Amed Abel Leiva Mederos	Universidad Central de las Villas, Cuba
Boris Villazón Terrazas	Tinámica, Madrid, Spain
Carlos Buil Aranda	Universidad Técnica Federico Santa María, Chile
Claudio Gutierrez	Universidad de Chile, Chile
Demian Abrego Almazán	Universidad Autónoma de Tamaulipas, Mexico
Diego Collarana	Enterprise Information System (EIS), Germany
Edelweis Rohrer	Universidad de la República, Uruguay
Edgar Tello	Universidad Autónoma de Tamaulipas, Mexico
Erick Antezana	Bayer Crop Science, Belgium
Erik Mannens	iMinds, Ghent University, Belgium
Francisco Edgar Castillo Barrera	Autónoma de San Luis Potosí, Mexico
Fernando Ortíz Rodríguez	Universidad Autonoma de Tamaulipas, Mexico
Freddy Priyatna	Universidad Politécnica de Madrid, Spain
Gerardo Haces Atondo	Universidad Autonoma De Tamaulipas, Mexico
Ghislain Auguste Atemezing	Mondeca, France
Harry Halpin	World Wide Web Consortium, USA
Harshvardhan J. Pandit	ADAPT Centre, Trinity College Dublin, Ireland
Irlan Grangel	BOSCH, Germany

Ismael Navas-Delgado	University of Malaga, Spain
Ivan Lopez-Arevalo	Cinvestav, Mexico
Jean-Paul Calbimonte	University of Applied Sciences and Arts, Switzerland
Jorge De La Calleja	Universidad Politécnica de Puebla, Mexico
Jose Senso	University of Granada, Spain
Jose Mora	Universidad Politécnica de Madrid, Spain
Jose Emilio Labra Gayo	Universidad de Oviedo, Spain
José Lázaro Martínez Rodríguez	Universidad Autónoma de Tamaulipas, Mexico
José Luis Redondo García	Amazon Research, UK
Jose María Alvarez Rodríguez	Carlos III University of Madrid, Spain
José Melchor Medina Quintero	Universidad Autónoma de Tamaulipas, Mexico
Juan Antonio Lossio-Ventura	Stanford University, USA
Leticia Arco	Vrije Universiteit Brussel, Belgium
Manuel-Enrique Puebla-Martínez	Universidad de las Ciencias Informáticas, Cuba
Maria Hallo	Escuela Politécnica Nacional, Ecuador
Maria Esther Vidal	Universidad Simon Bolivar, Colombia
Maria Keet	University of Cape Town, South Africa
Maricela Bravo	Universidad Autónoma Metropolitana, Mexico
Michael Benedikt	University of Oxford, UK
Nandana Mihindukulasooriya	Universidad Politécnica de Madrid, Spain
Nelson Piedra	Universidad Técnica Particular de Loja, Peru
Nicholas Beliz-Osorio	Universidad Tecnológica de Panamá, Panama
Panos Alexopoulos	Textkernel B.V., The Netherlands
Pascal Hitzler	Kansas State University, USA
Rafael S. Gonçalves	Stanford University, USA
Regina Motz	Universidad de la República, Uruguay
Sanju Tiwari	Universidad Autónoma de Tamaulipas, Mexico
Takanori Ugai	Fujitsu Laboratories Ltd., Japan
Victor Saquicela	Universidad de Cuenca, Ecuador
Yusniel Hidalgo Delgado	Universidad de las Ciencias Informáticas, Cuba
Alejandro Rodríguez-González	Universidad Politécnica de Madrid, Spain

Program Committee Indo-American Conference

Abhishek Bhattacharya	IEMIS Kolkata, India
Adolfo Antonio-Bravo	Universidad Politécnica de Madrid, Spain
Amadis Martinez	Universidad de Carabobo, Venezuela
Amit Sheth	University of South Carolina, USA
Ana Aguilera	Universidad de Valparaiso, Chile

Anna Fensel   University of Innsbruck, Austria
Antonio Di Nola   University of Salerno, Italy
Ayush Goyal   Texas A&M University, USA
Deepjyoti Kalita   Cotton University, India
Dimitris Kontokostas   Diffbot, USA
Eric Pardede   La Trobe University, Australia
Fatima N. Al-aswadi   Hodeidah University, Yemen
Filip Radulovic   SEPAGE, France
Hari Prabhat Gupta   IIT (BHU) Varanasi, India
Jennifer D'Souza   TIB, L3S, Germany
Juan F. Sequeda   Data World, USA
Kumar Abhishek   NIT Patna, India
M. A. Jabbar, Vardhaman   Vardhman College of Engineering, India
María Poveda Villalón   Universidad Politécnica de Madrid, Spain
Marlene Goncalves   Universidad Simon Bolívar, Colombia
Mukta Sharma   TIPS Delhi, India
Oscar Corcho Garcia   Universidad Politécnica de Madrid, Spain
Patience Usoro Usip   University of Uyo, Nigeria
Raghava Muthuraju   IIIT New Delhi, India
Raul Garcia Castro   Universidad Politécnica de Madrid, Spain
Sailesh Bajpai   Regional Center for Biotechnology, India
Shikha Mehta   JIIT Noida, India
Soren Auer   TIB, L3S, Germany
Sourav Banerjee   Kalyani Government Engineering College, India

Contents

A Domain Ontology for Task Instructions

Aaron Eberhart[1]([envelope])[ID], Cogan Shimizu[1][ID], Christopher Stevens[2],
Pascal Hitzler[1][ID], Christopher W. Myers[2][ID], and Benji Maruyama[3]

[1] DaSe Lab, Kansas State University, Manhattan, KS, USA
{aaroneberhart,coganmshimizu,hitzler}@ksu.edu
[2] Air Force Research Laboratory, Wright-Patterson AFB, OH, USA
{christopher.stevens.28,christopher.myers.29}@us.af.mil
[3] Air Force Research Laboratory, Materials and Manufacturing Directorate,
Wright-Patterson AFB, OH, USA
benji.maruyama@us.af.mil

Abstract. Knowledge graphs and ontologies represent information in a
variety of different applications. One use case, the Intelligence, Surveillance, & Reconnaissance: Mutli-Attribute Task Battery (ISR-MATB),
comes from Cognitive Science, where researchers use interdisciplinary
methods to understand the mind and cognition. The ISR-MATB is a
set of tasks that a cognitive or human agent perform which test visual,
auditory, and memory capabilities. An ontology can represent a cognitive
agent's background knowledge of the task it was instructed to perform
and act as an interchange format between different Cognitive Agent tasks
similar to ISR-MATB. We present several modular patterns for representing ISR-MATB task instructions, as well as a unified diagram that
links them together.

1 Introduction

Knowledge graphs facilitate data integration across highly heterogeneous sources
in a semantically useful way. Knowledge graphs may be equipped with a schema,
frequently an ontology, that combines the associative power of the knowledge
graph with the semantics of the ontology. Due to this, they are uniquely suited
to support research in cognitive science, where it is often necessary to incorporate information from fields like computer science, psychology, neuroscience,
philosophy, and more.

Cognitive agents are a sub-field of cognitive science and an application of
the more broad study of cognitive architectures. Cognitive architectures, like
ACT-R [1] for example, are an approach to understanding intelligent behavior
and cognition that grew out of the idea of Unified Theories of Cognition [8].
These systems have their roots in AI production systems and some types use
rules-based cognition. Many in Computer Science are familiar with inductive
themes from a different type, called Connectionism, due to its historic ties with
artificial neural networks. Symbolic cognitive architectures, by contrast, are less
widely known outside of cognitive science, and are abstracted and explicit like
logic programming.

© Springer Nature Switzerland AG 2020
B. Villazón-Terrazas et al. (Eds.): KGSWC 2020, CCIS 1232, pp. 1–13, 2020.
https://doi.org/10.1007/978-3-030-65384-2_1

Both ontologies and cognitive architectures deal with symbolic knowledge. Symbolic cognitive architectures typically focus on the plausibility of knowledge and the way in which that knowledge is translated into human behavior within a specific task. Ontologies offer a set of robust mechanisms for reasoning over complex knowledge bases and could help cognitive architectures adapt to tasks in novel environments. One way the two may be integrated is by leveraging the ontology to reduce the specificity of a cognitive agent.

In general, cognitive agents are often specialized, or *differentiated*, to perform a specific task or set of tasks. An *undifferentiated* agent is one that has no specialization. The purpose of such an agent is to be adaptable to new tasks as needed. As part of initial work to develop such an undifferentiated cognitive agent, we have developed a modular ontology that captures instructions for a specific cognitive agent task called ISR-MATB. We discuss this platform in more detail in the next section.

Currently, the ontology supports the memory of a cognitive agent by adding structure to its knowledge and providing new varieties of query-like recall. And due to design methodology used during the modeling process, the ontology is general enough that it could model other cognitive agent experiments, which could then be evaluated against each other in a structured way. This allows the ontology to act as an invaluable interchange format between researchers developing cognitive agents.

The rest of this paper is organized as follows. Section 2 provides a brief overview of the use-case: ISR-MATB. Section 3 provides an in-depth examination of the ontology. Finally, in Sect. 4, we briefly conclude and discuss next steps.

2   ISR-MATB

ISR-MATB is a series of cognitive tasks that could be completed by a Cognitive Agent or a human [3]. A trial starts with one very simple task, the evaluation then branches into two sub-tasks that relate back to the first task. After the two sub-tasks are complete the agent completes one final task requiring integration of remembered information from all previous tasks. The final task is made more difficult by the possibility of incorrect feedback as the agent learns. ISR-MATB is intended to be repeated for a fixed time so that researchers can observe changes in the agent's response time and develop better computational cognitive agents.

2.1 Psychomotor Vigilance Test

The Psychomotor Vigilance Test is one of the more basic cognitive tasks [2]. In this task, there is an area of the screen where a letter could appear. The letter will be drawn with a specific color. When the letter does appear an agent must press a button that acknowledges they have seen it. If the agent pushes the button too soon a false start is recorded and the task continues normally. If too much time passes before the agent pushes the button then the task will continue

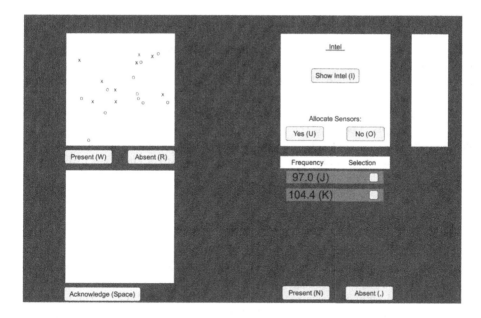

Fig. 1. An example depicting the four ISR-MATB tasks in a single interface.

with the letter unacknowledged. The next two tasks reference this letter and color, so the agent is instructed to remember them (Fig. 1).

2.2 Visual Search

The Visual Search task requires that the agent determine if the letter they remember is among a group of many letters that appear on the screen [10]. The other letters are distractors, and may be the same letter as the target with a different color, or the same color as the target with a different letter, or both color and letter different. The target may or may not appear among the distractors, and never appears more than once. The agent pushes a button to indicate whether the letter is present or absent.

2.3 Auditory Search

The Auditory Search task is very similar to the Visual Search, except of course that the agent must listen instead of look. In this task there are between one and four audio messages that each include a spoken color and letter. If one of the messages is the same as the letter and color from the first task the agent pushes a button to indicate that it is present, otherwise they indicate that it is absent.

2.4   Decision Making

The final task, Decision Making, requires agents to infer a relationship between the outcomes of the Visual and Auditory Search tasks together with a new binary piece of information called "Intelligence" that appears after choosing whether to hypothetically allocate sensors or not. The rule the agent must guess is not too hard, but it is complex enough that it must be learned by trial-and-error over multiple attempts. Learning the rule is made more difficult by the unlikely but not impossible event that the program responds incorrectly even when a correct answer is given. Responding 'yes' or 'no' to this sub-task ends one ISR-MATB trial.

3   Ontology Description

In this section we present the Instruction Ontology, a domain ontology built for use with the ISR-MATB experiment platform. This ontology was produced by following the Modular Ontology Modeling (MOM) methodology, outlined in [6,7] MOM is designed to ensure the high quality and reusability of the resulting ontology, both in terms of scope and in terms of granularity, which is a desired outcome.

The ontology consists of six modules: ISR-MATB Experiment, Instruction, SituationDescription, ItemRole, Action, and Affordance. For each module, we describe its purpose, provide a schema diagram,[1] and state its axiomatization in both description logic syntax and natural language. The OWL file for this ontology can be found online[2] as well as the official documentation.[3] Figure 5 shows the schema diagram for the entire ontology.

3.1   ISR-MATB Experiment

The ISR-MATB Experiment module is the core module for the ontology. The two main classes are ISR-MATB Experiment and ISR-MATB Task. As noted in Sect. 2, an experiment consists of up to four tasks that may require that information be carried between them, where each Task resides in a specific quadrant of the interface. Each Task provides roles to different Items, as well as a set of Instructions for the agent to carry out. We discuss these classes in more detail in their respective Module sections. The schema diagram for this module is shown in Fig. 2c.

---

[1] A schema diagram is an informal, but intuitive way for conveying information about the structure and contents of an ontology. We use a consistent visual syntax for convenience, detailed in Fig. 2.

[2] See   https://raw.githubusercontent.com/undiffagents/uagent/develop/ontology/ uagent.owl.

[3] See https://daselab.cs.ksu.edu/content/domain-ontology-instruction.   .

Axiomatization:

$$\top \sqsubseteq \forall \text{affords.Affordance} \qquad (1)$$

$$\text{ISR-MATBTask} \sqsubseteq \geq 1 \text{ hasInstruction.Instruction} \qquad (2)$$

$$\text{ISR-MATBExperiment} \sqsubseteq \leq 4 \text{ hasTask.ISR-MATBTask} \qquad (3)$$

$$\top \sqsubseteq \forall \text{hasLocation.Location} \qquad (4)$$

$$\top \sqsubseteq \forall \text{hasName.xsd:string} \qquad (5)$$

$$\text{ISR-MATBTask} \sqsubseteq =1 \text{ hasName.xsd:string} \qquad (6)$$

$$\text{ISR-MATBTask} \sqsubseteq \forall \text{providesRole.ItemRole} \qquad (7)$$

$$\text{ISR-MATBTask} \sqsubseteq \forall \text{informs.ISR-MATBTask} \qquad (8)$$

Explanation of Axioms Above:

1. Range. The range of affords is Affordance.
2. Minimum Cardinality. An ISR-MATBTask has at least one Instruction.
3. Maximum Cardinality. An ISR-MATBExperiment consists of at most four ISR-MATBTasks.
4. Range. The range of hasLocation is Location.
5. Range. The range of hasName is xsd:string.
6. Scoped Range. The range of providesRole is ItemRole when the domain is ISR-MATBTask.
7. Scoped Range. The range of informs is ISR-MATBTask when the domain is ISR-MATBTask.

3.2   Action

The Action module is an instantiation of the Explicit Typing meta-pattern described in [9].[4]

In this case, we use a class, ActionType, to represent a controlled vocabulary. We believe that using a controlled vocabulary to represent this type information is less invasive to the ontology. This way, adding or removing types of actions from the controlled vocabulary does not actually change the ontology. Some instances of the controlled vocabulary are listed in Fig. 5.

An Action, in this context, is the physical, actual action that takes place to transition between different states of the experiment, e.g. 'the action of clicking a button'. The schema diagram for this module is shown in Fig. 2a.

Axiomatization:

$$\text{Action} \sqsubseteq =1 \text{ofType.ActionType} \qquad (9)$$

---

[4] [9] is a modular ontology design library; it contains a set of frequently used patterns and respective documentation.

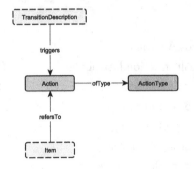

The schema diagram for the **Action** module.

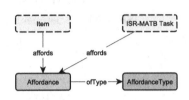

The schema diagram for the **Affordance** module.

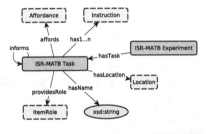

The schema diagram for the **ISR-MATB Experiment** module.

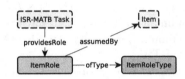

The schema diagram for the **ItemRole** module.

Fig. 2. Orange boxes are classes and indicate that they are central to the diagram. Blue dashed boxes indicate a reference to another diagram, pattern, or module. Gray frames with a dashed outline contain modules. Arrows depict relations and open arrows represent subclass relations. Yellow ovals indicate data types (and necessarily, arrows pointing to a datatype are data properties). Finally, purple boxes represent controlled vocabularies. That is, they represent a controlled set of IRIs that are of that type. (Color figure online)

Explanation of Axioms Above:

1. Exact Cardinality. An Action has exactly one ActionType.

3.3   Affordance

The Affordance module is also instantiated from the Explicit Typing meta-pattern, explained in more detail in Sect. 3.2 and [9]. An Affordance is essentially some quality of an Item that indicates that "something" may be done with it. Familiar examples might include *clickable* buttons or text highlighted in blue (perhaps indicating that it's a hyperlink). Instances of the AffordanceType can be found in Fig. 5. The schema diagram for this module is shown in Fig. 2b.

Axiomatization:

$$\text{Affordance} \sqsubseteq =1\text{hasAffordanceType.AffordanceType} \qquad (1)$$

Explanation of Axioms Above:

1. Exact cardinality. An Affordance has exactly one AffordanceType.

3.4 ItemRole

The ItemRole module is an instantiation of the AgentRole pattern, which may also be found in [9]. We also equip it with an explicit type, in the same manner as Action and Affordance.

Each ISR-MATB Task may provide roles to Items. That is, certain items may be a target or distractor, but not always. This allows us to assign certain roles to items that may, if they were qualities, be ontologically disjoint. The schema diagram for this module is shown in Fig. 2d.

Axiomatization:

$$\text{ISR-MATBTask} \sqsubseteq \forall\text{providesRole.ItemRole} \qquad (1)$$
$$\top \sqsubseteq \forall\text{hasItemRoleType.ItemRoleType} \qquad (2)$$
$$\text{ItemRole} \sqsubseteq \forall\text{assumedBy.Item} \qquad (3)$$
$$\text{ItemRole} \sqsubseteq \exists\text{assumedBy.Item} \qquad (4)$$

Explanation of Axioms Above:

1. Scoped Range. The range of providesRole is ItemRole when the domain is ISR-MATBTask.
2. Range. The range of hasItemRoleType is ItemRoleType.
3. Scoped Range. ItemRoles are assumedBy Items.
4. Existential. Every ItemRole is assumedBy an Item.

3.5 SituationDescription

For this module, we opted to use the Situation and Description approach. We chose to use this conceptualization due to the non-linear nature of the instructions.[5] That is, an ISR-MATB Task is not a sequence of instructions, but a collection of directions or descriptions.

An Instruction, is a description of a way to transition between two states. In order to follow out an instruction the state described in the pre-SituationDescription would need to be met. Following through would result in a new state, the Post-Situation Description.

---

[5] For a deeper discussion on Descriptions, Situations, and Plans, see [4].

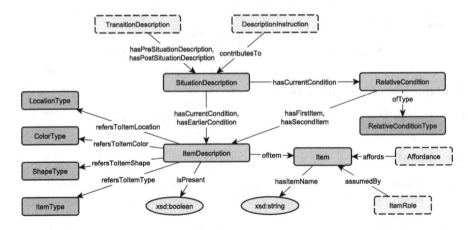

Fig. 3. The schema diagram for the SchemaDiagram module. Color and shape usage is the same as in previous diagrams.

Furthermore, the SituationDescription will indicate the presence, or absence, of an item, as well as its description. Descriptions, in this case, are relegated to controlled vocabularies in the same manner as Affordance or Action. We call this an ItemDescription because it is inherent to the Instruction and not the Item, itself. The schema diagram for this module is shown in Fig. 3.

Axiomatization:

$$\text{SituationDescription} \sqsubseteq \forall \text{hasCurrentCondition.}(\text{RelativeCondition} \sqcup \text{ItemDescription}) \quad (1)$$

$$\text{SituationDescription} \sqsubseteq \forall \text{hasEarlierCondition.ItemDescription} \quad (2)$$

$$\top \sqsubseteq \forall \text{hasRelativeConditionType.RelativeConditionType} \quad (3)$$

$$\text{RelativeCondition} \sqsubseteq \forall \text{hasFirstItem.ItemDescription} \quad (4)$$

$$\text{RelativeCondition} \sqsubseteq \forall \text{hasSecondItem.ItemDescription} \quad (5)$$

$$\text{ItemDescription} \sqsubseteq \forall \text{ofItem.Item} \quad (6)$$

$$\text{ItemDescription} \sqsubseteq \ =1 \ \text{isPresent.xsd:boolean} \quad (7)$$

$$\top \sqsubseteq \forall \text{refersToItemLocation.LocationType} \quad (8)$$

$$\top \sqsubseteq \forall \text{refersToItemColor.ColorType} \quad (9)$$

$$\top \sqsubseteq \forall \text{refersToShapeType.ShapeType} \quad (10)$$

$$\top \sqsubseteq \forall \text{refersToItemType.ItemType} \quad (11)$$

$$\text{ItemDescription} \sqsubseteq \ \geq 0 \ \text{refersToItemLocation.LocationType} \quad (12)$$

$$\text{ItemDescription} \sqsubseteq \ \geq 0 \ \text{refersToItemColor.ColorType} \quad (13)$$

$$\text{ItemDescription} \sqsubseteq \ \geq 0 \ \text{refersToItemShape.ShapeType} \quad (14)$$

$$\text{ItemDescription} \sqsubseteq \ \geq 0 \ \text{refersToItemType.ItemType} \quad (15)$$

$$\top \sqsubseteq \forall \text{hasItemName.xsd:string} \quad (16)$$

$$\exists \text{hasItemName.} \top \sqsubseteq \text{Item} \quad (17)$$

Explanation of Axioms Above:

1. Scoped Range. The range of hasCurrentCondition is a RelativeCondition or ItemDescription when the domain is SituationDescription.
2. Scoped Range. The range of hasEarlierCondition is ItemDescription when the domain is SituationDescription.
3. Range. The range of hasRelativeConditionType is RelativeConditionType.
4. Scoped Range. The range of hasFirstItem is ItemDescription when the domain is RelativeCondition.
5. Scoped Range. The range of hasSecondItem is ItemDescription when the domain is RelativeCondition.
6. Scoped Range. The range of ofItem is Item when the domain is ItemDescription.
7. Scoped Range. An ItemDescription has exactly one Boolean flag indicating whether or not it is present.
8. Range. The range of refersToItemLocation is LocationType.
9. Range. The range of refersToItemColor is ColorType.
10. Range. The range of refersToItemShape is ShapeType.
11. Range. The range of refersToItemType is ItemType.
12. Structural Tautology. An ItemDescription may refer to a LocationType.
13. Structural Tautology. An ItemDescription may refer to a ColorType.
14. Structural Tautology. An ItemDescription may refer to a ShapeType.
15. Structural Tautology. An ItemDescription may refer to an ItemType.
16. Range. The range of hasItemName is xsd:string.
17. Domain Restriction. The domain of hasItemName is restricted to Items.

3.6 Instruction

Instructions are the atomic units of a task. They come in two varieties: descriptions and actions. The former are instructions that are prescriptive or descriptive. They are statements that indicate information about the environment or the task. They may, in natural language, take such form as "There is a button named 'Present'". The latter type of instruction instructs when or where to do something. For example, "Press the button if a high-pitched tone is heard". An Action-Instruction prescribes some transition between descriptions of situations, whereas Description-Instructions directly contribute to said SituationDescription. The module also uses a data property to capture the natural language formulation of the Instruction. The schema diagram for this module is shown in Fig. 4.

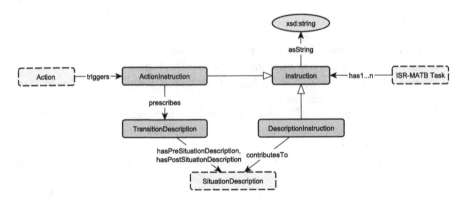

Fig. 4. The schema diagram for the Instruction module. Color and shape usage is the same as in previous diagrams.

Axiomatization:

$$\text{ActionInstruction} \sqsubseteq \text{Instruction} \tag{1}$$

$$\text{ActionInstruction} \sqsubseteq \forall\text{prescribes.TransitionDescription} \tag{2}$$

$$\top \sqsubseteq \forall\text{asString.xsd:string} \tag{3}$$

$$\text{Instruction} \sqsubseteq \geq 0 \text{ asString.xsd:string} \tag{4}$$

$$\text{DescriptionInstruction} \sqsubseteq \text{Instruction} \tag{5}$$

$$\text{DescriptionInstruction} \sqsubseteq \forall\text{contributesTo.SituationDescription} \tag{6}$$

$$\top \sqsubseteq \forall\text{hasPreSituationDescription.SituationDescription} \tag{7}$$

$$\top \sqsubseteq \forall\text{hasPostSituationDescription.SituationDescription} \tag{8}$$

Explanation of Axioms Above:

1. Subclass. Every ActionInstruction is an Instruction.
2. Scoped Range. The range of prescribes is TransitionDescription when the domain is ActionInstruction.
3. Range. The range of asString is xsd:string.
4. Structural Tautology. An Instruction may have a string representation.
5. Subclass. Every DescriptionInstruction is an Instruction.
6. Scoped Range. The range of contributesTo is SituationDescription when the domain is DescriptionInstruction.
7. Range. The range of hasPreSituationDescription is SituationDescription.
8. Range. The range of hasPostSituationDescription is SituationDescription.

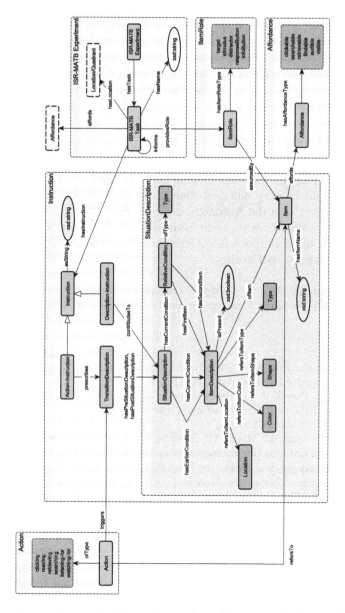

Fig. 5. The schema diagram for the entire ontology. Note that the SituationDescription module is nested in the Instruction Module. Color and shape usage is the same as in previous diagrams.

4   Conclusion

In this paper we have presented an ontology for modeling the ISR-MATB cognitive agent task instructions. This ontology can be used, as we have, to directly support the memory of a cognitive agent performing tasks. It also could support experiment design, irrespective of any agent, by providing a structured basis for evaluating similar tasks. The modular structure facilitates adapting the ontology to other use cases and scenarios by replacing or adapting the existing modules. It is also possible to create new modules from the referenced patterns via template-based instantiation [5].

4.1 Future Work

In the future we plan to extend this ontology so that it can support a fully undifferentiated agent. This will include tasks like ISR-MATB, but also many others that could be very different. One such task is supporting materials science research that uses the Autonomous Research System (ARES) framework. An undifferentiated cognitive agent could operate a robotic system that performs research, using software like ARES, saving materials researchers hours of potentially hazardous lab work.

Acknowledgement. This material is based upon work supported by the Air Force Office of Scientific Research under award number FA9550-18-1-0386.

References

1. Anderson, J.R.: How Can The Human Mind Occur in the Physical Universe? Oxford University Press, Oxford (2007)
2. Dinges, D.F., Powell, J.W.: Microcomputer analyses of performance on a portable, simple visual RT task during sustained operations. Behav. Res. Methods Instrum. Comput. **17**(6), 652–655 (1985)
3. Frame, M., Lopez, J., Myers, C., Stevens, C., Estepp, J., Boydstun, A.: Development of an autonomous management system for human-machine teaming with multiple interdependent tasks. In: Presented to the Annual Meeting of the Psychonomic Society Conference, Montreal, QC, Canada, November 2019 (2019)
4. Gangemi, A., Mika, P.: Understanding the semantic web through descriptions and situations. In: Meersman, R., Tari, Z., Schmidt, D.C. (eds.) OTM 2003. LNCS, vol. 2888, pp. 689–706. Springer, Heidelberg (2003). https://doi.org/10.1007/978-3-540-39964-3_44
5. Hammar, K., Presutti, V.: Template-based content ODP instantiation. In: Hammar, K., Hitzler, P., Krisnadhi, A., Lawrynowicz, A., Nuzzolese, A.G., Solanki, M. (eds.) Advances in Ontology Design and Patterns [Revised and Extended Versions of The Papers Presented at the 7th edition of the Workshop on Ontology and Semantic Web Patterns, WOP@ISWC 2016, Kobe, Japan, 18th October 2016]. Studies on the Semantic Web, vol. 32, pp. 1–13. IOS Press (2016). https://doi. org/10.3233/978-1-61499-826-6-1
6. Hitzler, P., Krisnadhi, A.: A tutorial on modular ontology modeling with ontology design patterns: the cooking recipes ontology. CoRR abs/1808.08433 (2018). http://arxiv.org/abs/1808.08433
7. Krisnadhi, A., Hitzler, P.: Modeling with ontology design patterns: chess games as a worked example. In: Hitzler, P., Gangemi, A., Janowicz, K., Krisnadhi, A., Presutti, V. (eds.) Ontology Engineering with Ontology Design Patterns - Foundations and Applications, Studies on the Semantic Web, vol. 25, pp. 3–21. IOS Press (2016)

8. Newell, A.: Unified Theories of Cognition. Harvard University Press, Cambridge (1994)
9. Shimizu, C., Hirt, Q., Hitzler, P.: MODL: a modular ontology design library. In: WOP@ISWC. CEUR Workshop Proceedings, vol. 2459, pp. 47–58. CEUR-WS.org (2019)
10. Treisman, A.M., Gelade, G.: A feature-integration theory of attention. Cogn. Psychol. **12**(1), 97–136 (1980)

Axiomatic Relation Extraction from Text in the Domain of Tourism

Ana B. Rios-Alvarado[1]([☒]), Jose L. Martinez-Rodriguez[2],
Tania Y. Guerrero-Melendez[1], Adolfo J. Rodriguez-Rodriguez[2],
and David T. Vargas-Requena[2]

[1] Faculty of Engineering and Science, UAT, Ciudad Victoria, Mexico
{arios,tyguerre}@docentes.uat.edu.mx
[2] UAM Reynosa - Rodhe, UAT, Reynosa, Mexico
lazaro.martinez@uat.edu.mx, {arodriguez,dvargas}@docentes.uat.edu.mx

Abstract. Tourism is one of the most important activities in the economic sector. Thus, text about this topic coming from diverse data sources such as the Web should be analyzed to get information and knowledge that can be represented and consumed by people and applications. Such tasks are part of the Ontology Learning and Population (OLP) field, where the goal is to find elements of information (named entities) and their associations to create a knowledge base. In this regard, OLP deals with the discovery of named entities and how they are grouped, related, and subdivided according to their characteristics (class). However, the association between entities has not been studied in the same way, particularly axiomatic relations that exploit the type of the named entities. Therefore, this paper proposes a strategy for the extraction of axiomatic relations from text. It is based on the identification of named entities, their class, and their co-occurrence in the text to define lexical-syntactic patterns that support the extraction of axiomatic relations such as equivalence and disjointness between classes. The results demonstrate the usefulness of the strategy to produce new statements that enrich ontologies and knowledge bases.

Keywords: Semantic web · Ontology learning · Axiom extraction · Entity co-occurrence

1 Introduction

Due to the easy way to access digital resources, the Web has become one of the most important data sources for several information domains. One of the domains that gained spread in the Web is Tourism, which is an important activity for the economic sector, where the data increasing in such domain is in part due to government sectors, Tourism agencies, journalists, and people in general. Even though the Web has the HTML format as standard for the presentation of data, the content is mainly provided as unstructured text[1], typically disseminated in

---

[1] Unstructured text refers to the one presented as natural language, which contains no structure or linguistic annotations that can be exploited by computers.

© Springer Nature Switzerland AG 2020
B. Villazón-Terrazas et al. (Eds.): KGSWC 2020, CCIS 1232, pp. 14–28, 2020.
https://doi.org/10.1007/978-3-030-65384-2_2

sources such as web pages, social media, emails, and so on, which difficult the publishing and consumption of data. In this regard, to take advantage of the data from such resources, it is recommended to follow a representation that allows people and machines to get information facts that can be associated to obtain knowledge.

Along these lines, ontologies are helpful to define a set of concepts and categories in a domain of information and to show their properties and relations between them. Ontologies play an important role in getting a formal representation of the information to later be easily consumed or used for infering new data. However, an ontology is commonly crafted by knowledge engineers and domain experts, resulting in a long and tedious development process [3]. In this regard, an area that supports the automatic development of ontologies from text is the *Ontology Learning and Population* (OLP) [7]. OLP involves the analysis of a large number of unstructured text documents to extract useful knowledge and to get the vocabulary of a domain and the relationships between concepts so that it is possible to create (hierarchical) structures and rules to describe the information. Thus, OLP requires the implementation and development of different tasks based on natural language processing (e.g., part-of-speech tagging, phrase chunking, and stemming) and information extraction. In this context, methods for extracting plain text, splitting text into sentences, deleting stopwords, tagging, and parsing sentences need to be applied.

Several ontology learning approaches have been proposed so far, they are commonly focused on extracting specific elements of the hierarchical structure [6–8], non-taxonomic relations [10,12], or axioms [2,4,11,14,15,17] in an independent manner. In this regard, axioms[2] have not been tackled in the same way, which would be useful to enrich ontologies with more expressive representation elements (useful for reasoning tasks). Although there are approaches addressing the axiom extraction problem, they are focused mainly on description logic rules applied over classes to discover facts and terminological axioms. For example, based on patterns [11], or based on rules [14,15]. However, the analysis of class and instance axioms is also required to enrich the ontology so that the level of expressivity would allow people and applications to describe additional rules for reasoning and data inferencing.

This paper proposes an approach for axiomatic relation extraction from unstructured text in English regarding the domain of Tourism. It is based on the extraction of vocabulary and semantic relationships from textual resources. In order to achieve such a goal, we consider the identification of named entities[3], their class, and their co-occurrence in text to define lexical-syntactic patterns to characterize classes and to identify axiomatic relations such as sameAs, differentFrom, instanceOf, disjointWith, and equivalentClass.

---

[2] Axioms refer to assertions (in a logical form) as the smallest unit of knowledge within an ontology that defines formal relations between ontology components.

[3] A *named entity* is an information unit such as the name of a person, an organization, a location, a brand, a product, or a numeric expression found in a sentence.

2   Background

Axioms are important in the development of ontologies for providing additional expressiveness. In this sense, axioms can be commonly classified into the following categories: *terminological axioms*, *facts*, and *annotations*.

- Terminological axioms refer to concepts and the relationships between them, where concepts may involve either named entities or general thing concepts. There are two common types of terminological axioms: *class axioms* and *property axioms*. Class axioms can be a subsumption ($\sqsubseteq$), equivalence ($\equiv$), or disjunction ($\sqcup$). For example, $S \sqsubseteq O$ means that the concept S is a subclass and O is the superclass. On the other hand, property axioms span particularities of properties. For example, functional properties, subproperties, and equivalent properties, to mention a few.
- A *fact* or individual axiom is an assertion on individuals. The instantiation is expressed with the relation `instanceOf(C, a)`, where C represents a class and a being an individual name. Semantically this means that the individual with the name a is an extension of the set described by C. There are two subtypes of fact axioms:
  - *Individual equality* is an axiom that describes two names referring to the same individual. According to OWL[4], it is expressed using the sintax `sameAs`(a_1,a_2), where a_1 and a_2 are different names for the same individual
  - *Individual inequality* makes explicit that the names do not refer to the same individual. It is expressed through `differentFrom(a,c)`, where a and c are names of two different individuals
- Annotations are descriptions that include a subject and classes of an ontology. For example, for describing a photo of a place, it is possible to include the name of the place and the type of that place (beach, river, or city).

3   Related Work

There are different works focused on class expression axioms [2,4,16,17]. Völker *et al.* [16] proposed the tool LEDA, which allows the automated generation of disjointness axioms based on machine learning classification. They trained a classifier with lexical and logical features (e.g., subsumption, taxonomic overlap of subclasses and individuals, and document-based lexical context similarity) to predict disjointness of unseen pairs of classes. Lehmann *et al.* [2] described a semi-automatic method for learning OWL class expressions using machine learning for the generation of suggestions from instance data. Zhang *et al.* [17] proposed an unsupervised method for mining equivalent relations from Linked Data. It consists of two components: 1) a measure of equivalency between pairs of relations of a concept and 2) a clustering process to group equivalent relations. Ma *et al.* [4] introduced an approach to discover disjointness between two

---

[4] Web Ontology Language (OWL) http://www.w3.org/TR/owl-features/.

concepts. In such work, the task of association rule mining is to generate patterns of the form $A \rightarrow \neg B$, and then transform them to disjointness axiom "A `owl:disjointWith` B".

In relation to the type of axioms, Völker *et al.* [14,15] focus on the class expression axioms using logic and transformation rules. For extraction of object property axioms, the approaches use lexical patterns and lexical/statistical analysis [11]. Recent proposals use unsupervised algorithms for learning disjointness axioms. For example, Nguyen *et al.* [5] use DBpedia and an evolutionary algorithm for learning disjointness OWL 2 axioms. Rizzo *et al.* [9] use distance-based clustering and the divide-and-conquer strategy for obtaining terminological cluster trees that can be used to detect candidate disjointness axioms from emerging concept descriptions. These proposals have shown the existence of an association between lexical relations into the text and axioms. However, they do not select in an automatic way the relevant individuals and their classes to obtain axiomatic relations. Moreover, axiomatic relations are not often contained in several existing ontologies in the Tourism domain, which is desirable for organizing and querying the data in such a domain.

4   Proposed Method

We propose the acquisition of axiomatic class relations from unstructured text in English, obtaining lexical evidence, and instantiating classes from the input text. Our proposed method for the extraction of Axiomatic Relations is depicted in Fig. 1.

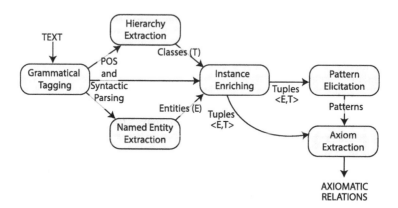

Fig. 1. Method for the extraction of axiomatic relations from text

The steps in the proposed method are described as follows:

– **Grammatical Tagging**. This step is aimed at the identification and tagging of the grammatical role of words in the input text. Particularly, this step performs the Part-Of-Speech (POS) tagging and syntactic parser.

- **Named Entity extraction**. In this stage the named entities are detected and classified into categories such as *Person, Organization, Country, City*, among others. This step is performed through a tool able to detect named entities and associated them to a type in a taxonomy of types (for named entities).
- **Hierarchy Extraction**. The goal of this step is to obtain the relation between classes and subclasses from text. In this sense, we followed a bottom-up approach as proposed by Rios-Alvarado *et al.* [7] to define a hierarchical structure from unstructured text. Such an approach is based on unsupervised learning (clustering) and an information retrieval strategy (based on web search engine's results) to provide the class labeling of the hierarchy.
- **Instance Enriching**. Named entities are assigned to either of the possible types. Additionally, according to the classes provided in the hierarchy extraction, this step associates individuals to such classes. Additional details of this process are later presented.
- **Pattern Elicitation**. This step refers to the creation of patterns that describes axioms according to the lexical-syntactic context of the entities.
- **Axiom Extraction**. According to the defined patterns, this final step extracts the axiomatic relations between entities and organizes the information using OWL tags.

In general, the idea is to identify individuals (named entities) from the text and the class they belong to in a hierarchical structure to later exploit lexical-syntactic features to obtain the relation between classes. Our general intuition is that the individuals have diverse features according to the class containing them. Thus, we can make the following assumptions:

- A **disjoint** class is assumed when individuals are different from one class to another
- An **equivalent** class occurs when the individuals (leaves in the hierarchy) are similar
- Additionally, entities that co-occurs together in a sentence can be associated as **same/different** elements.

For example, in the *instance level*, the set of leaves for `country` class includes the instances `Mexico`, `Canada`, and `Brazil`, but the set of leaves for `city` class contains the instances `Mexico City`, `Ottawa`, and `Sao Paulo`. Then, `country` class and `city` class are disjoint (expressed as `disjointWith(country,city)`). Likewise, the individuals `Mexico City` and `Sao Paulo` are different resources (`differentFrom(MexicoCity,SaoPaulo)`).

Therefore, our approach is focused on two main blocks, the exploiting of entities and the definition of axioms and patterns to extract them. Thus, we provide additional details of such blocks in the following subsections.

4.1   Definition of Axioms

Our approach exploits the occurrence of named entities into the input text as a support for the axiom extraction. This is because named entities have been traditionally considered for the OLP field [7]. Thus, for detecting the occurrence of named entities and the `instanceOf` relation, the following axioms have been defined:

- **Axiom 1.** A *class* (often denoted by C) is composed of a set of individuals with similar properties.
- **Axiom 2.** An instance x is an individual for a specific class.
- **Axiom 3.** An instantiation or `instanceOf` relation is expressed by the form `instanceOf(C,x)`, where C denotes a class and x represents an individual (named entity). Real-world entities are referred by instances established by this Axiom. For example, $C = city$ and $x = Montreal$, that means `instanceOf(city, Montreal)`.
- **Axiom 4.** Let C and D be classes, C and D are disjoint classes if the set of instances of C is different to the set of instances of class D.
- **Axiom 5.** Let C and D be classes, C and D are equivalent classes if the set of instances of C is the same to the set of instances of class D.

While the first three axioms are useful for establishing the instantiation of concepts, the last two of them are helpful for establishing the relations `disjoint-With` and `equivalentClass`. Therefore, the collection of named entities obtained from text is important for providing the instances belonging to a specific class (defining such a class in an extensional manner), allowing the establishment of axiomatic relations.

4.2 Entity Extraction and Enriching

Named entities (individuals) represent one of the core components in the definition of axiomatic relations. In this regard, we use an existing tool to perform named entity recognition, returning tuples composed of the entity mention and its type (categories such as *Person, Organization, Country, City*, among others).

Once the individuals (named entities) have been identified, the following step consists of the enrichment of instances. That is, according to the concepts representing the classes and subclasses in a hierarchy extracted from text [7], our goal is to capture the correspondence of named entities (and nouns) to one of those concepts (classes). This task is performed through the definition of wildcards that describes the structure of named entities belonging to one of the derived (sub) classes. To do so, we use the syntactic tree of the input text to determine the constituents and, together with the named entities (previously collected too), we manually define the wildcards of the form $<NE$ is an $NP> | <NP (NE)>$, where NE corresponds to a named entity detected by the NER tool and NP represents the label of a concept (*NounPhrase*). The Axioms 1, 2, and 3 were considered to establish the concept instantiation.

4.3 Pattern Elicitation

We define patterns that describe the relation between concepts expressed as an axiom. In other words, the sentences where a set of instances and its corresponding classes co-occur are grouped to determine if there exists a relation between the contexts of two classes. This process is supported by the linguistic context of the input text, previously obtained by the Part-Of-Speech (POS) tagger and a syntactic parser (i.e., representative elements such as *nouns, verbs, adjectives*, and their grammatical relations) upon which some lexical-syntactic patterns are defined. Such a process is also supported by the patterns defined by Hearst [1] and Snow *et al.* [13]. The linguistic context supports the identification of relations based on the named entities used to derive one of the following axiomatic relations:

1. `sameAs/differentFrom`. In this case, at the instance level, two (or, sometimes, more than two) different named entities identify the same individual. Those named entities refer to the same individual, and so they can assign objects to the `sameAs` constructor. For the identification of this relation, `sameAs` relations manually annotated were used together with some lexical patterns, for example <*NE, also called NE*> were identified. The lexical patterns used are *NE (NE)*, *NE* named *NE*, *NE* known as *NE*, *NE* (also known as *NE*), *NE* called *NE*, and *NE* also called *NE*, where *NE* is a named entity. In this case, the Axiom 2 is applied.

2. `disjointWith`. Considering that a `disjointWith` relation states that one class does not have an instance member in common with another class, we consider named entities co-occurring in the same context by using Axiom 4. For each NER (`class1, class2`) duple, the list of instances was compared. If there is not a common named entity between the two classes then the `disjointWith(class1, class2)` relation is established.

3. `equivalentClass`. This relation is established between two classes when the class descriptions include the same set of individuals; the Axiom 5 is used. It is important to note that the equivalent class means that classes have the same intensional meaning (i.e. denoting the same concept).

The learned axioms from text are included in the ontology for evaluation of human understanding. For this, a set of questions for identifying equivalence, disjoint and instantiation relationships were proposed. For example, the `festival` class does not share a context (a sentence) with `museum`, `theatre` or `church`. On the contrary, `festival` class occurs with the class `time` or `event` that indicates a kind of relation between them. The following sentences provide evidence for the relation `subClassOf` between `festival` and `event` based on the lexical-pattern "is a" and the `instanceOf` relation:

1. "In Wexford the November Opera Festival is an international event."
2. "The Elephanta Festival is a classical dance and music event on Elephanta Island usually held in February."
3. "The Grenada National Museum in the center of town incorporates an old French barracks dating from 1704."

From the text, the annotated relations of `festival` class are: `instanceOf(No-vember Opera Festival, festival)`, `instanceOf(The Elephanta Festival, festival)`, `subClassOf(festival, event)`, and `disjointClass(festival, museum)`.

5   Experiments and Results

The experiments were conducted to evaluate the axiom extraction and the accuracy of the extracted named entities. Additionally, some examples of the validation of learned axioms are included. A brief description of the scenario used in the experiments is as follows:

- Dataset. The dataset used in the experiments was Lonely Planet[5], which consists of 1801 files about Tourism and covers a list of 96 classes and a taxonomy with 103 hierarchical relations manually annotated.
- Grammatical tagging. In this step, the Stanford POS-tagging tool was used for processing the dataset.
- Hierarchy extraction. As previously mentioned, the hierarchy of classes and subclasses was obtained through the implementation of an existing approach based on unsupervised learning and web search engine results [7].
- NER. Three Named Entity Recognition tools were used for identifying named entities: Watson Natural Language Understanding (NLU)[6], DBpedia Spotlight[7], and OpenCalais[8]. We use such tools due to their availability, performance, and because they do not require human intervention.
- Evaluation. For the evaluation of the obtained results, manual annotations were done by human experts in the Semantic Web domain (regarding the ontology learning process and with high English understanding) who selected if a relation was learned correctly or not.

5.1   Instance Identification Evaluation

The first activity is the identification of instances. In this stage the objective was to evaluate the identification of the `instanceOf` relation by the three NER tools that define a taxonomy of types of named entities. Table 1 presents the results of *Precision*, *Recall*, and *F-measure* values on 277 `instanceOf` relations that were manually annotated (from the LonelyPlanet dataset). According to the evaluation, Watson NLU had better precision than other tools in this experiment.

Table 1. Performance of NER tools - identifying instances

Tool	Precision	Recall	F-measure
Watson NLU	0.6910	0.4036	0.5095
OpenCalais	0.6022	0.3513	0.4437
DBpedia Spotlight	0.0318	0.2166	0.0555

---

[5] http://www.cimiano.de/doku.php?id=olp.

[6] https://cloud.ibm.com/catalog/services/natural-language-understanding.

[7] https://www.dbpedia-spotlight.org/.

[8] https://developers.refinitiv.com/open-permid/intelligent-tagging-restful-api.

The Table 2 presents the performance of the three previous NER tools for the identification of instances belonging to the following classes: *City, Country, Holiday, Natural Feature*, and *Region*. The obtained results were compared against 156 `instanceOf` relations from the Lonely Planet dataset, where 12 correspond to *City*, 35 to *Country*, 10 to *Holiday*, 85 to *Natural Feature*, and 14 to *Region*. Watson NLU showed the best F-measure for the *City, Country*, and *Region* classes; Open Calais had better F-measure for the *Holiday* and *Natural Feature* classes; and DBpedia Spotlight demonstrated encouraging results regarding the recall for the *Country* and *Region* classes. For *Country* class, the DBpedia Spotlight tool has 97% of recall value, that means that 34 of the individuals annotated manually were identified correctly.

Table 2. Performance of the selected NER tools - identified instances by class

Class	Tool	Precision	Recall	F-measure
City	Watson NLU	0.4000	0.5000	**0.4445**
	OpenCalais	0.3529	0.5000	0.4137
	DBpedia Spotlight	0.0081	0.2500	0.0157
Country	Watson NLU	0.7631	0.8285	**0.7945**
	OpenCalais	0.7000	0.8000	0.7466
	DBpedia Spotlight	0.0906	**0.9714**	0.1658
Holiday	Watson NLU	0.4285	0.3000	0.3529
	OpenCalais	0.4000	0.4000	**0.4001**
	DBpedia Spotlight	0.0139	0.2000	0.0261
Natural Feature	Watson NLU	0.3846	0.2941	0.3333
	OpenCalais	0.5438	0.3647	**0.4366**
	DBpedia Spotlight	0.0215	0.1647	0.0380
Region	Watson NLU	0.4000	0.1428	**0.2105**
	OpenCalais	0.2000	0.0714	0.1052
	DBpedia Spotlight	0.0138	0.2142	0.0260

The identification of `instanceOf` relations plays a very important role in the approach because such relations were used for the learning of axiomatic relations: `sameAs/differentFrom`, `disjointWith`, and `equivalentClass`. In addition, it can be seen that using the context of instances, in some cases, the instances of different classes appear in the same sentence, i.e. they co-occur. The linguistic context for each one of the named entities was analyzed and some lexical patterns were obtained. Examples of the most frequent patterns obtained for identifying the `instanceOf` relation (in the Lonely Planet dataset) are:

1. "Nyhavn, long a haunt for sailors and *writers* (including *Hans Christian Andersen*), is now more gentrified than seedy ...."

2. "Some of the island's prettiest *beaches* and calmest waters include *Paynes Bay, Sandy Bay* and *Mullins Bay.*"
3. "In addition to the parks and reserves, the *Elephant Marsh* is an excellent *place* for birding."

According to the first example, *Hans Christian Andersen* is an instance of *writer* class and the pattern associated is *<NP (including NE)>*[9]. Regarding the example 2, *Paynes Bay, Sandy Bay*, and *Mullins Bay* are instances of *beaches* class where the pattern is *<NP include NE, NE, and NE>*. Finally, in the example 3, *Elephant Marsh* is an instance of *place* and the pattern is *<NE is a NP>*.

It is worth mentioning that the context analysis is useful for dealing with the problem of ambiguous named entities. For example, given the *Country* class and *Luxembourg* individual, if both elements co-occur in the same sentence, then *Luxembourg* as instance of *Country* is resolved, like in the sentence *"A highly developed country, Luxembourg is Europe's 10th-largest economy"*. Whereas, if *Luxembourg* co-occurs with the *City* class in the sentence *"Luxembourg is a city with a mixture of ancient fortresses and cutting-edge architecture"*, then *Luxembourg* is established as instance of *City*.

5.2   Analysis of Axiom Identification

In order to demonstrate the identification of axioms, we present the analysis of examples regarding the three type of relations obtained: `sameAs/differentFrom`, `disjointWith`, `equivalentClass`.

Identification of sameAs Relations. To illustrate the identification of `sameAs/ differentFrom` relations, some instances of the more frequent patterns where this relation occurs are:

1. "The elegant *Beit el-Ajaib (House of Wonders)* was rebuilt after the British made their displeasure felt and bombed the area in the late-19th century."
2. "*Massive Lake Malawi* (also called *Lake Nyasa*) forms part of the border with Malawi."

In the first case, the *House of Wonders* is named as *Beit el-Ajaib* and in the second example, the *Massive Lake Malawi* is also called *Lake Nyasa*. The most common identified patterns are *<NE (NE)>* and *<NE called NE>*. On the contrary, when the `sameAs` relation is not found between two or more named entities, then the `differentFrom` relation is established. For instance, in the two examples the relation `sameAs(Beit el-Ajaib, House of Wonders)` is found, as well as `differentFrom(House of Wonders, Massive Lake Malawi)` relation is established.

---

[9] NE is a named entity and NP is a noun phrase.

Identification of disjointWith Relations. To demonstrate the identification of `disjointWith` relation, it was used a sample of the Lonely Planet dataset composed of 700 files. After the files were processed, we obtained 15 types showing no entity overlapping between their set of instances. That is, there is an overlapping when an instance is contained in more than one entity class. Some examples recovered by the Watson NLU tool denoting a `disjointWith` relation between classes are: *City, Organization, Person, HealthConditon, Country, Hoilday, Organization, NaturalDisaster, Person,* and *Region.* Table 3 shows some `disjointWith` relations learned for the *City* class and their corresponding named entities.

Table 3. Examples of learned `disjointWith` relations and their named entities (instances)

Class1/Class2	Class1's NE	Class2's NE
City/Organization	Belfast, San Juan, Iraklio, Brussels, Dakar	UNESCO, Forest Department River Club, EU
City/Region	Belfast, San Juan, Iraklio, Brussels, Dakar	Antarctic, Mediterranean, Caribbean, West Africa
City/Holiday	Belfast, San Juan, Iraklio, Brussels, Dakar	New Year, Easter, Christmas, Ramadan, Bastille Day
City/River	Belfast, San Juan, Iraklio, Brussels, Dakar	The Gambia River, Shire River, Orange River
City/Sport	Belfast, San Juan, Iraklio, Brussels, Dakar	Swimming, baseball skiing, sailing

We noted that in cases where an instance appears in more than one class, the disjoint rule is not often demonstrated. For example, the instance *Mediterranean* belongs to the *Natural Feature* and *Region* classes, which are not necessary disjoint classes. We also noted that although the NER tool results indicate that the set of instances were very different between *Region* and *Natural Feature,* such classes are associated in a `subClassOf` relation. The same case occurs with *Region/Country* and *Organization/Company.* This fact is supposed to be solved by the hierarchy extraction strategy and thus, it is not within the focus of this paper.

Identification of equivalentClass Relations. For illustrating the process of learning `equivalentClass` relations, the types of the entities extracted by Watson NLU and OpenCalais were selected because they obtained the highest values of F-measure in the identification of instances. For each class, its set of obtained instances were compared. If the intersection of the set of instances between two different classes is (almost) complete then an `equivalentClass(class1,` `class2`) relation is established (according to Axiom 5). Although the ideal situation to define such a relation is where the total of instances are overlapped between classes, we established a threshold of 90% of overlapping considering that the NER tools are not always completely precise.

Table 4. Examples of equivalentClass relations and their named entities

Class1/Class2	Class1's NE	Class2's NE
Watson:Organization/ OpenCalais:Organization	UNESCO, River Club, EU, Nature Reserve	UNESCO, River Club, EU, Nature Reserve
Watson:Country/ OpenCalais:Country	Scotland, Honduras, Niger, GrecceNiger, Grecce El Salvador, ...	Scotland, Honduras, Niger, Grecce, El Salvador, ...
Watson:Sports/ OpenCalais:SportsGame	Swimming, baseball, sailing skiing	Swimming, baseball, sailing skiing
Watson:HealthCondition/ OpenCalais:MedicalCondition	Fever, hepatitis, malaria, dehydration	Fever, hepatitis, malaria, dehydration
Watson:Organization/ OpenCalais:Company	UNESCO, EU, River Club, Nature Reserve	Forest Department, River Club, Nature Reserve

For instance, in the case of classes such as *Watson:Organization/OpenCalais: Organization, Watson:Country/OpenCalais:Country, Watson:Sport/OpenCalais: SportsGame,* and *Watson:HealthCondition/OpenCalais:MedicalCondition,* it can be determined an equivalence relationship between them. On the contrary, there are cases where different classes with similar individuals do not demonstrate an equivalence relation. For example, the classes *Watson:Organization/OpenCalais: Company* and *Watson:Person/OpenCalais:Holiday* have similar individuals but are not equivalent classes. Table 4 shows some examples of learned equivalent relations and their named entities, where it can be observed that the set of named entities is similar or dissimilar (last row) in both classes.

5.3   Question Validation

An axiom is often used for producing new knowledge from an existing knowledge base, or to check the knowledge base compliance with the description and semantics of the considered domain. In our case, we validate the axiom schemata checking the semantics in the domain. Taking into account the evidence of semantic information from text and a set of queries, we observed that the learned axioms correspond to knowledge in text that can verify the responses for each query.

Table 5. Examples of queries for validating the obtained axioms

Query	Axiom	Fragment text
New Orleans is a city?	`instanceOf(New Orleans, city)`	*"...New Orleans is a great city for biking ..."*
French Guiana is a country?	`instanceOf(French Guiana, country)`	*"French Guiana is a wet country..."*
Donia is a festival?	`instanceOf(Donia, festival)`	*"The Donia, a traditional music festival,..."*
Voski Ashun is a festival?	`instanceOf(Voski Ashun, festival)`	*"The town of Hrazdan hosts an annual autumn festival, called Voski Ashun."*
New Year's Day is is a holiday?	`instanceOf(New Year's Day, holiday)`	*"Most businesses close on public holidays such as New Year's Day..."*
What is *pohutukawa*?	`instanceOf(pohutukawa, plant)`	*"...One of the most noticeable plant is the pohutukawa..."*
What is *Wogasia*?	`instanceOf(Wogasia, celebration)`	*"...marriage ceremonies take place in a celebration called Wogasia."*
Fort Louis is same to *Fort de Marigot*?	`sameAs(Fort Louis, Fort de Marigot)`	*"Fort Louis (also called Fort de Marigot) was built in 1789."*
Lake Malawi is same to *Lake Nyasa*?	`sameAs(Lake Malawi, Lake Nyasa)`	*"Lake Malawi (also called Lake Nyasa) forms part of the border with Malawi."*
Chinatown is same to *Hongkong Street*?	`sameAs(Chinatown, Hongkong Street)`	*"Chinatown is sometimes called Hongkong Street..."*

Table 5 shows some examples of queries, learned axioms (`instanceOf` and `sameAs`), and a fragment of text showing where the axiom was obtained for the Lonely Planet corpus. When the learned axioms are integrated into an ontology, these queries can be seen as competency questions wrote in natural language outlining and constraining the scope of knowledge represented in that ontology. Note that other method for validation consists of using a reasoner or test the ontology in an information system, axioms such as `subClassOf`, `disjointWith` or `equivalentClass` could use that method for their validation.

As previously mentioned, our approach covers diverse axiomatic relations. However, existing approaches are commonly focused on the extraction of only one type of axiomatic relation. Therefore, we compared our approach against the one proposed by Völker *et al.* [16] regarding the `disjointWith` relation. In this sense, Völker *et al.* obtained an average precision of 86.4% in the identification of disjoint classes. On the other hand, our approach shows a precision of 87.26% for the `disjointWith` relation. The results demonstrate the effectiveness of our approach. It is worth mentioning that our approach extracts axiomatic relations from texts without any human intervention.

6 Conclusions

This paper proposed an approach to discovery axiomatic relations from text. The approach is based on the extraction of named entities, identifying the instances of each class and compare their context to establish an axiomatic relation such as `sameAs`, `differentFrom`, `disjointWith`, and `equivalenceClass`. In consequence, the named entities and lexical patterns help to determine a disjoint relation between two classes. From texts in the Tourism domain, the identified lexical patterns benefits the classes such as *City, Country, Holiday, NaturalFeature*, and *Region*, which are important in that context.

Regarding the evaluation, current NER tools such as Watson NLU demonstrate good performance in the identification of instances. It is important to note that some relations could not be identified correctly in the process of building the representation model due to imprecision in the process of extracting lexical relations. In this sense, recent NER approaches based on Linked Data can be useful in the process of extracting axiomatic relations due to the formal representation and availability of diverse classes. In addition, the problem of ambiguity in named entities must be addressed. For example, if one term is associated with different classes, an umbral can be considered to determine if a term belongs to one class or another.

Although the Lonely Planet dataset has been a reference dataset used in experiments of ontology learning evaluation, it is limited regarding the concepts and type of relations between classes. Therefore, as a future work, we plan to extend it with the new axiomatic relations and to add quantitative evaluation on automatic relation axiom extraction. Moreover, in the process of axiom learning, some lexical resources could be added to build the context for a specific class and then other kind of lexical-syntactic dependencies could be identified. Some of the main challenges in axiom learning are associated with synonyms and ambiguous class that will be addressed in further experiments.

References

1. Hearst, M.: Automatic acquisition of hyponyms from large text corpora in proc. In: 14th International Conference Computational Linguistics, Nantes France (1992)
2. Lehmann, J., Auer, S., Bühmann, L., Tramp, S.: Class expression learning for ontology engineering. J. Web Semant. **9**(1), 71–81 (2011). https://doi.org/10.1016/j.websem.2011.01.001
3. Ma, C., Molnár, B.: Use of ontology learning in information system integration: a literature survey. In: Sitek, P., Pietranik, M., Krótkiewicz, M., Srinilta, C. (eds.) ACIIDS 2020. CCIS, vol. 1178, pp. 342–353. Springer, Singapore (2020). https://doi.org/10.1007/978-981-15-3380-8_30

4. Ma, Y., Gao, H., Wu, T., Qi, G.: Learning disjointness axioms with association rule mining and its application to inconsistency detection of linked data. In: Zhao, D., Du, J., Wang, H., Wang, P., Ji, D., Pan, J.Z. (eds.) CSWS 2014. CCIS, vol. 480, pp. 29–41. Springer, Heidelberg (2014). https://doi.org/10.1007/978-3-662-45495-4_3

5. Nguyen, T.H., Tettamanzi, A.G.B.: Learning class disjointness axioms using grammatical evolution. In: Sekanina, L., Hu, T., Lourenço, N., Richter, H., García-Sánchez, P. (eds.) EuroGP 2019. LNCS, vol. 11451, pp. 278–294. Springer, Cham (2019). https://doi.org/10.1007/978-3-030-16670-0_18

6. Ponzetto, S.P., Strube, M.: Deriving a large scale taxonomy from Wikipedia. In: Proceedings of AAAI 2007, pp. 1440–1445 (2007). https://dl.acm.org/doi/abs/10.5555/1619797.1619876

7. Rios-Alvarado, A.B., Lopez-Arevalo, I., Sosa-Sosa, V.J.: Learning concept hierarchies from textual resources for ontologies construction. Expert. Syst. Appl. **40**(15), 5907–5915 (2013)

8. Ritter, A., Soderland, S., Etzioni, O.: What is this, anyway: automatic hypernym discovery. In: Proceedings of AAAI-09 Spring Symposium on Learning by Reading and Learning to Read, pp. 88–93 (2009)

9. Rizzo, G., d'Amato, C., Fanizzi, N., Esposito, F.: Terminological cluster trees for disjointness axiom discovery. In: Blomqvist, E., Maynard, D., Gangemi, A., Hoekstra, R., Hitzler, P., Hartig, O. (eds.) ESWC 2017. LNCS, vol. 10249, pp. 184–201. Springer, Cham (2017). https://doi.org/10.1007/978-3-319-58068-5_12

10. Sánchez, D.: Domain ontology learning from the web. Knowl. Eng. Rev. **24**(04), 413 (2009)

11. Sánchez, D., Moreno, A., Del Vasto-Terrientes, L.: Learning relation axioms from text: an automatic Web-based approach. Expert. Syst. Appl. **39**(5), 5792–5805 (2012). https://doi.org/10.1016/j.eswa.2011.11.088

12. Schutz, A., Buitelaar, P.: *RelExt*: a tool for relation extraction from text in ontology extension. In: Gil, Y., Motta, E., Benjamins, V.R., Musen, M.A. (eds.) ISWC 2005. LNCS, vol. 3729, pp. 593–606. Springer, Heidelberg (2005). https://doi.org/10.1007/11574620_43

13. Snow, R., Jurafsky, D., Ng, A.Y.: Learning syntactic patterns for automatic hypernym discovery. In: Advances in Neural Information Processing Systems, pp. 1297–1304 (2005)

14. Völker, J., Hitzler, P., Cimiano, P.: Acquisition of OWL DL axioms from lexical resources. In: Franconi, E., Kifer, M., May, W. (eds.) ESWC 2007. LNCS, vol. 4519, pp. 670–685. Springer, Heidelberg (2007). https://doi.org/10.1007/978-3-540-72667-8_47

15. Völker, J., Rudolph, S.: Lexico-logical acquisition of OWL DL axioms. In: Medina, R., Obiedkov, S. (eds.) ICFCA 2008. LNCS (LNAI), vol. 4933, pp. 62–77. Springer, Heidelberg (2008). https://doi.org/10.1007/978-3-540-78137-0_5

16. Völker, J., Vrandečić, D., Sure, Y., Hotho, A.: Learning disjointness. In: Franconi, E., Kifer, M., May, W. (eds.) ESWC 2007. LNCS, vol. 4519, pp. 175–189. Springer, Heidelberg (2007). https://doi.org/10.1007/978-3-540-72667-8_14

17. Zhang, Z., Gentile, A.L., Augenstein, I., Blomqvist, E., Ciravegna, F.: Mining equivalent relations from linked data. In: Proceedings of the 51st Annual Meeting of the Association for Computational Linguistics, pp. 289–293. The Association for Computer Linguistics (2013)

Making Neural Networks FAIR

Anna Nguyen[1(✉)], Tobias Weller[1], Michael Färber[1], and York Sure-Vetter[2]

[1] Karlsruhe Institute of Technology (KIT), Karlsruhe, Germany
anna.nguyen@kit.edu
[2] National Research Data Infrastructure (NFDI), Karlsruhe, Germany

Abstract. Research on neural networks has gained significant momentum over the past few years. Because training is a resource-intensive process and training data cannot always be made available to everyone, there has been a trend to reuse pre-trained neural networks. As such, neural networks themselves have become research data. In this paper, we first present the neural network ontology *FAIRnets Ontology*, an ontology to make existing neural network models *findable, accessible, interoperable,* and *reusable* according to the FAIR principles. Our ontology allows us to model neural networks on a meta-level in a structured way, including the representation of all network layers and their characteristics. Secondly, we have modeled over 18,400 neural networks from GitHub based on this ontology, which we provide to the public as a knowledge graph called *FAIRnets*, ready to be used for recommending suitable neural networks to data scientists.

1 Introduction

Researchers of various sciences and data analysts reuse but also re-train neural network models according to their needs.[1] Providing pre-trained neural network models online has the following advantages. First, as a provider, you can benefit from users improving your neural network and circulating your research. Second, as a user of an already trained neural network, you can overcome the cold start problem as well as save on training time and costs. Furthermore, providing trained neural network models gets increasingly important in the light of the research community efforts to make research results more transparent and explainable (see FAIR principles [21]). As a result, more and more trained models are provided online at source code repositories such as GitHub. The models provided serve not only to reproduce the results but also to interpret them (e.g., by comparing similar neural network models). Lastly, providing and using pre-trained models gets increasingly important via transfer learning in other domains.

To ensure the high-quality reuse of data sets and infrastructure, the *FAIR Guiding Principles for scientific data management and stewardship* [21] have

---

[1] https://trends.google.com/trends/explore?date=all&q=transfer%20learning

---

A. Nguyen and T. Weller—These authors contributed equally to the work.

© Springer Nature Switzerland AG 2020
B. Villazón-Terrazas et al. (Eds.): KGSWC 2020, CCIS 1232, pp. 29–44, 2020.
https://doi.org/10.1007/978-3-030-65384-2_3

been proposed. These guidelines are designed to make digital assets **F**indable, **A**ccessible, **I**nteroperable, and **R**e-usable. They have been widely accepted by several scientific communities nowadays (e.g., [22]). Making digital assets FAIR is essential to deal with a data-driven world and thus keeping pace with an increasing volume, complexity, and creation speed of data. So far, the FAIR principles have been mainly applied when providing data sets and code [3, 22], but not machine learning models, such as neural network models. In this paper, we bring the FAIR principles to neural networks by (1) proposing a novel schema (i.e., ontology) which enables semantic annotations to enhance the information basis (e.g., for search and reasoning purposes) and (2) representing a wide range of existing neural network models with this schema in a FAIR way. As we outline in Sect. 3.1, extracting metadata from neural networks automatically is a nontrivial task due to heterogeneous code styles, dynamic coding, and varying versioning. The key idea is that the information contained in these networks should be provided according to the FAIR principles. This comprises several steps which not only consist of having identifiers but providing (meta)data in a machine-readable way in order to enable researchers and practitioners (e.g., data scientists) easy access to the data. We facilitate this by using semantic web technologies such as OWL and RDF/RDFS.

Overall, we provide the following contributions:

1. We provide an *ontology*, called FAIRNETS ONTOLOGY, for representing neural networks. It is made available using a persistent URI by w3id and registered at the platform Linked Open Vocabularies (LOV).
   Ontology URI: https://w3id.org/nno/ontology
   LOV: https://lov.linkeddata.es/dataset/lov/vocabs/nno
2. We provide a *knowledge graph*, called FAIRNETS, representing over 18,400 publicly available neural networks, following the FAIR principles. FAIRNETS is available using a persistent URI by w3id and is uploaded to Zenodo.
   Knowledge Graph URI: https://w3id.org/nno/data
   Zenodo: https://doi.org/10.5281/zenodo.3885249

Our contribution is beneficial in several application areas (see Sect. 5). For instance, we already provide an online search system called FAIRNETS SEARCH [13] by which users can explore and analyze neural network models.

The paper is structured as follows. Sect. 2 describes the structure of FAIRNETS ONTOLOGY and Sect. 3 describes the knowledge graph FAIRNETS. Sect. 4 explains the reason why the neural networks in FAIRNETS follow the FAIR principles. Sect. 5 describes the impact of FAIRNETS. Sect. 6 gives an overview of related work. Lastly, the contributions are summarized.

2   FAIRnets Ontology

2.1   Creation Process

The FAIRNETS ONTOLOGY is dedicated to model metadata for neural network models on a schema level. We developed the ontology by using Protégé [12].

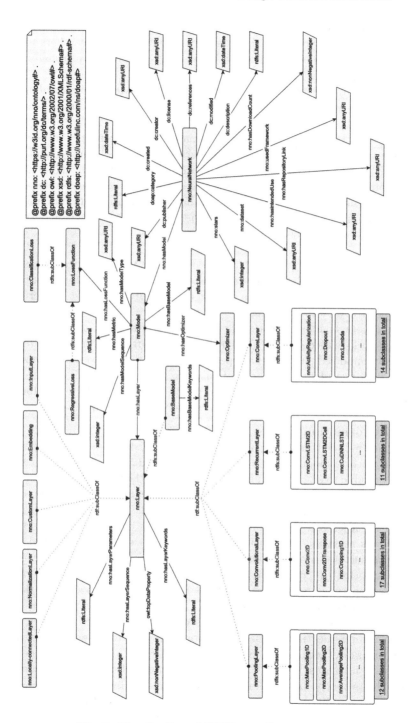

Fig. 1. Visualization of FAIRNETS ONTOLOGY.

To the best of our knowledge, there is no existing vocabulary for the specific description of neural networks. That is why several senior researchers use best practices [6] to construct the ontology. We identify researchers, especially beginners, as potential users. The use cases we envision can be found in Sect. 5.

In addition to the consideration of the Predictive Model Markup Language (PMML) in the development of the ontology (especially in describing the architecture), findings from further work were also considered. In particular, model cards [11] were taken into account to validate relevant concepts. Model cards encourage transparent model reports concerning machine learning models and are used for outlining the intended use of a model. These cards define minimal information needed to sufficiently describe a machine learning model (in our case, a neural network) that is relevant to the intended application domains. As suggested from model cards, we included model details such as person developing model, model date, model type, and licenses.

Characteristics. The structure of the FAIRNETS ONTOLOGY can be seen in Fig. 1. Overall, the ontology consists of a total of 516 axioms and uses a total of 77 classes where 70 are sub-classes. It also consists of four object properties, 23 data properties, and 29 individuals.

The ontology enables representing three different aspects of information. (1) Neural network-related general metadata and (2) neural network-dependent features can be modeled, such as the type of layer, loss function, and optimizer. (3) Layer-specific metadata is used to enhance the information basis of the specific layers, e.g., its keywords and parameters. In the following, we will describe these three components of the FAIRNETS ONTOLOGY correspondingly.[2]

General information describe general components of the neural network, as well as the intended use. For instance, the owner/developer of the (trained) neural network is modeled by using the property `dc:creator`. This attribute makes it possible to search for repositories by the author in the domain of neural networks. Following the Linked Data Principles, the author is represented via a URI. In this way, the authors are uniquely identified. Therefore, it is possible to link it to the Microsoft Academic Knowledge Graph [5] which models scholarly data such as scientific publications in which some of the represented neural network models are proposed and evaluated. Moreover, a name (`rdfs:label`) and a description (`dc:description`) of the trained neural network are stored. The data property `nno:dataset` of type URI allows us to specify the data set that was used to train the neural network. This information already gives a more detailed insight into the neural network as well as the intended use of it.

Furthermore, the timestamp of creation date (`dc:created`) or last modification (`dc:modified`) allows assessing the currency of the neural network. `dc:license` indicates the rights to modify and redistribute that network. Besides, the property `nno:hasRepositoryLink` allows linking to the repository in which the neural network is located. Likewise, references to published papers can be included using `dc:references`.

---

[2] We will use `nno` as the prefix for the namespace https://w3id.org/nno/ontology#.

Model-specific information covers model-specific components of the neural network, such as optimization function denoted by `nno:hasOptimizer`. The ontology covers modeling various loss functions, such as binary cross-entropy and mean squared error, via the property `nno:hasLossFunction`. Loss functions are subdivided into classification and regression loss functions in the ontology to further indicate the intended use of the neural network. The information about existing layers of the neural network can be linked via the property `nno:hasLayer`. The loss functions and layer types available in Keras, an open-source deep learning framework to model neural networks, served as a basis to model available loss functions and layers.

Layer-specific metadata outline additional information about the individual layer. The layers of neural networks are subdivided into subclasses such as core, recurrent, and convolutional layer. These classes are further subdivided into more specific layer classes. This specification derived from Keras enables to categorize the neural networks. For example, a neural network with a layer from class convolutional layer can be assigned to the type convolutional neural network. Furthermore, the hyperparameters (e.g., kernel size, stride, and padding) are denoted by `nno:hasLayerKeywords` and saved as a dictionary. Additional values in the layer are denoted by `nno:hasLayerParameter`.

Most of the categories, properties, and instances are annotated with a label (`rdfs:label`), a description (`rdfs:comment`), and, if given, a link (`rdfs:seeAlso`) which make it easy for ontology users to identify the intended use of categories, properties, and instances, therefore supporting the reusability.

2.2 Provisioning

The World Wide Web Consortium (W3C) Permanent Identifier Community Group service is used to provide secure and permanent URL forwarding to the ontology. The FAIRNETS ONTOLOGY in syntax turtle is accessible under https://w3id.org/nno/ontology. Moreover, the ontology has been registered at LOV.[3] The ontology is licensed under Creative Commons BY 4.0[4] which allows its wide usage. Furthermore, the ontology follows the 5-Star Linked Data Principles[5] and can, therefore, be easily reused. A VoID file is provided under https://w3id.org/nno/fairnetsvoid including provisioning information.

3   FAIRnets Knowledge Graph

Apart from the ontology, we provide the FAIRNETS knowledge graph, which is based on the FAIRNETS ONTOLOGY. The knowledge graph allows us to store knowledge (in our case, detailed metadata for neural network models) intuitively as a graph. Existing and widely used W3C standards and recommendations,

---

[3] https://lov.linkeddata.es/dataset/lov/vocabs/nno, last acc. 2020-10-15.
[4] https://creativecommons.org/licenses/by/4.0/, last acc. 2020-10-15.
[5] https://5stardata.info/en/, last acc. 2020-10-15.

such as RDF and SPARQL, can be used to query the knowledge graph and to integrate relatively easily into existing frameworks and systems. For instance, FAIRNETS is already integrated into KBox [10] which is a data management framework, allowing users to share resources among different applications.

3.1 Creation Process

The previous online available neural network repositories such as Keras,[6] Caffe Model Zoo,[7] and Wolfram Alpha[8] are rather small (under one hundred neural networks) and not sufficient to present trends in the development and usage of neural networks. General-purpose online code-sharing services, such as GitHub[9] and Bitbucket,[10] in contrast, contain many repositories of different nature. We, thus, decided to use GitHub since it is the largest host of repositories. Details about the nontrivial extraction process are given in the following.

Data Source. We extract and represent metadata of publicly available, trained neural network models in RDF* (i.e. RDF and RDFS) based on the FAIRNETS ONTOLOGY. Information from SemanGit [9] and GHTorrent [7] can be used to identify GitHub repositories. SemanGit and GHTorrent provide a collection of data extracted from GitHub. In total there are more than 119 million repositories available in the GHTorrent data collection. However, SemanGit and GHTorrent have a different focus and do not provide all the information which we wanted to provide in the FAIRNETS knowledge graph. For instance, information about the architectures of neural networks within the repositories, the creation date of the repositories, as well as the watcher count is not included. We, therefore, directly accessed the GitHub Repository API and queried available neural network repositories. We used the search term 'neural network' and filtered for repositories that use Python as a programming language. We accessed these repositories[11] and extracted the neural network metadata.

Extraction Process. The difficulty lies in the extraction of the architecture information from the code. We narrowed our extraction down on neural networks implemented in Python. Still, it is difficult to identify the Python file which models a neural network. Therefore, we started with h5 files which are an open-source technology for storing trained machine learning models. Neural networks that have been trained with Keras, for example, can be stored in this format. The h5 file contains information about the neural network, e.g., the sequence of layers, used activation functions, optimization function, and loss function. Accessing the information in the h5 file makes it easier to identify and extract

---

[6] https://keras.io, last acc. 2020-10-15.
[7] https://github.com/BVLC/caffe/wiki/Model-Zoo, last acc. 2020-10-15.
[8] https://resources.wolframcloud.com/NeuralNetRepository, last acc. 2020-10-15.
[9] https://www.github.com, last acc. 2020-10-15.
[10] https://www.bitbucket.org, last acc. 2020-10-15.
[11] Exemplary GitHub API Request: https://api.github.com/repos/dmnelson/sentiment-analysis-imdb, last acc. 2020-10-15..

Table 1. Mapping of GitHub REST API values to the general components in FAIR-NETS.

GitHub API	FAIRnets ontology
created_at	`dc:created`
description, readme	`dc:description`
html_url	`nno:hasRepositoryLink`
license	`dc:license`
owner ['html_url']	`dc:creator`
updated_at	`dc:modified`
watchers_count	`nno:stars`
name	`rdfs:label`
topics ['names']	`doap:category`

the architecture of the neural network. However, not every repository contains trained neural networks in h5 files. The reason is that trained neural networks often take up a lot of storage space. Thus, our contribution is the information extraction from the code directly which will be described below.

General Information: The mapping of the values from the Github API with the corresponding general component properties in FAIRNETS can be seen in Table 1. We use the *full_name* of the GitHub REST API as a unique identifier (e.g., 'dmnelson/sentiment-analysis-imdb' in note (see Footnote 11)). The *full_name* consists of the GitHub username combined with the name of the repository. The owner of the repository is also the owner of the neural network. Moreover, we store the link (`nno:hasRepositoryLink`), the time of creation (`dc:created`), and the last modification (`dc:modified`) of the repository. As a description of the neural network (`dc:description`), we extracted automatically the description and readme file of the GitHub repository. This gives a summary of the possible use of the neural network. Furthermore, license information about the neural network is extracted and modeled in the knowledge graph, if available. This information is crucial regarding the reusability of neural networks. Given this information, it is possible to filter neural networks by license – which is often an important constraint in industrial settings. To enrich the knowledge graph FAIRNETS with information according to the usage of a neural network, we extract the topics[12] of each repository from the GitHub repositories and store them as `doap:category`.

Additionally, we extract arXiv HTTP links within the readme file and map them to `dc:references`. If BibTex file codes can be found in the readme file, we extract the URL information from the BibTex entry and link it by using the property `dc:references`. The property `dc:references` is only intended for scientific contributions. By linking it with URLs from BibTex entries and arXiv

---

[12] https://developer.github.com/v3/repos/#list-all-topics-for-a-repository, last acc. 2020-10-15.

links, we ensure this condition. Other links in the readme file are linked to the neural network using `rdfs:seeAlso`.

Model and Technical Information: The main feature of FAIRNETS is the modeling of neural networks. We can model the structure and technical components of neural networks by employing the FAIRNETS ONTOLOGY. To extract the neural network information from the repositories we consider all Python files in the repositories. Each repository can contain several models of a neural network. In general, it is difficult to extract the architecture information automatically without executing the source code. By executing the code, you can save the neural network model, for example in h5, and retrieve the information easier. We seek a more elegant way by saving execution costs and use language processing to extract the information. Due to that, we focus on Python files with static variables. Despite this restriction, there are still challenges because of various programming styles such as inconsistent naming of variables, complex loop constructions, different structures of code, and other logic statements. Another challenge is changing parameter naming due to different framework versions which are usually not stated. To solve these tasks, a general method is generated using Python Abstract Syntax Trees (AST) module.[13] The AST module helps Python applications to process trees of the Python abstract syntax grammar. We focused on Keras applications of neural networks to extract the architecture because it is the most used deep learning framework among the top-winners on Kaggle (see Footnote 6). The information on the architecture of the neural network is then modeled by using the schema and properties provided by the FAIRNETS ONTOLOGY. Also, the individual layers and their hyperparameters are stored in our knowledge graph. Likewise, the used optimization function and loss function are stored, among other things, allowing us to infer whether the neural network is used for classification or regression. Our code can be found on GitHub.[14]

Evaluation. To evaluate the accuracy of our information extraction, we manually went through 50 examples where we judged the extraction of the GitHub Repository API in Table 1. The evaluation was in all cases correct. In the case of the neural network architecture, we used the h5 files, if available, in the repositories. We were able to evaluate over 1,343 h5 files with architecture information (i.e., layer information) which overlap with the architecture extracted from the code with 54% accuracy. Due to later modifications in the code it is possible that the overlap with the h5 file does not apply anymore (e.g., if a layer is commented out).

3.2   Provisioning

Just like the FAIRNETS ONTOLOGY, the knowledge graph FAIRNETS is also based on the 5-Star Linked Data Principles. The knowledge graph is accessible under a persistent URI from w3id and additionally provided on Zenodo.

---

[13] https://docs.python.org/3/library/ast.html, last acc. 2020-10-15.
[14] https://github.com/annugyen/FAIRnets.

Table 2. Statistical key figures about FAIRNETS.

Key figure	Value
Repositories	9,516
Unique users	8,637
Neural networks	18,463
FFNN	8,924 (48%)
CNN	6,667 (36%)
RNN	2,872 (16%)

In combining FAIR principles and Linked Data Principles using URIs to identify things, providing information using RDF*, and linking to other URIs, it is possible to easily reference and use FAIRNETS (see Sect. 5). Machine-readable metadata allows us to describe and search for neural networks. The knowledge graph FAIRNETS, like the ONTOLOGY, is published under the Creative Commons BY 4.0 license (see Footnote 4). A VoID file describing the knowledge graph in a machine-readable format is provided under https://w3id.org/nno/fairnetsvoid.

3.3 Statistical Analysis of the FAIRnets Knowledge Graph

Table 2 shows some key figures about the created knowledge graph. It consists of 18,463 neural networks, retrieved from 9,516 repositories, and provided by 8,637 unique users. The creation time of the neural networks in our knowledge graph ranges from January 2015 to June 2019. All these networks have a link to the respective repository and owner. Based on the used layers, we can infer the type of neural network. If a network uses a convolutional layer, it is inferred that the network is a convolutional neural network (CNN). Likewise, if a network contains a recurrent layer, it is inferred that the network is a recurrent neural network (RNN). For simplicity, if none of those two layer types are used, the default claim for the network is a feed-forward neural network (FFNN). Of the total 18,463 neural networks, FFNN is most represented in the knowledge graph comprising half of the neural networks. CNNs follows with 36% and RNN with 16% of the total number of neural networks.

4 FAIR Principles for Neural Networks

With FAIRNETS, we treat neural networks as research data. As such, to ensure good scientific practice, it should be provided according to the FAIR principles, that is, the data should be findable, accessible, interoperable, and reusable. While the GitHub repositories themselves do not satisfy the FAIR principles (e.g., the metadata is not easily searchable and processable by machines), the modeling of the neural networks in the FAIRNETS knowledge graph is made *FAIR* as we show

Table 3. Evaluation of FAIRNETS according to the Generation2 FAIRMetrics (Note: ✓ = passed, (✓) = should pass, ✗ = not passed).

Principle	FAIRMetric	Name	Result
Findable	Gen2_FM_F1A	Identifier uniqueness	✓
	Gen2_FM_F1B	Identifier persistence	✓
	Gen2_FM_F2	Machine-readability of metadata	✓
	Gen2_FM_F3	Resource identifier in metadata	✓
	Gen2_FM_F4	Indexed in a searchable resource	✗
Accessible	Gen2_FM_A1.1	Access protocol	✓
	Gen2_FM_A1.2	Access authorization	✓
	Gen2_FM_A2	Metadata longevity	(✓)
Interoperable	Gen2_FM_I1	Use a knowledge representation language	✓
	Gen2_FM_I2	Use FAIR vocabularies	✓
	Gen2_FM_I3	Use qualified references	✓
Reusable	Gen2_FM_R1.1	Accessible usage license	✓
	Gen2_FM_R1.2	Detailed provenance	(✓)
	Gen2_FM_R1.3	Meets community standards	(✓)

in the following. Specifically, in this section, we identify the factors that make the neural network representations in FAIRNETS *FAIR*. This was achieved by following the *FAIRification process*.[15] Our FAIRification process is aligned with the *FAIRMetrics*[16] outlined in Table 3. In the following, we point out how the single FAIR metrics are met by our knowledge graph.

Findable describes the property that metadata for digital assets is easy for both humans and machines to find. Our approach ensured that, firstly, by retrieving the metadata available in the repository, secondly, structuring its metadata in the readme file, and thirdly, obtaining the architecture information from the code file according to the FAIRNETS ONTOLOGY. The neural networks we model have unique identifiers (i.e., fulfilling *Gen2_FM_F1A*) and a persistent URI (*Gen2_FM_F1B*). As a result, the process for a human to find a suitable neural network through resource identifiers in the metadata (*Gen2_FM_F3*) is improved. By using RDF as the data model and by providing a schema in OWL as well as a VoID file as a description of the knowledge graph, the metadata is machine-readable (*Gen2_FM_F2*). Thus, the knowledge graph can be automatically filtered and used by services. An exemplary service supporting this statement is presented in Sec. 5. FAIRNETS allows for querying information about and within the architecture of the neural networks which was not possible previously. Now, complex queries are feasible (e.g., list all recurrent neural networks published in 2018), which cannot be solved by traditional keyword searches.

---

[15] https://www.go-fair.org/fair-principles/fairification-process/, last acc. 2020-10-15.
[16] https://fairmetrics.org, last acc. 2020-10-15.

The metric $Gen2\_FM\_F4$[17] – 'indexed in a searchable resource' – was not passed by FAIRNETS although we indexed it on Zenodo. The reason is that the resource on Zenodo is not findable in the search engine Bing which the authors of the FAIRMetrics use as ground truth. However, FAIRNETS is indexed by the search engine Google.

Accessible describes that users can access (meta)data using a standardized communication protocol. The protocol must be open, free, and universally implemented. FAIRNETS ONTOLOGY AND KNOWLEDGE GRAPH is located on a web server and can be accessed using the HTTPS protocol ($Gen2\_FM\_A1.1$). The neural networks in the repositories can also be accessed using the HTTPS protocol ($Gen2\_FM\_A1.2$). In addition to the open protocol, the accessible property requires that metadata can be retrieved, even if the actual digital assets are no longer available. Due to the separation of the information in FAIRNETS and the actual neural networks on GitHub, this property is fulfilled, since the information in FAIRNETS is preserved even if the neural networks on GitHub are no longer available ($Gen2\_FM\_A2$). The service to evaluate the metric $Gen2\_FM\_A2$ – 'metadata longevity' – could not be executed because it only tests files that are less than $300\,\text{kb}$[18] whereas FAIRNETS has more than $80\,\text{MB}$. This test checks for the existence of the 'persistence policy' predicate. This predicate is available in FAIRNETS, which should pass the test.

Interoperable refers to the capability of being integrated with other data as well as being available to applications for analysis, storage, and further processing. We make use of Linked Data by applying RDF ($Gen2\_FM\_I1$) and SPARQL to represent the information. This makes the data machine-readable, even without the specification of an ad-hoc algorithm or mapping. Additionally, the FAIRNETS ONTOLOGY and the respective KNOWLEDGE GRAPH use well-established and commonly used vocabularies to represent the information. Among others, Dublin Core, Vocabulary of a Friend (VOAF), Creative Commons (CC), and a vocabulary for annotating vocabulary descriptions (VANN) are used for annotations and descriptions ($Gen2\_FM\_I2$). As a further requirement of the FAIR guideline, qualified references to further metadata are required. This requirement is fulfilled by `rdfs:seeAlso` and `dc:references` ($Gen2\_FM\_I3$). `dc:references` statements provide scientific references between the neural networks and scientific contributions. These references to the scientific contributions are provided via globally unique and persistent identifiers, such as DOIs.

Reusable aims at achieving well-defined digital assets. This facilitates the replicability and usage in other contexts (i.e., reproducibility), as well as findability. Due to the architecture and metadata extraction, the process of finding and reusing a neural network by an end-user becomes significantly easier and can now be performed systematically. By using best practices in ontology building, the

---

[17] https://github.com/FAIRMetrics/Metrics/blob/master/FM_F4, last acc. 2020-10-15.

[18] https://github.com/FAIRMetrics/Metrics/blob/master/FM_A2, last acc. 2020-10-15.

properties and classes of FAIRNETS ONTOLOGY provided are self-explanatory with labels and descriptions (*Gen2_FM_R1.3*). The neural networks in FAIRNETS contain structured detailed metadata such as creator and GitHub link (see *Gen2_FM_R1.2*) for easy findability and reuse. At the same time, most neural networks in FAIRNETS have an assigned license which is important for reusability (*Gen2_FM_R1.1*). For passing *Gen2_FM_R1.2*, (meta)data must be associated with detailed provenance reusing existing vocabularies such as Dublin Core which we included in our knowledge graph. *Gen2_FM_R1.3* tests a certification saying that the resource is compliant with a minimum of metadata. FAIRNETS is described by using LOV standards for publication. Therefore, we assume that these metrics are fulfilled. Overall, the neural networks modeled in FAIRNETS fulfill all requirements of the FAIR principles, see Table 3.

5   Impact

We see high potential of FAIRNETS ONTOLOGY and the knowledge graph FAIRNETS in the areas of *transparency, recommendation, reusability, education,* and *search.* In the following, we outline these application areas in more detail.

Transparency. Neural networks are applied in many different areas such as finance [16], medical health [8], and law [14]. Transparency plays a major role in these areas when it comes to trust the output of a used neural network model. We claim that our contribution which makes neural networks more transparent can increase trust and privacy [17]. Additionally, using semantic annotations can even enhance interpretability by distributional semantics [18].

Another aspect is the transparency of scientific work regarding neural networks. Researchers publishing a model should provide it according to the FAIR principles to strengthen their scientific contribution. Our knowledge graph FAIRNETS can pave the way for this.

Recommendation. Neural Architecture Search (NAS) is used to find the best suitable neural network architecture based on existing architectures [4]. However, the search is performed purely based on metrics like accuracy ignoring explainability aspects concerning the best fitting model. Our knowledge graph allows us to have a search for the best suitable neural network models on a meta-level, using modeled use-cases, data sets, and scientific papers. Knowledge graphs have also been used to provide explanations for recommendation to the user [19,23].

Additionally, we can apply explainable reasoning [20] given the ontology and the knowledge graph and infer some rules. Doing this, we might reason which neural network models are reasonable or which components of the architecture stand in conflict with each other.

Reusability. Transfer learning is a method in deep learning to reuse pre-trained models on new tasks. Our contribution facilitate the search of pre-trained neural networks and provide metadata needed to choose a specific neural network. We can envision FAIRNETS linked with other knowledge bases to enrich reusability of neural networks by applying Linked Data Principles (see Footnote 5). For example, training data sets can be linked with Neural Data Server,[19] Wikidata,[20] and Zenodo[21] through schema.org,[22] scientific papers can be linked with the Microsoft Academic Knowledge Graph [5], and metadata can be extended with OpenAIRE.[23]

On the other hand, providing a model and encouraging its reuse can improve it by revealing limitations, errors, or suggestions to other tasks.

Education. Our FAIRNETS knowledge graph can be used for educational purposes [2], for instance, to learn best practices regarding designing a neural network model. Another aspect is to learn the usages of different architectures and their approaches (e.g., via linked papers). Our knowledge graph includes training parameters that can help setting up the training process of a neural network (e.g., when facing the cold start problem).

Search. We provide online the search system FAIRNETS SEARCH[24] [13], which is based on the proposed FAIRNETS ONTOLOGY and KNOWLEDGE GRAPH. Users can search for neural network models through search terms. Additional information can be retrieved by using SPARQL as query language on top of our knowledge graph, which enables faceted and semantic search capabilities. The SPARQL endpoint is also available to the public. The search system shows how a semantic search system can be realized which improved the limited capabilities of keyword searches on GitHub. Furthermore, developers can provide their GitHub repository to run the FAIRification process on their neural networks. Until now, we have over 550 visits to the website FAIRNETS SEARCH with over 4,800 page views, 1,400 searches on our website with an average duration of twelve minutes, and the maximal actions in one visit is 356.

6   Related Work

Information of Neural Network Models. Mitchell et al. [11] suggest which information about neural networks should be considered as relevant when modeling them. Information such as description, date of the last modification, link to papers, or other resources to further information, as well as the intended purpose of a neural network, are taken into account. Storing such information makes the neural networks more transparent. We follow this suggestion by defining a

---

[19] http://aidemos.cs.toronto.edu/nds/, last acc. 2020-10-15.
[20] https://www.wikidata.org, last acc. 2020-10-15.
[21] https://zenodo.org, last acc. 2020-10-15.
[22] https://schema.org, last acc. 2020-10-15.
[23] https://www.openaire.eu, last acc. 2020-10-15.
[24] https://km.aifb.kit.edu/services/fairnets/, last acc. 2020-10-15.

semantic representation which, to the best of our knowledge, does not exist for neural network models so far.

The knowledge extraction from neural networks can point out relevant features or redundancies [1]. We extract neural network information to build a knowledge graph to better evaluate the causal relationships between different neural network architectures.

Representing and Provisioning Neural Network Models. There exist several standards for the exchange of neural network information on the instance level. The Predictive Model Markup Language (PMML)[25] is an XML-based standard for analytic models developed by the Data Mining Group. PMML is currently supported by more than 30 organizations. The Open Neural Network eXchange format (ONNX)[26] is a project by Facebook and Microsoft that converts neural networks into different frameworks. These two formats serve as an exchange format for neural networks on instance level. We are less interested in the exchange of formats, but rather the reusability of the neural networks on a meta-level. Therefore, our FAIRNETS ONTOLOGY lifts it's elements to a semantic level, i.e. to RDF/S, following a methodology for reusing ontologies [15] and applying the Linked Data Principles (see Footnote 5). Thus, we incorporate information on the instance and meta-level in the knowledge graph FAIRNETS.

Neural Network Repositories. Many pre-trained neural networks are available online. The well-known Keras framework offers ten pre-trained neural networks for reuse (see Footnote 6). The Berkeley Artificial Intelligence Research Lab has a deep learning framework called Caffe Model Zoo (see Footnote 7) which consists of about fifty neural networks. Wolfram Alpha has a repository with neural networks (see Footnote 8) which consists of approximately ninety models. These pre-trained neural networks are represented in different formats making it, for instance, difficult to compare or reuse neural networks. Besides, a larger number of neural networks can be found in code repositories such as GitHub. These neural networks are typically coded in one of the major programming frameworks such as Keras, TensorFlow, or PyTorch. Our approach aims to consider such neural networks and make them available as FAIR data.

7   Conclusion and Future Work

This paper was dedicated to make neural networks FAIR. To this end, we first proposed the FAIRNETS ONTOLOGY, an ontology that allows us to model neural networks on a fine-grained level and that is easily extensible. Second, we provided the knowledge graph FAIRNETS. This graph contains rich metadata of 18,463 publicly available neural network models using our proposed ontology

---

[25] http://dmg.org/pmml/v4-0-1/NeuralNetwork.html, last acc. 2020-10-15.
[26] https://onnx.ai, last acc. 2020-10-15.

as knowledge schema. Both the FAIRNETS ONTOLOGY as well as the FAIR-
NETS knowledge graph show a high potential impact in fields like recommender
systems and education.

For the future, we plan to connect the FAIRNETS ONTOLOGY and KNOWL-
EDGE GRAPH with scholarly data. Specifically, we will work on linking pub-
lications, authors, and venues modeled in knowledge graphs like the Microsoft
Academic Knowledge Graph [5] or Wikidata to the FAIRNETS knowledge graph.
This will require to apply sophisticated information extraction methods on sci-
entific publications.

References

1. Boger, Z., Guterman, H.: Knowledge extraction from artificial neural network models. In: Proceedings of the SMC 1997, pp. 3030–3035 (1997)
2. Chen, P., Lu, Y., Zheng, V.W., et al.: KnowEdu: a system to construct knowledge
   graph for education. IEEE Access **6**, 31553–31563 (2018)
3. Devarakonda, R., Prakash, G., Guntupally, K., et al.: Big federal data centers
   implementing FAIR data principles: ARM data center example. In: Proceedings of
   BigData 2019, pp. 6033–6036 (2019)
4. Elsken, T., Metzen, J.H., Hutter, F.: Neural architecture search: a survey. J. Mach.
   Learn. Res. **20**, 55:1–55:21 (2019)
5. Färber, M.: The microsoft academic knowledge graph: a linked data source with
   8 billion triples of scholarly data. In: Ghidini, C., et al. (eds.) ISWC 2019. LNCS,
   vol. 11779, pp. 113–129. Springer, Cham (2019). https://doi.org/10.1007/978-3-
   030-30796-7_8
6. Gangemi, A., Presutti, V.: Ontology design patterns. In: Staab, S., Studer, R.
   (eds.) Handbook on Ontologies. IHIS, pp. 221–243. Springer, Heidelberg (2009).
   https://doi.org/10.1007/978-3-540-92673-3_10
7. Gousios, G.: The GHTorrent dataset and tool suite. In: Proceedings of MSR 2013,
   pp. 233–236 (2013)
8. Khan, J., Wei, J.S., Ringnér, M., et al.: Classification and diagnostic prediction of
   cancers using gene expression profiling and artificial neural networks. Nat. Med.
   7(6), 673–679 (2001)
9. Kubitza, D.O., Böckmann, M., Graux, D.: SemanGit: a linked dataset from `git`.
   In: Ghidini, C., Hartig, O., Maleshkova, M., Svátek, V., Cruz, I., Hogan, A., Song,
   J., Lefrançois, M., Gandon, F. (eds.) ISWC 2019. LNCS, vol. 11779, pp. 215–228.
   Springer, Cham (2019). https://doi.org/10.1007/978-3-030-30796-7_14
10. Marx, E., Soru, T., Baron, C., Coelho, S.A.: KBox: distributing ready-to-query
    RDF knowledge graphs. In: Blomqvist, E., Hose, K., Paulheim, H., Ławrynowicz,
    A., Ciravegna, F., Hartig, O. (eds.) ESWC 2017. LNCS, vol. 10577, pp. 54–58.
    Springer, Cham (2017). https://doi.org/10.1007/978-3-319-70407-4_11
11. Mitchell, M., Wu, S., Zaldivar, A., et al.: Model cards for model reporting. In:
    Proceedings of the FAT 2019, pp. 220–229 (2019)
12. Musen, M.A.: The Protégé project: a look back and a look forward. AI Matters
    1(4), 4–12 (2015)
13. Nguyen, A., Weller, T.: FAIRnets search - a prototype search service to find neural
    networks. In: Proceedings of SEMANTICS 2019, vol. 2451 (2019)
14. Palocsay, S.W., Wang, P., Brookshire, R.G.: Predicting criminal recidivism using
    neural networks. Socio Econ. Plan. Sci. **34**(4), 271–284 (2000)

15. Pinto, H.S., Martins, J.P.: Reusing ontologies. AAAI Technical report SS-00-03, pp. 77–84 (2000)
16. Qi, S., Jin, K., Li, B., et al.: The exploration of internet finance by using neural network. J. Comput. Appl. Math. **369**, 112630 (2020)
17. Schwabe, D.: Trust and privacy in knowledge graphs. In: Proceedings of WWW 2019, pp. 722–728 (2019)
18. Silva, V.D.S., Freitas, A., Handschuh, S.: On the semantic interpretability of artificial intelligence models. CoRR abs/1907.04105 (2019)
19. Wang, X., He, X., Cao, Y., et al.: KGAT: knowledge graph attention network for recommendation. In: Proceedings of KDD 2019, pp. 950–958 (2019)
20. Wang, X., Wang, D., Xu, C., et al.: Explainable reasoning over knowledge graphs for recommendation. In: Proceedings of AAAI 2019, pp. 5329–5336 (2019)
21. Wilkinson, M.D., Dumontier, M., Aalbersberg, I.J., et al.: The FAIR guiding principles for scientific data management and stewardship. Sci. Data **3**, 1–9 (2016)
22. Wise, J., de Barron, A.G., Splendiani, A., et al.: Implementation and relevance of FAIR data principles in biopharmaceutical R&D. Drug Discov. Today **24**(4), 933–938 (2019)
23. Xian, Y., Fu, Z., Muthukrishnan, S., et al.: Reinforcement knowledge graph reasoning for explainable recommendation. In: Proceedings of SIGIR 2019, pp. 285–294 (2019)

Creating Annotations for Web Ontology Language Ontology Generated from Relational Databases

Matthew Wagner🄳 and Dalia Varanka$^{(\boxtimes)}$🄳

U.S. Geological Survey, Rolla, MO 65401, USA
matthewwagner57@gmail.com, dvaranka@usgs.gov

Abstract. Many approaches that have been proposed that allow users to create a Web Ontology Language (OWL) ontology from a relational database fail to include metadata that are inherent to the database tables. Without metadata, the resulting ontology lacks annotation properties. These properties are key when performing ontology alignment. This paper proposes a method to include relevant metadata through annotation properties to OWL ontologies, which furthers the ability to integrate and use data from multiple unique ontologies. The described method is applied to geospatial data collected from The National Map, a data source hosted by the U. S. Geological Survey. Following that method, an ontology was manually created that used the metadata from The National Map. Because a manual approach is prone to human error, an automated approach to storing and converting metadata into annotation properties is discussed.

Keywords: Semantic Web · OWL ontology · Geographic information systems (GIS) · Geospatial data · Metadata

1 Introduction

The next generation of the World Wide Web, named the Semantic Web, focuses on increasing the accessibility and readability of data for machines. The Semantic Web uses concepts and data standards, such as Resource Description Framework (RDF) and Web Ontology Language (OWL) to accomplish that goal. By following Semantic Web guidelines and practices, data from multiple different sources can be accessed, leveraged, and integrated for any application. The research documented in this paper explores the process of adding annotation properties to an OWL ontology generated from a preexisting relational database.

The U.S. Geological Survey (USGS) publishes free geospatial data that cover the United States. Data are published in layers, each referring to a specific geospatial feature set. These data layers include structures, transportation, hydrography, geographic names, boundaries, elevation, land cover, and orthographic images. Whereas the USGS generates some data, a significant portion is

B. Villazón-Terrazas et al. (Eds.): KGSWC 2020, CCIS 1232, pp. 45–60, 2020.
https://doi.org/10.1007/978-3-030-65384-2_4

collected from third-party sources including individual States, the U.S. Census Bureau, and other organizations. The USGS collects these data, standardizes them, and publishes the data as a single dataset. This process results in a major challenge since the data are not USGS created. In some cases, constraints are imposed by the standards of the collecting agencies. Thus, the USGS acts as a data steward and publisher for data acquired from a variety of different sources.

The data published by the USGS provide an opportunity to bring a large-scale data source to the Semantic Web. Multiple other data sources such as Wikidata, DBPedia, and Geonames.org have brought geospatial data to the Semantic Web [3,5,24]; however, this work examines a process to align data with Semantic Web standards, unlike other data sources in which data are directly in the RDF format.

Various research projects have proposed techniques and workflows that generate an OWL ontology and convert data contained in a relational database into RDF. A major problem with past approaches is the lack of useful annotation properties in an OWL ontology. An annotation property is a property that has a data literal, URI reference, or an individual as the object [15]. These properties fully define entities in an ontology such as classes, properties, datatypes, and even the ontology itself. By adding information to these entities, users can determine the relationships among them. Five different annotation properties are predefined by OWL: owl:versionInfo, rdfs:label, rdfs:comment, rdfs:seeAlso, and rdfs:isDefinedBy. This basic information allows classes, properties, and instances to be compared and contrasted resulting in ontology alignment. Ontology alignment is an important feature of OWL ontologies since they are rarely uniform. The Semantic Web encourages users to build ontologies to fit their needs, resulting in the lack of a complete standard for ontologies to exist. Unique classes, properties, and instances from different ontologies must be linked if their data are going to be used together. Annotation properties provide one method for doing so.

Since the Semantic Web is designed with machines in mind, this problem needs to be examined from a machine perspective. A machine would only be able to use the data at hand to match instances. Common data properties for geospatial data include human readable names and coordinate information. Both Wikidata and DBpedia use the widely accepted rdfs:label[1] datatype property to describe entities. However, the GeoNames ontology uses the geonames:name[2] annotation property. The issue for a machine is not comparing the data from those two properties, but rather knowing which two properties to compare. Since the same attribute exists in both Wikidata and DBpedia, a machine would have no problem finding similarities on an instance level for these two data stores. With the introduction of the GeoNames' ontology, a problem arises. For datatype properties, the machine could use annotation properties to draw a comparison between two or more instances. Common properties such as rdfs:comment, rdfs:range, and rdfs:seeAlso can be used to look for similarities. However, the

---

[1] The rdfs namespace is http://www.w3.org/2000/01/rdf-schema#.

[2] The geonames namespace is http://www.geonames.org/ontology#.

geonames:name property only possesses the rdfs:domain field, something entirely dependent on the ontology of Geonames. Thus, a machine would be unable to make any real comparison this way and would be forced to compare the instances of each datatype property to align any instances.

A similar situation occurs if the machine examines the description of an object in the form of a geometry. These geometries take the form of a point, polyline, and polygon. In all three data stores, geometries are represented with coordinate points of latitude and longitude. GeoNames and DBpedia uses geo:lat and geo:long[3] whereas Wikidata uses custom datatype properties wikibase:geoLatitude[4] and wikibase:geoLongitude. The geo:lat and geo:long datatype properties have annotations such as rdfs:domain, rdfs:label, and rdfs:comment. The wikibase:geoLatitude and wikibase:geoLongitude have an rdfs:label, rdfs:comment, rdfs:domain, and rdfs:range. Plain text comparison of both sets of rdfs:label and rdfs:comment would be able to provide some links for a machine. However, the lack of an rdfs:range annotation for the geo namespace becomes a hurdle since coordinates can be represented in a variety of formats. The machine would have to again rely on comparing the instances to affirm the contents rather than being able to draw this link from the ontology alone.

A machine needs to accurately analyze datatype and object properties to align different ontologies. Whereas some annotation properties are present, many ontologies lack complete descriptions. Many authors have previously proposed methods for converting relational databases to OWL ontologies. However, a method for converting metadata to annotation properties and adding these to OWL ontology has not been proposed. Without annotation properties to fully define entities within an OWL ontology, Semantic Web data sources will struggle to be used in conjunction with other data sources.

Section 2 of this paper presents background information on the research area being presented. Section 3 discusses past proposed solutions to converting relational database to Semantic Web formats and cases that are inadequate. In Sect. 4, the approach used to manually create an OWL ontology for USGS data is presented. Section 5 presents the resulting ontology created after applying the proposed approach. Challenges faced and the verification of the ontology are also discussed. Section 6 discusses the proposed approach and potential automated conversion solutions. Lastly, in Sect. 7, conclusions from this work are presented.

2   Background

An OWL ontology is a formal method to describe the taxonomy and relationships that exist within data. It consists of classes, properties, and datatypes, and instances that are comparable to the table and key structure for a relational database and instance data that are comparable to individual records. When converting a relational database to an OWL ontology, the structure of the

---

[3] The geo namespace is http://www.w3.org/2003/01/geo/wgs84_pos#.

[4] The wikibase namespace is http://wikiba.se/ontology#.

database is stored in an OWL ontology whereas the data records are converted into instances.

Classes are an abstract method for grouping instances with similar characteristics. This grouping is the same as a table in a relational database. All of the records in the table have similar attributes, with some characteristics being common among them. Labeling an instance with a class in an OWL ontology allows that instance to inherit the attributes and additional properties of that class. In a relational database, the records in a table are constrained by any overriding rules of that table. This results in those records inheriting the rules of the table.

Properties for OWL ontologies consist of three types: object properties, data properties, and annotation properties. Object properties define relationships between objects, each with a unique Universal Resource Identifier (URI). These properties are comparable to foreign keys in a relational database. For example, geo:hasGeometry is an object property that connects a geographic feature (the subject) to an object describing its coordinate representation (the object). Data properties define relationships between objects and literals. Literal data, which are classified using datatypes, are the plain text data that connect additional information to an object. In a relational database, literal data are the data that are not foreign keys attached to an individual record. A popular example of a data property is geo:asWKT, which links a geometry object (the subject) to a geo:wktLiteral representation of the geometry (the object). Annotation properties are akin to the metadata within a relational database. They describe the restrictions placed on attributes and allow users to understand the contents of that attribute. For example, rdfs:label links a URI (the object) to a human-readable label describing the entity (the subject).

Instance level semantics are the overwhelming majority of links between ontologies [10]. They generally take the form of object properties, such as owl:sameAs. The owl:sameAs relationship indicates that the two instances it links refer to the same thing. Whereas the owl:sameAs relationship is an effective method for drawing connections between instance data, two issues currently exist. First, these relationships must be determined ahead of time and the triples must be stored. Typically, this process is done manually by experts with in-depth knowledge on those ontologies. Secondly, some authors argue that owl:sameAs is often inaccurate when comparing instances [8].

Ontology alignment examines the different ontologies and determines relationships between classes and properties. With these relationships present, direct comparisons of the instance-level data can be performed using string comparisons to determine instance-level relationships. Properties used in ontology alignment can bring in relevant information without needing to state the exact relationship between the instance. This on-the-fly process can avoid the argument about the semantics of such relationships and remove the need to manually link ontologies. However, to perform this task, annotation properties must be defined and used to provide enough depth of information for different ontologies to be aligned successfully. With this background information, previous research in this area is discussed in the next section.

3   Related Work

Significant research has examined approaches to convert a relational database to the Semantic Web standards. Proposed methods to convert a relational database to an OWL ontology include [1,9,12,18]. Each of these references suggests slight variations to achieve similar results. Li et al. [12] proposed a set of 12 rules that were grouped into five categories: rules for learning classes, rules for learning properties and property characteristics with rules for learning hierarchy, cardinality, and instances.

Similarly, Sequeda et al. [18] present a solution to mapping relational databases to RDF that focuses on maintaining information preservation and query preservation during their conversion process. Information preservation refers to the ability to recreate the relational database from the OWL ontology after the mapping process has occurred. Query preservation is the notion that every query that can be performed on the relational database can be translated into an equivalent query on the data post mapping to OWL.

Hu et al. [9] propose an approach to discovering simple mappings between a relational database schema and an ontology. The authors construct a special type of semantic mapping called a contextual mapping, which holds the subsumption relationships existing within the relational database.

The most intuitive of these approaches is one proposed by Astrova et al. [1] for automatic transformation of relational databases to ontologies in which the quality of the transformation is also considered. They created a set of rules for mapping tables, columns, datatypes, constraints, and rows.

The major drawback of these previous approaches is that annotation properties are not discussed. Without annotation properties, the OWL ontologies created by the proposed approaches suffer from the drawbacks discussed in Sect. 1 and Sect. 2.

Other work examined the inverse relationship; converting an OWL ontology to a relational schema. Gali et al. [4] present a set of techniques to provide a lossless mapping of an OWL ontology to a relational schema and the corresponding instances to data. They presented a set of mapping rules for converting an OWL ontology to a relational schema. Similar to the approaches that developed mappings from a relational database to an OWL ontology, the work does not discuss annotation properties.

4   Approach

The Protege tool was used to manually create an OWL ontology for USGS The National Map (TNM) data [14]. Data dictionaries describing the metadata properties of different layers were referenced to build the OWL ontology. These references are not downloaded or incorporated with the datastores. Instead, the USGS is in the process of building a specifications library, SpecX, to store detailed data dictionaries about the USGS products [23]. The Domestic Geographic Names layer was added to the ontology even though its data dictionaries are not currently available in SpecX. Instead, the file format for the data can be accessed online [22].

Data from the USGS TNM is downloaded in datasets that consist of multiple layers grouped. For example, the Transportation dataset contains layers including trails, roads, railways, and airways. In each dataset, each layer is stored as a table. Since all data are downloaded from TNM, a class called topo:TNM[5] was created with two subclasses: topo:Attribute and topo:Feature. Topo:Attribute refers to data belonging to static tables in the database. These include tables containing feature names, feature codes, resolution types, and more. This is separate from the topo:Feature class since the data are referenced across different datasets and layers. By making these static tables a set of static classes, redundant information regarding each instance of these classes can be removed and replaced with object properties referring to these classes, reducing data storage requirements.

Topo:Feature refers to the dynamic tables in the database that contain instance data. The topo:Feature was made equivalent to the geosparql:Feature class. GeoSPARQL was used to leverage preexisting query capabilities that exceed SPARQL, the current standard for performing queries on Semantic Web compliant data [16]. GeoSPARQL is the Open Geospatial Consortium standard for representing and querying geospatial data in the Semantic Web. It adds additional query capabilities that allow users to perform comparisons between geometries. This added equivalence relationship allows the ontology created in this work to leverage the feature geometry relationship and the set of geometry properties, including geosparql:asWKT and geosparql:asGML. This relationship removed the need to create custom definitions of the attributes. It also increased the set of operations that can be performed on the ontology by users.

4.1 Creating Class

The following rules were used to generate classes for the OWL ontology.

- Each database will have its own class. The database's class will be a subclass of topo:Feature.
- Each dynamic table in the database will have its own class. This class will be a subclass of the class for its database.
- Each class referring to a dynamic table belonging to the same database is disjoint from all other classes referring to a dynamic table in the same database.
- Each static table will have its own class. This class will be a subclass of topo:Attribute. Static tables shared across multiple databases shall not be duplicated.

---

[5] TNM is a spatial data infrastructure for topographic data. The namespace http://data.usgs.gov/lod/topo/ was used for the ontology describing TNM data.

- Each class representing a static table will be disjoint from all other subclasses of topo:Attribute.
- Each record in a static table will have its own class. This class will be a subclass of the class for its table.
- Each record in a static table will be disjoint from all other classes resulting from records in the same static table.

The tables in the Structures data dictionary is split into four categories: Feature Classes, NonSpatial Tables, Feature Code (FCode) Domains, and Non-FCode Domains. The Feature Class tables are dynamic and contain instance data. The NonSpatial Tables contain data that refer to the internal workflows used to publish the data. They are purposely excluded from this work since that information, whereas important, cannot be linked easily to other ontologies. Both the FCode and NonFCode categories refer to sets of static tables. FCode tables are used to explicitly label geographic features.

4.2   Creating Object Properties

The following rules are implemented to generate object properties. The major difference between an object property and a data property is the link to another class. In TNM data, a large volume of data are located in a static table. Thus, object properties are leveraged to decrease the number of instances of that information, overall decreasing the space required to store all the data.

- If an attribute in a table links to another table, that is, it is a foreign key, then it is an object property. In SpecX, this can be seen as the existence of a value in the Domain field. The FCode and FType fields are also considered object properties regardless of the lack of data in the domain field.
- The class representing the table that contains the foreign key becomes the object property's domain.
- The class representing the table to which the foreign key links becomes the object property's range.
- If the foreign key exists in multiple tables, the domain of the object property is the union of those tables.
- If the foreign key has a one-to-one relationship, the object property is a functional property.

The rdfs:subPropertyOf relationship was leveraged to reduce the size of the ontology.

4.3   Creating Data Properties

The following rules are implemented to generate data properties. These properties contain the bulk of the data published by the USGS TNM.

- If an attribute does not link to another table, then it is a data property. In the SpecX database, this means that the domain field is blank.

- The table that contains the attribute becomes the data property's domain.
- The data type of the attribute becomes the data property's range.
- Any unique datatypes that are not defined in geosparql, xsd, rdf, or rdfs become a unique data type.
- If the attribute exists in multiple tables, the domain of the data property is the union of those tables.
- If the attribute has a one-to-one relationship, the data property is a functional property.

Only one unique datatype, topo:objectID, was created for the TNM ontology. The rest of the datatypes were mapped to preexisting datatypes in the rdfs ontology.

4.4 Creating Annotation

While changes were added to previous approaches to create classes, object properties, and data properties, creating annotation properties is an entirely new aspect.

- Any description of the table located in the data dictionary becomes an rdfs:comment for the class representing that table.
- Any metadata attribute located in the data dictionary description become an annotation property.
- The description of the metadata attribute becomes an rdfs:comment of the annotation property.
- The datatype for the metadata attribute becomes the range of that annotation property.
- Any metadata attribute located in the data dictionary description for an attribute becomes an annotation property for that class, object property, or data property.
- If attributes contain different metadata, they must be considered different, unique properties and labeled accordingly.

The results of applying these rules can be seen in the example RDF/XML shown below generated by Protege from applying the rules to create annotation properties.

```
<owl:AnnotationProperty rdf:about="http://data.usgs.gov/lod/topo/description">
    <rdfs:comment>Description of a property.</rdfs:comment>
    <rdfs:range rdf:resource="http://www.w3.org/2001/XMLSchema#string"/>
</owl:AnnotationProperty>
<owl:Class rdf:about="http://data.usgs.gov/lod/topo/Structure/Struct_Point">
    <rdfs:subClassOf rdf:resource="http://data.usgs.gov/lod/topo/Structure"/>
    <rdfs:comment>A feature class representing the location of a building or
        other structure as a point.</rdfs:comment>
</owl:Class>
<rdf:Description rdf:about="http://data.usgs.gov/lod/topo/objectID">
    <comments></comments>
    <default_Value></default_Value>
    <definition>Internal feature or event number.</definition>
    <precision></precision>
    <allows_Nulls rdf:datatype="http://www.w3.org/2001/XMLSchema#boolean">
        false</allows_Nulls>
    <length></length>
</rdf:Description>
```

4.5 Creating Geometries

Geometries are unique geospatial data. When coupled with GeoSPARQL, geometries allow users to find unique relationships among instances that otherwise would not exist.

– The geometry field for all tables is not converted to a data property or object property. Instead, it is converted to a geosparql:Geometry.

Since this paper does not cover converting instance data in depth, example geometry data are not included.

4.6 URI Naming Conventions

Due to the size of the datasets published in the USGS TNM, a formal naming convention was created. For classes representing a dataset or attribute table, the name of the table was appended to the namespace for the TNM ontology. For the classes representing dynamic tables, the name of the table was appended to the URI of the class representing the dataset of which it is a part. Similarly, for the content of the static table, the name of the record is appended to the class representing the table in which it is contained. For object properties, data properties, annotation properties, and datatype properties the name of the attribute was appended to the URI for the namespace. The only exception to the rule is properties incorporated from the Geographic Names dataset. Instead, those were appended to the URI for the class representing the Geographic Names dataset. The conventions can be seen in Table 1.

Table 1. URI naming conventions for TNM ontology

Entity	Convention
Dataset classes Static table classes Object properties Data properties Annotation properties Datatype properties	Topo namespace + **Entity name**
Dynamic table classes Static tables contents	Topo namespace + **Dataset name** + "/" + **Entity name**
All geographic name entities	topo namespace + "GNIS/" + **Entity name**

5 Results

The resulting metrics produced by the Protege tool can be seen in Table 2 through Table 6. Protege produces five different metric tables for various parts

Table 2. Protege ontology metrics

Metric	Count
Axiom	6682
Logical axioms	2135
Declaration axioms	1241
Classes	909
Object properties	87
Data properties	225
Annotation properties	33

Table 4. Protege ontology object property axioms

Metric	Count
SubObjectPropertyOf	59
EquivalentObjectProperties	0
InverseObjectProperties	4
DisjointObjectProperties	0
FunctionalObjectProperty	43
InverseFunctionalObjectProperty	0
TransitiveObjectProperty	3
SymmetricObjectProperty	4
AsymmetricObjectProperty	0
ReflexiveObjectProperty	0
IrrefexiveObjectProperty	0
ObjectPropertyDomain	74
ObjectPropertyRange	70
SubProprtyChainOf	0

Table 3. Annotation axioms

Metric	Count
AnnotationAssertion	3288
AnnotationPropertyDomain https://www.overleaf.com/project/5f85d900cbe2ca0001b11f7b	0
AnnotationPropertyRagneOf	9

of the ontology including general metrics, class metrics, object property metrics, data property metrics, and annotation metrics. In looking at these results, it is important to note that some entities are added automatically to an ontology created using Protege. Additionally, the GeoSPARQL ontology was imported into the ontology as a result of the approach discussed in Sect. 4. Thus, some of the relationships not mentioned in the approach were inherent within that ontology.

Table 4 and Table 6 both show interesting results in terms of the Disjoint-ObjectProperties and the DisjointDataProperties. Both tables show that none of those relationships were generated during ontology creation. In several of the data layers that were incorporated into the system, there were multiple places where multiple fields for a single entity related to a static type with multiple object properties. A primary example of this phenomenon is the trails layer in the transportation dataset. In this trails layer table, a majority of the attributes tell a user whether a certain mode of transportation is allowed on a trail. All of the fields then link to the TrailYesNoDomain. Thus, these relations break the formal definition of DisjointObjectProperty [7]. For the DisjointDataProperty, there is no way to determine if one data instance would be linked to an entity with multiple relationships. This is especially true if multiple data objects share a common DataPropertyRange. Thus, no DisjointDataProperties were added to the system (Tables 3 and 5).

Table 5. Protege ontology class axioms

Metric	Count
SubClassOf Properties	921
Equivalent Classes	1
Disjoint Classes	62
GCI Count	0
Hidden GCI Count	2

Table 6. Data property axioms

Metric	Count
SubDataPropertyOf	219
EquivalentDataProperties	0
DisjointDataProperties	0
FunctionalDataProperty	211
DataPropertyDomain	229
DatatPropertyRange	235

5.1   Challenges

When manually creating this ontology, two major challenges were faced. The first challenge to create an OWL ontology from preexisting data is the reuse of attribute labels. Across all datasets published by the USGS, attribute names are shared whereas their meaning and attached metadata are changed. One primary example is the use of the attribute "Name". Working exclusively with the five layers mentioned earlier, twelve different sets of metadata were associated with this attribute. These attributes have a variety of different definitions, field lengths, and some nullable values. Whereas some may consider generalizing the attribute metadata and associating all of these with the same data property in an OWL ontology, that would be a mistake. Each attribute fundamentally has a different definition and could be referring to semantically different things. Manually expanding the ontology, careful attention was paid to ensure all unique pairings of attribute names and metadata were found. A unique entity was created for each pairing. However, this resulted in the second major challenge—naming conventions.

Whereas all of these unique pairings have the same attribute name, each pairing must result in a unique URI. This resulted in the creation of a custom naming convention. For naming these attributes, a combination of the namespace and the metadata difference was used. A shorthand for the table containing the unique pairing was appended if the only major difference between pairings is the description metadata field. Otherwise, the different metadata attribute was appended to the original attribute.

5.2   Validation

The plugin OntoDebug was used to validate the formal logic contained within the OWL ontology [17]. This plugin uses the preexisting reasoners to determine whether the ontology is coherent and consistent. For an ontology to be coherent, all classes must be satisfiable. For an ontology to be consistent, one of its classes must be satisfiable.

To validate the logic contained within the ontology, three different reasoners were used: Pellet, ELK, and HermiT.

Pellet is a popular reasoner created to support OWL Description Logic (OWL-DL) [19]. It is implemented in Java and is free to download as a plugin for the Protege tool. Version 2.2.0 was used within this work. When OntoDebug is run with the Pellet reasoner on the created ontology, it is both coherent and consistent.

ELK is another reasoner available for use through the Protege tool [11]. Version 0.4.3 was used in this work. Although efficient, it does not support a significant number of axioms including DataPropertyRange, ObjectPropertyRange, FunctionalDataProperty, SubDataPropertyOf, and more. With the axioms it does support, ELK produces coherent and consistent results when run on the generated ontology.

HermiT version 1.4.3 is the reasoner shipped with the installation of Protege [6]. This was the only reasoner out of the three that produced an error. However, this error was the result of a restriction on the set of acceptable datatypes allowed in the reasoner. The reasoner only allows datatypes of the OWL 2 datatype map. The xsd:date and topo:objectID datatypes both resulted in errors since they are not present in the standard. A test version of the ontology without either of these datatypes was created and validated using this reasoner. HermiT produced a coherent and consistent validation result.

6   Discussion

The only requirement for applying the manual approach proposed in this work is the existence of metadata information for the database. For the USGS, these are currently presented in the SpecX database and previously described using large data model posters [21]. The proposed rules could be used to create an OWL ontology for all datasets from the USGS. Furthermore, it could be extended to any database outside of the USGS as long as metadata exists. Without the metadata, the created ontology would match previously proposed approaches.

Applying the approach manually is time consuming. The human error involved in the process required multiple rounds of revisions to ensure that all the proposed rules were followed correctly for the example OWL ontology created. To overcome this challenge, an automated approach to generating the metadata needs to be created. A significant amount of research has been done that proposed automated approaches for generating OWL ontologies from relational databases [2,13,20,25].

Cullot et al. presented a tool called DB2OWL that automatically generates ontologies from database schemas [2]. They break the mapping process into six steps that cover mapping classes, subclasses, object properties, and datatype properties. Additionally, they include how additional relationships such as inverse, domain, and range are determined. In [20], Trinh et al. propose RDB2ONT, a tool that describes a formal algorithm to use relational database metadata and structural constraints to construct an OWL ontology preserving the structural constraints of the underlying relational database system. A tool called Ontology Automatic Generation System based on Relational Database (OGSRD) was proposed in [25] as a method for automatic ontology building using the relational database resources. Lastly, Mogotlane & Fonou-Dombeu

[13] performed a study applying two different tools, DataMaster and OntoBase, that automatically construct ontologies from a relational database. Definitions of a class, object properties, datatype property, and instances are given. Nine different rules are drawn from previous work to map a relational database to an OWL ontology.

All of these works present methods to correctly create OWL ontologies that avoid the time-consuming and error-prone process of manually creating them. However, all of the reviewed works fail to discuss the implementation of annotation properties. One possible reason for this is the lack of metadata for the databases used. The existence of metadata describing the data model is often known and maintained by the data provider; however, these metadata generally are not attached to the database. Whereas this does not present a challenge for manual approaches, it does for automated approaches. The previous approaches look exclusively at the relational database and its structure. Requiring the process to examine a website, such as SpecX, and get the requisite information provides its own challenges.

One potential solution to overcoming this challenge is to create metadata tables as part of a relational database. These tables would contain all metadata information for the classes, data property, object properties, and even annotation properties. Rather than creating a new approach, this could leverage the technology already in use in these relational database systems. Additionally, this extension could be added to previously proposed automated ontology creation approaches. Example metadata tables are shown in Fig. 1.

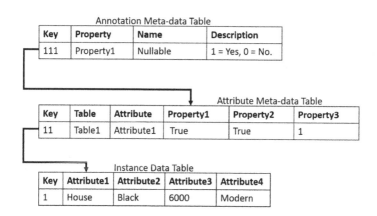

Annotation Meta-data Table

Key	Property	Name	Description
111	Property1	Nullable	1 = Yes, 0 = No.

Attribute Meta-data Table

Key	Table	Attribute	Property1	Property2	Property3
11	Table1	Attribute1	True	True	1

Instance Data Table

Key	Attribute1	Attribute2	Attribute3	Attribute4
1	House	Black	6000	Modern

Fig. 1. Example automated metadata database

In Fig. 1, there are three tables: instance data, attribute metadata, and annotation metadata. Attributes refer to the columns in the instance data table and are converted to object and data properties based on the approach used in this work. Annotations refer to the annotation properties used to describe the attribute metadata. This second level of annotations is important to describe custom metadata used in a system. Many of the properties for the USGS TNM datasets can be seen in the SpecX database including name, definition, type, allow nulls, domain, default value, comments, and many more. Whereas some of these annotations may seem intuitive, fields such as precision and length which are generated by third-party software are not. Thus, exact definitions need to be provided to allow for accurate comparisons of classes and properties between ontologies.

7   Conclusion

This work highlights the need for annotation properties to properly align and use instance data from different ontologies. Additional rules to create an OWL ontology directly from a relational database that addresses the need for these properties is proposed. An ontology was manually created using the Protege tool to show the results of implementing the proposed approach. It incorporated multiple different datasets and data layers produced by the USGS TNM. The ontology excluded instance data due to the size of the datasets. Furthermore, the OntoDebug plugin was used to validate the formal logic present within the OWL ontology. The results from three different reasoners prove that the formal logic in the results of the proposed approach is coherent and consistent.

An automated solution for storing metadata attributes within the database with the instance data was introduced, which addresses the inherent issues of a manual approach. If metadata attributes are stored within the database, they could be converted to annotation properties. This approach could serve as an extension to previously created solutions instead of requiring new solutions to be generated. However, the actual creation of this automated tool is left to future research.

Any use of trade, firm, or product names is for descriptive purposes only and does not imply endorsement by the U.S. Government.

References

1. Astrova, I.: Rules for mapping SQL relational databases to OWL ontologies. In: Sicilia, M.A., Lytras, M.D. (eds.) Metadata and Semantics, pp. 415–424. Springer, Boston (2007). https://doi.org/10.1007/978-0-387-77745-0_40
2. Cullot, N., Ghawi, R., Yétongnon, K.: DB2OWL: a tool for automatic database-to-ontology mapping. SEBD **7**, 491–494 (2007)
3. DBpedia (2020). https://wiki.dbpedia.org/. Accessed July 2020
4. Gali, A., Chen, C.X., Claypool, K.T., Uceda-Sosa, R.: From ontology to relational databases. In: Wang, S., et al. (eds.) ER 2004. LNCS, vol. 3289, pp. 278–289. Springer, Heidelberg (2004). https://doi.org/10.1007/978-3-540-30466-1_26
5. GeoNames: Geonames ontology (2019). http://www.geonames.org/ontology/documentation.html. Accessed July 2020
6. Glimm, B., Horrocks, I., Motik, B., Stoilos, G., Wang, Z.: HermiT: an OWL 2 reasoner. J. Autom. Reasoning **53**(3), 245–269 (2014). https://doi.org/10.1007/s10817-014-9305-1

7. Golbreich, C., Wallace, E.K., Patel-Schneider, P.F.: Owl 2 web ontology language new features and rationale. W3C working draft, W3C (2009). http://www.w3.org/TR/2009/WD-owl2-new-features-20090611
8. Halpin, H., Hayes, P.J.: When owl:sameAs isn't the same: an analysis of identity links on the semantic web. In: LDOW (2010)
9. Hu, W., Qu, Y.: Discovering simple mappings between relational database schemas and ontologies. In: Aberer, K., et al. (eds.) ASWC/ISWC -2007. LNCS, vol. 4825, pp. 225–238. Springer, Heidelberg (2007). https://doi.org/10.1007/978-3-540-76298-0_17
10. Jain, P., Hitzler, P., Sheth, A.P., Verma, K., Yeh, P.Z.: Ontology alignment for linked open data. In: Patel-Schneider, P.F., et al. (eds.) ISWC 2010. LNCS, vol. 6496, pp. 402–417. Springer, Heidelberg (2010). https://doi.org/10.1007/978-3-642-17746-0_26
11. Kazakov, Y.: Elk (2016). https://protegewiki.stanford.edu/wiki/ELK. Accessed July 2020
12. Li, M., Du, X.Y., Wang, S.: Learning ontology from relational database. In: 2005 International Conference on Machine Learning and Cybernetics. IEEE (2005). https://doi.org/10.1109/icmlc.2005.1527531
13. Mogotlane, K.D., Fonou-Dombeu, J.V.: Automatic conversion of relational databases into ontologies: a comparative analysis of protege plug-ins performances. Int. J. Web Semant. Technol. **7**(3/4), 21–40 (2016). https://doi.org/10.5121/ijwest.2016.7403
14. Noy, N., Sintek, M., Decker, S., Crubezy, M., Fergerson, R., Musen, M.: Creating semantic web contents with protege-2000. IEEE Intell. Syst. **16**(2), 60–71 (2001). https://doi.org/10.1109/5254.920601
15. Parsia, B., Patel-Schneider, P., Motik, B.: Owl 2 web ontology language structural specification and functional-style syntax. W3C, W3C Recommendation (2012)
16. Perry, M., Herring, J.: GeoSPARQL - a geographic query language for RDF data. Open Geospatial Consortium (2012). https://www.ogc.org/standards/geosparql
17. Schekotihin, K., Rodler, P., Schmid, W.: OntoDebug: interactive ontology debugging plug-in for protégé. In: Ferrarotti, F., Woltran, S. (eds.) Foundations of Information and Knowledge Systems. Lecture Notes in Computer Science, vol. 10833, pp. 340–359. Springer, Cham (2018). https://doi.org/10.1007/978-3-319-90050-6_19
18. Sequeda, J.F., Arenas, M., Miranker, D.P.: On directly mapping relational databases to RDF and OWL. In: Proceedings of the 21st International Conference on World Wide Web - WWW 2012. ACM Press (2012). https://doi.org/10.1145/2187836.2187924
19. Sirin, E., Parsia, B., Grau, B.C., Kalyanpur, A., Katz, Y.: Pellet: a practical OWL-DL reasoner. SSRN Electron. J. (2007). https://doi.org/10.2139/ssrn.3199351
20. Trinh, Q., Barker, K., Alhajj, R.: RDB2ONT: a tool for generating OWL ontologies from relational database systems. In: Advanced International Conference on Telecommunications and International Conference on Internet and Web Applications and Services (AICT-ICIW 2006). IEEE (2006). https://doi.org/10.1109/aict-iciw.2006.159
21. U. S. Geological Survey: The Best Practices Data Model-Governmental Units (2006). https://services.nationalmap.gov/bestpractices/model/acrodocs/Poster_BPGovtUnits_03_01_2006.pdf. Accessed July 2020
22. U. S. Geological Survey: File Format for Domestic Geographic Names (2020). https://geonames.usgs.gov/docs/pubs/Nat_State_Topic_File_formats.pdf. Accessed July 2020

23. U. S. Geological Survey: Spec-X - Making Information Accessible (2020). https://usgs-mrs.cr.usgs.gov/SPECX/treeview/index. Accessed July 2020
24. Wikidata (2020). https://www.wikidata.org/wiki/Wikidata:Main_Page. Accessed July 2020
25. Zhang, L., Li, J.: Automatic generation of ontology based on database. J. Comput. Inf. Syst. **7**(4), 1148–1154 (2011)

Malware Detection Using Machine Learning

Ajay Kumar[1], Kumar Abhishek[1]([⊠]), Kunjal Shah[2], Divy Patel[2], Yash Jain[2], Harsh Chheda[2], and Pranav Nerurkar[2,3]

[1] NIT Patna, Patna, India
{ajayk.phd18.cs,kumar.abhishek.cse}@nitp.ac.in
[2] Veermata Jijabai Technological Institute, Matunga, Mumbai, India
{kshah_b18,panerurkar_p17}@ce.vjti.ac.in,
{dspatel_b17,ysjain_b17,hkchheda_b17}@it.vjti.ac.in
[3] NMIMS Mumbai, Mumbai, India
pranav.n@nmims.edu

Abstract. Decision making using Machine Learning can be efficiently applied to security. Malware has become a big risk in today's times. In order to provide protection for the same, we present a machine-learning based technique for predicting Windows PE files as benign or malignant based on fifty-seven of their attributes. We have used the Brazilian Malware dataset, which had around 1,00,000 samples and 57 labels. We have made seven models, and have achieved 99.7% accuracy for the Random Forest model, which is very high when compared to other existing systems. Thus using the Random Forest model one can make a decision on whether a particular file is malware or benign.

Keywords: Security · Malware · Machine learning

1 Introduction

Decision making is an important process today in almost all domains. Cyber security is a particular field wherein we need to make decision on files whether they are malware or benign. Malware is malicious software or a program or a script which can be harmful to any instance of computing. These malicious programs are capable of performing multiple tasks, including data theft, encoding, or straight-away deleting sensitive data, modifying or hijacking basic system functionalities, and keeping track of (spying on) the actions performed by humans/human driven software on the computers [7,26]. Malware is the short form for 'malicious software', a technical word for noting some particular computer program or code which undertakes illegal tasks without the owner's permission. In the last decade, the number of newly found malware has risen exponentially. As specified earlier, malware can have disastrous effects on the system if left uncontrolled. Therefore, we should always have a capable protection from

© Springer Nature Switzerland AG 2020
B. Villazón-Terrazas et al. (Eds.): KGSWC 2020, CCIS 1232, pp. 61–71, 2020.
https://doi.org/10.1007/978-3-030-65384-2_5

such malignant programs. Currently we can group prevalent anti-malware mechanisms into three kinds: signature, behaviour and heuristics-based techniques. However, they cannot handle malware whose definitions are not known or the latest, frequently developed post discovery of a zero-day exploit. The number and types of malware are multiplying daily, and a dynamic system is essentially required for the classification of files as "malware" or "benign". As per the statistics published by the Computer Economics 1, the fiscal damage caused by the various malware attacks has risen from 3.3 billion dollar in 1997 to 13.3 billion dollar in 2006. It is a huge jump. The definition of Year of Mega Breach must be manipulated every few years to inculcate protection to the attacks performed in that particular year [2].

The static features of malware when it is not in the running state are: overall characteristics, PE structure characteristics, binary code characteristics, and assembly code characteristics [8,21].

We now converge our discussions to a specific type of file called the PE file, which is usually executed on the Microsoft Windows Operating System. Windows Portable Executable Files (PE files) are those who stand for the main file format for executables that are binary in nature and DLLs under Windows. A PE file comprises DOS Header, PE Header, Section Headers (Section table), and several sections [7]. PE files can be classified as benign or malicious, depending on their nature and attributes [1].

We divide our paper into the following sections: Sect. 2 has a comprehensive literature survey on the existing systems, Sect. 3 describes the dataset, Sect. 4 explains in detail the proposed methodology and Sect. 5 highlights the conclusion.

We have built seven different models and concluded with saying that Random Forest Model has provided the highest accuracy of all. Our model has improved accuracy over several existing systems.

2   Literature Survey

Classifying malware has been of great interest to researchers throughout the world, owing to the blast in demand for cybersecurity. Cybersecurity issues have become national issues [9], and not only machine learning but also blockchain [22], IoT [13], and cloud technologies involving heterogeneous client networks [5,14] have been used for fighting against them. Android [30] requires protection from Malicious PE files can cause data leakage [25] and other dangers to the security level.

Ren and Chen [19] have devised a new graphical analysis technique for researching malware resemblance. This technique converts malignant PE files into local entropy images for observing internal features of malware and then normalizes local entropy images into entropy pixel images for classifying malware. Zhang and Luo [30] have proposed a behaviour based analysis technique based on the method-level correlation relationship of application's abstracted API calls.

Mahmood Yousefi-Azar has shown work quite similar to what we have done. He has put forward a technique that he named 'Malytics' which consists of three parts: extracting features, measuring similarity, and classifying everything. The three parts are presented by a neural network [15] with two hidden layers and one single output layer. The author could achieve an accuracy of 99.45% [28]. Rushabh Vyas has worked on four different types of PE files and has extracted 28 features, packing, imported DLLs and functions from them. He could achieve 98.7% detection rates using machine learning [27]. Erdogan Dogdu has presented a paper wherein a shallow deep learning-based feature extraction method named as word2vec is used to show any given malware based on its opcodes. Classification is done using gradient boost. They have used k-fold cross-validation for validating the model performance without compromising with a validation split. He has successfully achieved an accuracy of ninety-six percent (96%) [3].

Muhammad Ijaz has used two techniques: static and dynamic to extract the features of files. Under static mechanism he could achieve an accuracy of 99.36% (PE files) and under dynamic mechanism he could achieve an accuracy of 94.64% [17]. In static analysis, the executable file is analyzed on structure bases without executing it in controlled environment. In dynamic analysis, malware behavior is analyzed in dynamic controlled environment.

Beyond all this, in the latest technology domain, data fusion models have also been prepared for malware detection [12].

3 Dataset

We have used the Brazilian Malware Dataset [4] for the project. It contained about 1,21,000 rows and 57 columns corresponding to 57 different attributes of PE files. The classes that it had were malicious and benign. Here is a description of the data items given in Table 1. We have shown the column name(which is a characteristic of the PE file), the type of data (numeric or categorical), the number of distinct values in each, and the correlation of each feature with the target.

Table 1. Exploration of data

Column name	Type	Distinct count	Correlation with target
AddressOfEntryPoint	Columnar	23,110	0.072
BaseOfCode	Columnar	385	0.04
BaseOfData	Columnar	1,106	0.101
Characteristics	Columnar	104	0.13
DllCharacteristics	Columnar	74	0.107
ExportNb	Numeric	670	0.4
FileAlignment	Numeric	9	0.103
ImportsNb	Numeric	954	0.27
ImportsNbDLL	Numeric	48	0.252

(*continued*)

Table 1. (*continued*)

Column name	Type	Distinct count	Correlation with target
ImportsNbOrdinal	Numeric	337	0.19
Legitimate Target	Columnar	2	—
LoadConfigurationSize	Numeric	39	0173
LoaderFlags	Columnar	15	0.001
Machine	Columnar	3	0.078
MajorImageVersion	Columnar	38	0.079
MajorLinkerVersion	Columnar	41	0.099
MajorOperatingSystemVersion	Columnar	12	0.103
MajorSubsystemVersion	Columnar	6	0.089
MinorImageVersion	Columnar	70	0.108
MinorLinkerVersion	Columnar	62	0.045
MinorOperatingSystemVersion	Columnar	12	0.043
MinorSubsystemVersion	Columnar	10	0.049
NumberOfRvaAndSizes	Numeric	23	0.004
ResourcesMaxEntropy	Numeric	23,004	0.329
ResourcesMaxSize	Numeric	50	0.313
ResourcesMeanEntropy	Numeric	42,745	0.17
ResourcesMeanSize	Numeric	16,013	0.253
ResourcesMinEntropy	Numeric	17,929	0.361
ResourcesMinSize	Numeric	1,011	0.422
ResourcesNb	Numeric	496	0.396
SectionAlignment	Numeric	12	0.112
SectionMaxRawsize	Numeric	4796	0.186
SectionMaxVirtualsize	Numeric	29,123	0.268
SectionsMaxEntropy	Numeric	49,062	0.35
SectionsMeanEntropy	Numeric	58,807	0.222
SectionsMeanRawsize	Numeric	9,233	0.168
SectionsMeanVirtualsize	Numeric	36,811	0.251
SectionsMinEntropy	Numeric	25,505	0.343
SectionsMinRawsize	Numeric	694	0.376
SectionsMinVirtualsize	Numeric	6,515	0.27
SectionsNb	Numeric	28	0.259
SizeOfCode	Numeric	3,809	0.334
SizeOfHeaders	Numeric	30	0 092
SizeOfHeapCommit	Numeric	21	0.1
SizeOfHeapReserve	Numeric	30	0.101
SizeOfImage	Numeric	2,312	0.289
SizeOfInitializedData	Numeric	3,217	0.288
SizeOfOptionalHeader	Columnar	5	0.078
SizeOfStackCommit	Numeric	40	0 099
SizeOfStackReserve	Numeric	40	0.46
Subsystem	Columnar	4	0.096
VersionInformationSize	Numeric	20	0.473

4   Proposed Methodology

The dataset is first preprocessed, and then important features were selected, the model was trained on the selected features. The entire stages of the process can be shown in the block diagram Fig. 1. Each section can be elegantly described as:

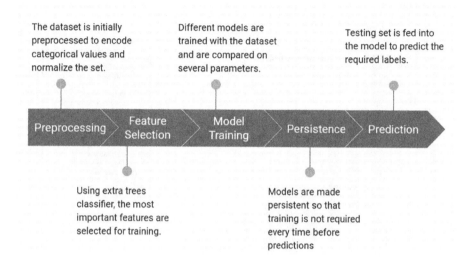

The dataset is initially preprocessed to encode categorical values and normalize the set.

Different models are trained with the dataset and are compared on several parameters.

Testing set is fed into the model to predict the required labels.

Preprocessing   Feature Selection   Model Training   Persistence   Prediction

Using extra trees classifier, the most important features are selected for training.

Models are made persistent so that training is not required every time before predictions

Fig. 1. Overall block diagram

4.1   Preprocessing

From the given PE file, about 56 features were extracted, for example, md5, ImageSize, etc. Some features were categorical, so we applied label encoding [10] followed by one-hot encoding to process those features. Some features were human-readable features like Name, so we manually discarded such features. The two tasks done were:

1. Label Encoding:
   It implies converting the labels to number format for changing it over to the machine-readable form. Machine learning algorithms [6] and calculations would then be able to choose in a superior manner on how those labels must be worked. It is a significant pre-handling step for the organized dataset in supervised learning [11].
2. One-Hot Encoding: It refers to splitting the column containing categorical data to several columns depending on the number of types in that column. Each column has "0" if it is not placed and "1" if it is placed [20] (Fig. 2).

4.2   Feature Section and Model Training

On the pre-processed set of features we applied ExtraTreesClassifier [24] from scikit learn [16] for feature selection. So we selected around 15 features from the set of features and trained our model using those features [29]. We trained several models on the dataset set; we used models provided by scikit learn with slight tweaks. The following Table 2 depicts the accuracies that we could attain for various models:

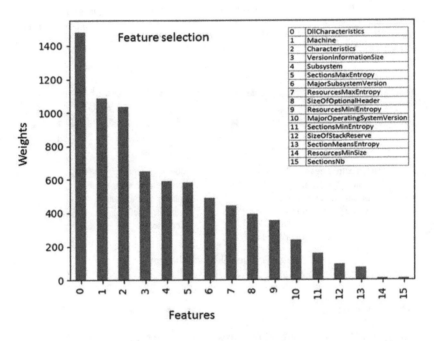

Fig. 2. Weights of top 15 features

Table 2. Accuracies

Key	Model	Accuracy
6	Decision Tree	99.7
1	Random Forest	99.7
4	Gradient Boost	98.48
2	SVM	96.9
0	Logistic Regression	96.8
5	XGBoost	96.7
3	AdaBoost	94.3

We also calculated precision, recall, training times and confusion matrices for the following figures. For the key please refer to Table 2 again (Figs. 3, 4, 5, 6).

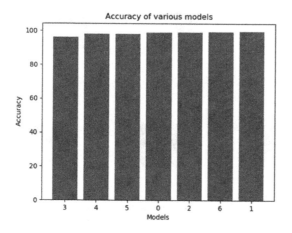

Fig. 3. Accuracies

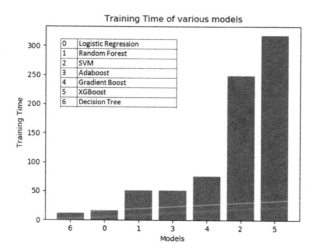

Fig. 4. Training times

In Fig. 7 we show various graphs for the model of Random Forest, for which we have received the highest accuracy. We show how the number of trees affects the training time as well as model accuracy.

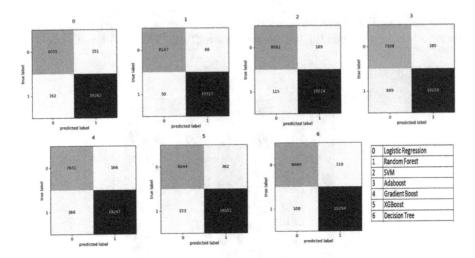

Fig. 5. Confusion matrices

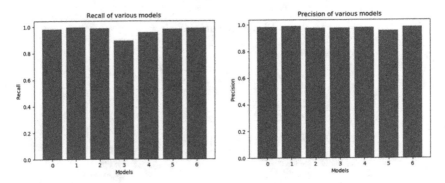

Fig. 6. Precision and Recall

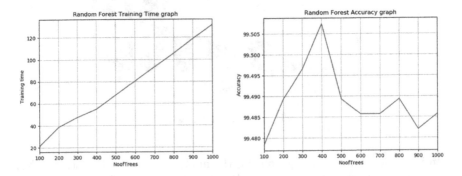

Fig. 7. Graphs for Random Forest

4.3 Persistence and Prediction

The models are made persistent so that training is not required every time before predictions. Persistence is very important for any machine learning model [18,23]. Finally, we feed in the testing set to predict the required labels. The results are compared with existing systems: 99.45% by Yousefi-Azar [28], 98.7% by Vyas [27] and 96% by Meng [3]. We show an accuracy of 99.7%.

5 Conclusion

From our analysis, we can conclude that the RandomForest model can give us the highest possible accuracy on the given dataset. Such machine learning methods can be used efficiently in cybersecurity in order to provide protection against malicious software around. In recent times viruses have become a very significant issue. Traditional protection methods (similar to those signature-based techniques) used by anti-virus will not be able to handle the latest malware issues. In our article, we have looked at malware analysis as an artificial intelligence-based problem. We have used state-of-the-art techniques in coding these models like cross-validation and feature selection. We have used feature selection methods. In the end, we could converge to the conclusion that the RandomForest model can give the highest possible accuracy. This model shows improvement over other systems.

References

1. Abdessadki, I., Lazaar, S.: New classification based model for malicious PE files detection. Int. J. Comput. Netw. Inform. Secur. **11**(6) (2019)
2. Belaoued, M., Mazouzi, S.: A real-time PE-malware detection system based on CHI-square test and PE-file features. In: Amine, A., Bellatreche, L., Elberrichi, Z., Neuhold, E.J., Wrembel, R. (eds.) CIIA 2015. IAICT, vol. 456, pp. 416–425. Springer, Cham (2015). https://doi.org/10.1007/978-3-319-19578-0_34
3. Cakir, B., Dogdu, E.: Malware classification using deep learning methods. In: Proceedings of the ACMSE 2018 Conference, pp. 1–5 (2018)
4. Ceschin, F., Pinage, F., Castilho, M., Menotti, D., Oliveira, L.S., Gregio, A.: The need for speed: an analysis of Brazilian malware classifers. IEEE Secur. Priv. **16**(6), 31–41 (2018)
5. Dey, S., Ye, Q., Sampalli, S.: A machine learning based intrusion detection scheme for data fusion in mobile clouds involving heterogeneous client networks. Inform. Fusion **49**, 205–215 (2019)
6. Gaurav, D., Tiwari, S.M., Goyal, A., Gandhi, N., Abraham, A.: Machine intelligence-based algorithms for spam filtering on document labeling. Soft Comput. **24**(13), 9625–9638 (2020)
7. Gheorghe, L., et al.: Smart malware detection on android. Secur. Commun. Netw. **8**(18), 4254–4272 (2015)
8. Han, W., Xue, J., Wang, Y., Liu, Z., Kong, Z.: MalInsight: a systematic profiling based malware detection framework. J. Netw. Comput. Appl. **125**, 236–250 (2019)
9. Kemmerer, R.A.: Cybersecurity. In: Proceedings of the 25th International Conference on Software Engineering, pp. 705–715. IEEE (2003)

10. Kumar, A., et al.: Multilabel classification of remote sensed satellite imagery. Trans. Emerg. Telecommun. Technol. e3988 (2020)

11. Lazzeri, F., Bruno, G., Nijhof, J., Giorgetti, A., Castoldi, P.: Efficient label encoding in segment-routing enabled optical networks. In: International Conference on Optical Network Design and Modeling (ONDM), pp. 34–38. IEEE (2015)

12. Meng, T., Jing, X., Yan, Z., Pedrycz, W.: A survey on machine learning for data fusion. Inform. Fusion **57**, 115–129 (2020)

13. Mishra, S., Sagban, R., Yakoob, A., Gandhi, N.: Swarm intelligence in anomaly detection systems: an overview. Int. J. Comput. Appl. 1–10 (2018)

14. Nerurkar, P., Chandane, M., Bhirud, S.: Survey of network embedding techniques for social networks. Turkish J. Electr. Eng. Comput. Sci. **27**(6), 4768–4782 (2019)

15. Nerurkar, P.A., Chandane, M., Bhirud, S.: Exploring convolutional auto-encoders for representation learning on networks. Comput. Sci. **20**(3) (2019)

16. Pedregosa, F., et al.: Scikit-learn: machine learning in python. J. Mach. Learn. Res. **12**, 2825–2830 (2011)

17. Raghuraman, C., Suresh, S., Shivshankar, S., Chapaneri, R.: Static and dynamic malware analysis using machine learning. In: Luhach, A.K., Kosa, J.A., Poonia, R.C., Gao, X.-Z., Singh, D. (eds.) First International Conference on Sustainable Technologies for Computational Intelligence. AISC, vol. 1045, pp. 793–806. Springer, Singapore (2020). https://doi.org/10.1007/978-981-15-0029-9_62

18. Rahul, M., Kohli, N., Agarwal, R., Mishra, S.: Facial expression recognition using geometric features and modified hidden Markov model. Int. J. Grid Utility Comput. **10**(5), 488–496 (2019)

19. Ren, Z., Chen, G.: EntropyVis: malware classification. In: 10th International Congress on Image and Signal Processing, BioMedical Engineering and Informatics (CISP-BMEI), pp. 1–6. IEEE (2017)

20. Rodríguez, P., Bautista, M.A., Gonzalez, J., Escalera, S.: Beyond one-hot encoding: lower dimensional target embedding. Image Vision Comput. **75**, 21–31 (2018)

21. Rudd, E.M., Rozsa, A., Günther, M., Boult, T.E.: A survey of stealth malware attacks, mitigation measures, and steps toward autonomous open world solutions. IEEE Commun. Surv. Tutor. **19**(2), 1145–1172 (2016)

22. Sengupta, J., Ruj, S., Bit, S.D.: A comprehensive survey on attacks, security issues and blockchain solutions for iot and iiot. J. Netw. Comput. Appl. **149**, 102481 (2020)

23. Shah, K., Bhandare, D., Bhirud, S.: Face recognition-based automated attendance system. In: Gupta, D., Khanna, A., Bhattacharyya, S., Hassanien, A.E., Anand, S., Jaiswal, A. (eds.) International Conference on Innovative Computing and Communications. AISC, vol. 1165, pp. 945–952. Springer, Singapore (2021). https://doi.org/10.1007/978-981-15-5113-0_79

24. Sharaff, A., Gupta, H.: Extra-tree classifier with metaheuristics approach for email classification. In: Bhatia, S.K., Tiwari, S., Mishra, K.K., Trivedi, M.C. (eds.) Advances in Computer Communication and Computational Sciences. AISC, vol. 924, pp. 189–197. Springer, Singapore (2019). https://doi.org/10.1007/978-981-13-6861-5_17

25. Shu, X., Yao, D., Bertino, E.: Privacy-preserving detection of sensitive data exposure. IEEE Trans. Inf. Forensics Secur. **10**(5), 1092–1103 (2015)

26. Udayakumar, N., Saglani, V.J., Cupta, A.V., Subbulakshmi, T.: Malware classification using machine learning algorithms. In: 2nd International Conference on Trends in Electronics and Informatics (ICOEI), pp. 1–9. IEEE (2018)

27. Vyas, R., Luo, X., McFarland, N., Justice, C.: Investigation of malicious portable executable file detection on the network using supervised learning techniques. In: IFIP/IEEE Symposium on Integrated Network and Service Management (IM), pp. 941–946. IEEE (2017)
28. Yousefi-Azar, M., Hamey, L.G., Varadharajan, V., Chen, S.: Malytics: a malware detection scheme. IEEE Access **6**, 49418–49431 (2018)
29. Zheng, W., Zhu, X., Wen, G., Zhu, Y., Yu, H., Gan, J.: Unsupervised feature selection by self-paced learning regularization. Pattern Recogn. Lett. **132**, 4–11 (2020)
30. Zhou, Y., Jiang, X.: Dissecting android malware: characterization and evolution. In: IEEE Symposium on Security and Privacy, pp. 95–109. IEEE (2012)

Wikipedia Knowledge Graph
for Explainable AI

Md Kamruzzaman Sarker[1(✉)], Joshua Schwartz[1], Pascal Hitzler[1], Lu Zhou[1],
Srikanth Nadella[3], Brandon Minnery[3], Ion Juvina[2], Michael L. Raymer[2,3],
and William R. Aue[2]

[1] Kansas State University, Manhattan, KS 66506, USA
mdkamruzzamansarker@ksu.edu
[2] Wright State University, Dayton, OH 45435, USA
[3] Kairos Research, Dayton, OH 45458, USA

Abstract. Explainable artificial intelligence (XAI) requires domain information to explain a system's decisions, for which structured forms of domain information like Knowledge Graphs (KGs) or ontologies are best suited. As such, readily available KGs are important to accelerate progress in XAI. To facilitate the advancement of XAI, we present the cycle-free Wikipedia Knowledge Graph (WKG) based on information from English Wikipedia. Each Wikipedia article title, its corresponding category, and the category hierarchy are transformed into different entities in the knowledge graph. Along with cycle-free version we also provide the original knowledge graph as it is. We evaluate whether the WKG is helpful to improve XAI compared with existing KGs, finding that WKG is better suited than the current state of the art. We also compare the cycle-free WKG with the Suggested Upper Merged Ontology (SUMO) and DBpedia schema KGs, finding minimal to no information loss.

Keywords: Knowledge graph · Wikipedia · Ontology · XAI

1 Introduction

Artificial intelligence (AI)—including the subfields of machine learning and deep learning—has advanced considerably in recent years. In tandem with these performance improvements, understanding how AI systems make decisions has become increasingly difficult due to many nonlinear transformations of input data and the complex nature of the algorithms involved. The research area explainable AI (XAI) [7,8,16] investigates techniques to examine these decision processes.

A main desideratum of XAI is user understandability [5,6], while explanations should take into account the context of the problem and relevant domain

This material is based upon work supported by the Defense Advanced Research Projects Agency (DARPA) under Agreement No. HR00111890019.

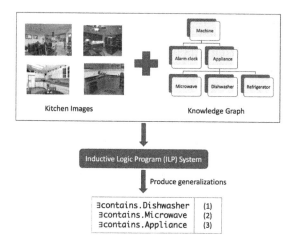

Fig. 1. Example of using knowledge graph to enhance explainability

knowledge [10]. Humans understand and reason mostly in terms of concepts and combinations thereof. A knowledge graph (KG) embodies such understanding in links between concepts; such a natural conceptual network creates a pathway to use knowledge graphs in XAI applications to improve overall understandability of complex AI algorithms. For an overview of some of the current discussion on utilizing knowledge graphs to enhance explanations, and possible limitations of existing approaches, see [9,12].

One of the primary elements of knowledge graphs to use in the XAI context is the notion of a concept hierarchy [4,18]. As illustrated in Fig. 1, consider a system trying to explain the decisions of an image classifier. It may determine that an image should be given the label "Kitchen" because it contains a dishwasher, refrigerator, and microwave, and with the help of a KG concept hierarchy, it may produce the more general explanation that the image contains items in the "Appliance" class. These kinds of explanation generation systems are based on inductive logic programming (ILP) [14], and rich concept hierarchies play an important role in the generation of satisfactory explanations. To advance the state of XAI research, we provide a readily available knowledge graph with a rich concept hierarchy.

Wikipedia is perhaps the largest high-quality free source of information on the web. Wikipedia articles are classified into human-managed categories, which form a hierarchy (albeit with cycles). These concepts embody humans' natural ways of thinking and are easily understood, providing a greater benefit in an XAI context.

DBpedia [1], Suggested Upper Merged Ontology (SUMO) [15], Freebase [2], and Yago [19] are among the many high-quality, publicly available knowledge graphs providing domain information. These KGs use information from many sources, including Wikipedia. The hierarchical category information of

Wikiped-ia, in which we are interested, is available in SUMO[1] but not in Free-base. It also exists in DBpedia and is accessible through SPARQL queries. Prob-lematically, though, the Wikipedia parts of SUMO and the DBpedia KG contain cycles. For example, consider the following two axioms from DBpedia.

I.   *1949_establishments_in_Asia skos:broader 1949_establishments_in_India*
II.   *1949_establishments_in_India skos:broader 1949_establishments_in_Asia*

These axioms form a cycle in the Wikipedia category hierarchy and hence also in DBpedia. The Wikipedia category hierarchy contains many such cycles, which complicates its use in XAI applications, as choosing parent concepts from the KG becomes nondeterministic.

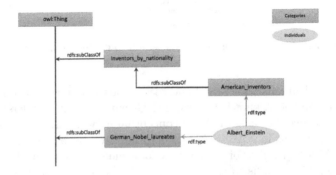

Fig. 2. Example architecture of the Wikipedia knowledge graph

To solve this problem, we provide a noncyclic version of the Wikipedia cat-egory hierarchy knowledge graph. We also empirically evaluate how the non-cyclic knowledge graph performs in an XAI context and whether breaking cycles degrades its quality, finding that the Wikipedia knowledge graph performs better in both scenarios than other existing knowledge graphs.

The rest of the paper is organized as follows. First, we describe the high level architecture of the knowledge graph in Sect. 2. Next, we describe the steps involved in building the knowledge graph. Then, in Sect. 4, we evaluate the knowledge graph before concluding.

2   Knowledge Graph Architecture

We want to make the knowledge graph as simple as possible to enable use within XAI applications with minimal preprocessing. In the knowledge graph, we will have entities (named individuals in OWL 2), their types (classes in OWL 2), and the types' hierarchy. Many relations can be extracted from Wikipedia, but

---

[1] http://www.adampease.org/OP/.

for simplicity we will use only two: *rdf:type* and *rdfs:subClassOf*. The relation *rdf:type* will be used to assign the individuals to their corresponding types, and the *rdfs:subClassOf* relation will be used to create the hierarchy. The title of a Wikipedia article (a.k.a. page) becomes an entity in our KG. Categories of a page become the types of the corresponding individual. A subcategory relationship becomes a *rdfs:subClassOf* relationship.

Figure 2 shows the architecture of our knowledge graph with an example. We can see that the article *Albert_Einstein* is mapped into the knowledge graph as an individual. This article belongs to many categories, including *German_Nobel_laureates* and *American_inventors*, which are converted into instances of *rdf:Class*. The category *American_inventors* is a subcategory of *Inventors_by_nationality*, among others, resulting in the relation.

American_inventors rdfs:subClassOf Inventors_by_nationality

in the KG.

3   Generating the Knowledge Graph

We now briefly describe a procedure for generating a knowledge graph like the one discussed above from the version of Wikipedia for a particular language; full details are in Appendix A. To construct the Wikipedia category hierarchy knowledge graph from scratch, we explored two alternative approaches: traversing and parsing the hierarchy page by page, and using a Wikipedia data dump.[2] To get all page and category information from Wikipedia through a traversal, we start at the top category[3] and exhaustively look through its subcategories and pages recursively, a time-consuming process complicated by the need to

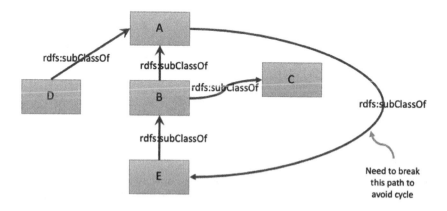

Fig. 3. Example of how cycles are broken

[2] http://dumps.wikimedia.org/enwiki/latest.
[3] https://en.wikipedia.org/wiki/Category:Main_topic_classifications.

parse each page to find the proper links to visit the next categories or pages. To determine how long this process takes in practice, we used Python to implement the visiting and scraping program and found that it took roughly five days on a 2.2 GHz Intel Core i5 machine with 32 GB memory. As taking five days to produce a knowledge graph is not reasonable, we will focus on the Wikipedia data dump option.

A Wikipedia data dump contains all the information for each article: full text, editor list, category, etc. As stated in Sect. 2, our knowledge graph includes article title, category name, and the hierarchy of categories. These data are stored in the *page* and *categorylinks* tables. Using the Wikipedia data dump is straightforward: we just need to download the dump, import it into a database, and access it through SQL queries. After importing it, producing the full knowledge graph took only one hour, on the order of 1% of the time of the previous approach.

3.1   Concrete Implementation

Following the steps mentioned in Appendix A, we can create a concrete Wikipedia knowledge graph, ensuring compliance with W3C standards to make it maintainable, reusable, and non-proprietary. Many tools are available for this; among the most popular are the OWL API [11], the Apache Jena[4] library, and Owlready2,[5], all of which are compliant with W3C's standards.

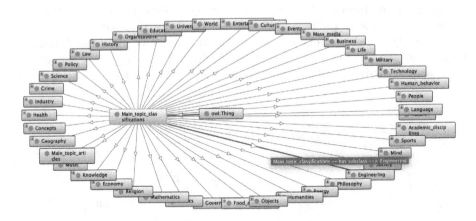

Fig. 4. Wikipedia knowledge graph

As discussed in Sect. 1, the raw Wikipedia hierarchy has cycles, resulting in cyclic relations in the knowledge graph. The Owlready2 library treats concepts as Python classes, representing subclass relationships through inheritance; since Python only supports inheritance without cycles, Owlready2 cannot handle these

---

[4] https://jena.apache.org/.

[5] https://pythonhosted.org/Owlready2/.

Table 1. Entity counts for Wikipedia, SUMO, and DBpedia knowledge graphs

Number of entities/facts	SUMO	DBpedia	Wikipedia cyclic	Wikipedia noncyclic
Concepts	4558	1183	1,901,708	1,860,342
Individuals	86,475	1	6,145,050	6,079,748
Object property	778	1144	2	2
Data property	0	1769	0	0
Axioms	175,208	7228	71,344,252	39,905,216
Class assertion axioms	167381	1	57,335,031	27,991,282
Subclass axioms	5330	769	5,962,463	3,973,845

cycles in relations. In contrast, the OWL API and Jena can support these cyclic relations; we use the former.[6]

While making the KG we face some practical issues, one being that many page titles on Wikipedia have non-ASCII characters, multiple spaces, and other peculiarities. For example, the article https://en.wikipedia.org/wiki/Polish_People %27s_Party_%22Piast%22_(1913%E2%80%931931) has title Polish_People%27s_ Party_%22Piast%22_(1913%E2%80%931931). From an ontological perspective, this title as an entity name seems bad. We decide to replace spaces and characters in the set

$$ ` \sim ! @ \# \$ \% \char94 \& * ( ) - + = \{ \} [ ] | \backslash ; ' " <> , . ? / $$

with underscores (_) and then trim leading and trailing underscores from the resulting string. Another technical issue consists in the fact that if proper Unicode rendering is not selected, some article names will be saved as non–Unicode-compliant names. For example, as of 20 January 2020, the article title *Fabian's Lizard* contains the additional character *0x92* just before the *s*. This character only exists in windows encoding cp1252 and not in Unicode.[7]

3.2 Breaking Cycles

As stated above, the Wikipedia category hierarchy contains cycles, which we break by visiting the categories using breadth-first search (BFS). Starting from the root—*Main topic classifications*—we go level by level. An example of breaking a cycle is shown in Fig. 3. In the example, if we start from A using BFS, we will get B and D as subclasses of A. On the next level, starting from B, we see that E is a subclass of B and store that information. On the next level, starting at E, we see that A is subclass of E; this results in a cycle, so we discard this information. Breaking cycles in this way results in some missing information in the final graph; however, it simplifies the knowledge graph considerably, allowing for efficient parent category determination, which is especially helpful in the XAI context.

---

[6] Our code is available at https://github.com/md-k-sarker/Wiki-KG.

[7] https://stackoverflow.com/q/29419322/1054358.

Entity counts for both the cyclic and noncyclic versions of the WKG are shown in Table 1. We see that breaking cycles results in losing 41,366 concepts (0.02% of the total 1,901,708 concepts) and 65,302 individuals (0.01% of the total 6,145,050 individuals). We further see that we lose a substantial number of class assertion axioms—29,341,749, or 0.5% of the total noncyclic axioms. Figure 4 shows a top-level view of the complete knowledge graph.[8]

4   Evaluation

The goal of our experimental evaluation was to test the hypothesis that the Wikipedia Knowledge graph produces XAI results comparable to or better than existing knowledge graphs. As to the best of our knowledge only SUMO has been used previously in a comparable context [18], to test this we compared the performance of our newly created WKG with that of the SUMO KG. We further hypothesized that breaking cycles in the Wikipedia knowledge graph results in minimal information loss and evaluated WKG relative to SUMO and the DBpedia schema.[9]

4.1   WKG's Effectiveness in XAI

To the best of our knowledge, there is no previously established quantitative measure of XAI quality, so we decided to use the accuracy metric of inductive logic programming (ILP)—the backbone of XAI [18]—to explain a supervised machine learning algorithm's decisions in terms of a KG. ILP provides many alternative solutions by using a KG. To measure a solution's performance, we used coverage score, described in Eq. (1), as the objective function. To measure the overall performance of a KG, we calculated the average of all scores of the produced solution for an experiment with Eq. (2).

$$Coverage(S) = \frac{P_S + N_{NS}}{P_S + P_{NS} + N_S + N_{NS}} \tag{1}$$

where

P_S = Number of positive individuals subsumed by the solution

P_{NS} = Number of positive individuals not subsumed by the solution

N_S = Number of negative individuals subsumed by the solution

N_{NS} = Number of negative individuals not subsumed by the solution

$$Average\ coverage = \sum_{i=1}^{n} Coverage(S_i) \tag{2}$$

---

[8] Available for download at https://osf.io/3wbyr/.
[9] http://downloads.dbpedia.org/2014/dbpedia_2014.owl.bz2.

Following [18], we used the ADE20K dataset [20], which contains over 20,000 images classified by scene type and annotated with contained objects, to compare the results. We cast the ADE20k dataset, with annotations, into an OWL ontology and aligned it with SUMO, as in [18]; in the present context, we also aligned the ontology with WKG. We use all five experiments mentioned in [18], but expand the range of the experiments. While the previous paper used only 3–10 images for each experiment, we took all the training images (around 100) of the relevant categories from the ADE20K dataset. To get the explanation, we use ECII [17] instead of DL-Learner [3] to avoid the latter's considerable time complexity.

Table 2. Comparison of average coverage for WKG and SUMO in XAI context

Experiment name	#Images	#Positive images	Wikipedia		SUMO	
			#Solution	Coverage	#Solution	Coverage
Market vs. WorkRoom and wareHouse	96	37	286	.72	240	.72
Mountain vs. Market and workRoom	181	85	195	.61	190	.53
OutdoorWarehouse vs. IndoorWarehouse	55	3	128	.94	102	.89
Warehouse vs. Workroom	59	55	268	.56	84	.24
Workroom vs. Warehouse	59	4	128	.93	93	.84

We will now briefly discuss each of the scenarios in turn, before we summarize; Table 2 and Fig. 5 provide an overview of the results.

The first experiment involved finding a generalization of market images from the market vs. workroom and warehouse images. The ADE20K training dataset has, for those three categories, a total of 96 images, all of which we used. The objective was to cover as *many* as possible of the 37 images of market scenes and as *few* as possible of the images of workroom and warehouse scenes. When using the Wikipedia knowledge graph, the explanation framework (ECII) produced 286 alternative rules to generalize the market images, while using the SUMO knowledge graph results in 240 alternative rules. Average coverage score for both Wikipedia and SUMO was 0.72, i.e. in this case the simple Wikipedia category hierarchy knowledge graph performs as well as SUMO.

To produce a generalized rule of mountain scenes was the objective of the second experiment. All 181 images from the ADE20K training set were taken in this mountain vs. market and workroom experiment, where 85 images were of mountain scenes. The average coverage for Wikipedia was 0.61, representing slightly better performance than the 0.53 coverage we obtained for SUMO.

In the ADE20K training data, only three images are of outdoor warehouse scenes, while 52 are of indoor warehouse scenes. We wanted to compare the

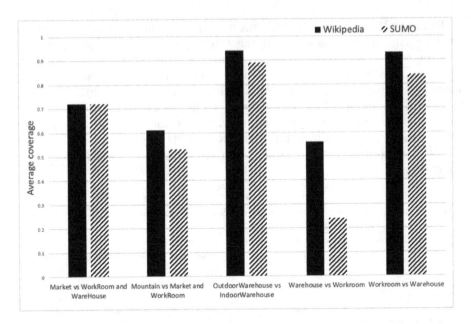

Fig. 5. Comparison of average coverage score between Wikipedia and SUMO knowledge graphs

performances of the WKG and SUMO given such skewed sizes of sets of positive and negative individuals, so we took the three images of outdoor warehouses and 52 images of indoor warehouses, aiming to produce a generalized rule to describe the outdoor warehouse scenes. As there are fewer images to describe, both SUMO and Wikipedia performed well: ECII produced average coverages of 0.89 from SUMO and 0.94 from Wikipedia, leading us to conclude that the Wikipedia KG again resulted in similar performance to the SUMO KG.

In the fourth and fifth experiments, we considered the case of warehouse vs. workroom. The ADE20K training set has 55 warehouse images and four workroom images. To produce a generalized rule to explain warehouse images SUMO returned average coverage of 0.24, while Wikipedia returned 0.56, a significantly larger difference than in previous cases. A large number of positive images compared to that of negative images (55 to 4) may explain the improved coverage score for the Wikipedia KG, as its depth and breadth of concepts exceeds those of SUMO. In the converse experiment (experiment 5)—describing the workroom scenes compared to the warehouse scenes—Wikipedia returned an average coverage score of 0.93 and SUMO returned 0.84. In this case, only four images were used to describe the workroom class, with 55 images on the negative side. Here Wikipedia and SUMO produced comparable average coverage scores.

The results are visualized in Fig. 5, showing the simple Wikipedia category hierarchy's superior performance in all experiments compared to the SUMO ontology.

4.2   Noncyclic WKG Information Loss

For the second type of experiment, we evaluated the noncyclic WKG class hierarchy with respect to the DBpedia schema and SUMO knowledge graph to see what proportion of subclass-superclass axioms remain in the WKG compared to the SUMO and DBpedia after breaking cycles. We expected that some subclass-superclass relations would be lost in the cycle-breaking process and hence not exist in our noncyclic WKG despite being present in other KGs. However, our experimental results show little to no information loss, with a substantial majority of the subclass-superclass relations in SUMO and DBpedia preserved in the noncyclic WKG.

The experiment involved first finding matching concepts in the WKG, SUMO, and DBpedia schema. To match the concepts we used a string similarity measurement algorithm (specifically Levenshtein [13] distance = 0), finding 22 matching concepts, shown in Table 3. We extracted the asserted superclasses of those concepts from all three KGs. Details of the parents are shown on Table 3. In the WKG, the number of asserted parents for some categories are quite large. For example, the category *Fish* has 114 asserted parent categories in the noncyclic WKG. As such, here we show only some of the parent concepts for each category.[10]

Table 3. Parents of all matching concepts in SUMO, DBpedia and noncyclic Wikipedia knowledge graph

Concept	Parent concepts			#Wikipedia parent concepts
	SUMO	DBpedia	Wikipedia	
Aircraft	Vehicle	MeanOfTransportation	Vehicles_by_type, Technology	5
Beer	AlcoholicBeverage	Beverage, Food	Food_and_drink	5
Birth	OrganismProcess	PersonalEvent, LifeCycleEvent, Event	Life	3
Boxing	Sport, ViolentContest	Sport, Activity	Sports	5
Brain	AnimalAnatomicalStructure, Organ	AnatomicalStructure	Human_anatomy, Physical_objects	15
Building	StationaryArtifact	ArchitecturalStructure, Place	Construction, Engineering	12
Cheese	PreparedFood, DairyProduct	Food	Foods	7
City	LandArea, GeopoliticalArea	Settlement, PopulatedPlace, Place	Human_habitats	42
Currency	FinancialInstrument	Thing	International_trade	60
Death	OrganismProcess	PersonalEvent, LifeCycleEvent, Event	Life	3
Fish	ColdBloodedVertebrate	Animal, Eukaryote, Species	Aquatic_organisms	114
Grape	Fruit	FloweringPlant, Plant, Eukaryote, Species	Edible_fruits	20
Language	LinguisticExpression	Thing	Culture	3
Medicine	BiologicallyActiveSubstance	Thing	Health_care, Health	4
Opera	DramaticPlay	MusicalWork, Work	Performing_arts, Entertainment	7
Painting	Coloring, Covering	Artwork, Work	Arts	7
Sales	Working	Activity	Marketing, Business	5
Sculpture	ArtWork	Artwork, Work	Visual_arts, Culture	7
Sound	BodyOfWater	Document, Work	Consciousness, Mind	5
Spacecraft	Vehicle	MeanOfTransportation	Spaceflight	13
Tax	ChargingAFee	TopicalConcept	Governmet_finances	4
Wine	AlcoholicBeverage, PlantAgriculturalProduct	Beverage, Food	Fermented_drinks	32

---

[10] See https://github.com/md-k-sarker/Wiki-KG for full results.

Due to space constraints, we discuss only a subset of the 22 concepts that matched across the three KGs. We can divide the 22 concepts into twelve subsets by using the first letter of those concepts; among these, the letter B has the largest subset, with five elements: *Beer*, *Birth*, *Boxing*, *Brain*, and *Building*.

The concept *Beer* is available in SUMO, DBpedia and WKG. The only SUMO axiom related to the concept *Beer* is *Beer* $\sqsubseteq$ *AlcoholicBeverage*, while in DBpedia we have *Beer* $\sqsubseteq$ *Beverage* and *Beer* $\sqsubseteq$ *Food*; finally, in the non-cyclic WKG we have the related axioms *Beer* $\sqsubseteq$ *Food_and_drink*. We see that all three KGs have semantically similar parents of varying specificity.

Axioms related to the concept *Birth* in DBpedia are *Birth* $\sqsubseteq$ *LifeCycleEvent*, *Birth* $\sqsubseteq$ *PersonalEvent* and *Birth* $\sqsubseteq$ *Event*; in SUMO we have *Birth* $\sqsubseteq$ *OrganismProcess*; and in the WKG, *Birth* $\sqsubseteq$ *Life*. We can see that these parent concepts are again similar in meaning.

In SUMO, axioms related to the concept *Boxing* are *Boxing* $\sqsubseteq$ *Sport* and *Boxing* $\sqsubseteq$ *ViolentContest*; DBpedia has *Boxing* $\sqsubseteq$ *Sport* and *Boxing* $\sqsubseteq$ *Activity*; WKG has *Boxing* $\sqsubseteq$ *Sports*, among others. The parent concepts of *Boxing* are *Sport*, *Sport*, and *Sports* in SUMO, DBpedia, and WKG, respectively; all of these clearly have the same meaning. Minor changes like the pluralization of the category name in Wikipedia are to be expected, as the SUMO and DBpedia schema are manually curated by domain experts and ontologists, while Wikipedia categories are editable by the general public.

Brain is another concept common to all three KGs. In SUMO we have *Brain* $\sqsubseteq$ *AnimalAnatomicalStructure* and *Brain* $\sqsubseteq$ *Organ*, and in DBpedia, *Brain* $\sqsubseteq$ *AnatomicalStructure*. Some related axioms in WKG are *Brain* $\sqsubseteq$ *Human_anatomy* and *Brain* $\sqsubseteq$ *Physical_objects*. We see that ontologically, there exist some differences between *Human_anatomy* and *AnatomicalStructure*, but similar differences also exist between SUMO and DBpedia.

Finally, axioms related to the *Building* concept are: in SUMO, *Building* $\sqsubseteq$ *StationaryArtifact*; in DBpedia, *Building* $\sqsubseteq$ *ArchitecturalStructure* and *Building* $\sqsubseteq$ *Place*; and in WKG, ten axioms dealing with direct parents of the concept, including *Building* $\sqsubseteq$ *Construction* and *Building* $\sqsubseteq$ *Society*. We again see that the parents are similar in semantics, though slight differences exist among the three ontologies.

Based on the above, we conclude that there is minimal information loss in the noncyclic Wikipedia KG with respect to DBpedia and SUMO. There exist some minor differences in an ontological sense with the WKG axioms, but such minor differences exist between SUMO and DBpedia as well.

5   Conclusion

The readily available Wikipedia category hierarchy and its corresponding named entities has great importance in artificial intelligence and its subfields. We make the Wikipedia Knowledge Graph (WKG), break its cycles, and make available both the original and cycle-free versions for public use. We evaluate the WKG in the context of XAI and compare it with the DBpedia and SUMO KGs, finding

WKG to be highly effective compared to the other two. We also evalute the noncyclic WKG relative to SUMO and the DBpedia schema, finding minimal information loss. Here we evaluate the WKG in a specific XAI application; further work should focus on evaluating it in other such applications and in different domains of artificial intelligence.

A   Steps for Building the Wikipedia Knowledge Graph

As of 20 January 2020, the *page* table[11] (containing article information) has around 49 million entries, while the *categorylinks* table[12] (containing category information) has around 140 million entries.

As these files are large (the larger is 24 GB), proper settings must be applied to the database before importing them to keep the import process from taking a prohibitively long time. In particular, we must disable foreign key checking and increase the buffer length.

There are different types of pages on Wikipedia: some pages are articles, some pages are categories, and some pages are for administrative use. Administrative pages are not of interest for the knowledge graph, so we omit them. Using the information from the table *categorylinks*, we can identify which pages are articles, which are categories, and so on. The column *page_namespace* holds the page type information; for categories, *page_namespace=14*, while for articles, *page_namespace=0*. This table also provides the category hierarchical information, in its columns *cl_from* and *cl_to*. The column *cl_from* is the article name or subcategory name, and column *cl_to* is the category or parent category name (depending on whether the page is an article or category). Each page has a unique ID and title. The table *page* gives us the needed information like ID of the page, title, etc.

The steps to create the knowledge graph are shown in Algorithm 1. By way of example, we demonstrate part of the execution of Algorithm 1 on the article Albert_Einstein.[13] Initially, we need to get the page_id for Albert_Einstein from the *page* table downloaded from the dump by executing the following query.

```
SELECT page_id, page_title, page_namespace FROM page
WHERE page_title = 'Albert_Einstein' and page_namespace = 0;
```

The result of this query is in Fig. 6, and we can see that the page_id of article Albert_Einstein is 736.

After getting the page_id, we need to get the page's category, which we can get using the following query.

---

[11] Available for download at http://dumps.wikimedia.org/enwiki/latest/enwiki-latest-page.sql.gz, with and described in detail at https://www.mediawiki.org/wiki/Manual:Page_table.

[12] Available for download at http://dumps.wikimedia.org/enwiki/latest/enwiki-latest-categorylinks.sql.gz, and described in detail at https://www.mediawiki.org/wiki/Manual:Categorylinks_table.

[13] https://en.wikipedia.org/wiki/Albert_Einstein.

Algorithm 1: Wikipedia knowledge graph construction algorithm

---

1 **Function** Iterate(A) :
2 | Find page_id pd, title t, page_namespace pn of page A;
3 | **if** $pn == 0$ **then**
4 | | Declare title t as an entity e;
5 | | Find categories ($c \in C$) of entity e;
6 | | **foreach** $c \in C$ **do**
7 | | | Declare category c as a rdf:type (class);
8 | | | Create facts: e rdf:type c;
9 | | | Find the pages ($p \in P$) which are entity of category c;
10 | | | **foreach** $p \in P$ **do**
11 | | | | Iterate(p) ;
12 | | | **end**
13 | | **end**
14 | **end**
15 | **else if** $pn == 14$ **then**
16 | | Declare title t a category (class) c;
17 | | Find all sub-categories ($sc \sqsubseteq c$) of category c;
18 | | **foreach** $sc \in C$ **do**
19 | | | Create relation: sc subClassOf c;
20 | | | Iterate(sc);
21 | | **end**
22 | **end**
23 **end**
24 Iterate(Main_topic_classifications)   /* start the process from root */

```
SELECT cl_from, cl_to FROM categorylinks WHERE cl_from = 736;
```

As of 20 January 2020, this page belongs to 148 different categories, a subset of which is shown in Fig. 7.

Using the results of these queries, we can create axioms like *Albert_Einstein rdf:type German_inventors* and incorporate them into our knowledge graph. To continue creating the full hierarchy, we must continue with the parent categories of each the article's categories.

To get the parent category of a category, we must find the page_id of that category and use that to find its parent. For example, if we want to find the parent category of German_inventors, we need to determine the page_id of the German_inventors page as follows.

```
SELECT page_id, page_title, page_namespace FROM page
WHERE page_title = 'German_inventors' and page_namespace = 14;
```

This will return the result shown in Fig. 8, where we see that the page_id of German_inventors is 1033282.

```
+----------+------------------+-----------------+
| page_id  | page_title       | page_namespace  |
+----------+------------------+-----------------+
|      736 | Albert_Einstein  |             0   |
+----------+------------------+-----------------+
```

Fig. 6. Page_id of the article Albert_Einstein

```
+----------+---------------------------------------+
| cl_from  | cl_to                                 |
+----------+---------------------------------------+
|      736 | German_Jews                           |
|      736 | German_Nobel_laureates                |
|      736 | German_agnostics                      |
|      736 | German_emigrants_to_Switzerland       |
|      736 | German_inventors                      |
|      736 | German_socialists                     |
+----------+---------------------------------------+
```

Fig. 7. Categories for the article Albert_Einstein

```
+----------+------------------+-----------------+
| page_id  | page_title       | page_namespace  |
+----------+------------------+-----------------+
| 1033282  | German_inventors |             14  |
+----------+------------------+-----------------+
```

Fig. 8. Page_id of category *German_inventors*

```
+----------+---------------------------------------+
| cl_from  | cl_to                                 |
+----------+---------------------------------------+
| 1033282  | Commons_category_link_is_on_Wikidata  |
| 1033282  | German_businesspeople                 |
| 1033282  | German_inventions                     |
| 1033282  | Inventors_by_nationality              |
| 1033282  | Science_and_technology_in_Germany     |
+----------+---------------------------------------+
```

Fig. 9. Parent categories of the category German_inventors

After getting this page_id, we can consult the *categorylinks* table for the parent category:

```
SELECT cl_from, cl_to FROM categorylinks WHERE cl_from = 1033282;
```

This will provide the parent results as shown in Fig. 9, where we see that the parent categories of *German_inventors* are *Inventors_by_nationality* and *Science_and_technology_in_Germany*, among others.[14] This kind of relationship creates cycles in the category hierarchy, as discussed in Sect. 3.2.

We now see the complete process of creating an entity and adding axioms for its types and supertypes. The example above is but one fragment of the knowledge graph creation adventure; to complete the knowledge graph, we need to start from the root of the category hierarchy and continue with Algorithm 1 until all pages have been processed to yield article titles with their categories, along with the resulting category hierarchy.

References

1. Bizer, C.: DBpedia–a crystallization point for the web of data. J. Web Semant. **7**(3), 154–165 (2009)
2. Bollacker, K., Evans, C., Paritosh, P., Sturge, T., Taylor, J.: Freebase: a collaboratively created graph database for structuring human knowledge. In: In SIGMOD Conference, pp. 1247–1250 (2008)

---

[14] It may seem odd to have *Science_and_technology_in_Germany* and similar as parent categories of *German_inventors* in an ontology; this reflects the somewhat messy nature of Wikipedia.

3. Bühmann, L., Lehmann, J., Westphal, P.: DL-learner - a framework for inductive learning on the semantic web. J. Web Sem. **39**, 15–24 (2016)
4. Confalonieri, R., et al.: An ontology-based approach to explaining artificial neural networks (2019)
5. Doran, D., Schulz, S., Besold, T.R.: What does explainable AI really mean? A new conceptualization of perspectives. In: Besold, T.R., Kutz, O. (eds.) Proceedings of the First International Workshop on Comprehensibility and Explanation in AI and ML 2017, CEUR Workshop Proceedings, Bari, Italy, vol. 2071. CEUR-WS.org (2017)
6. Doshi-Velez, F., Kim, B.: Towards a rigorous science of interpretable machine learning. arXiv preprint arXiv:1702.08608 (2017)
7. Guidotti, R., Monreale, A., Ruggieri, S., Turini, F., Giannotti, F., Pedreschi, D.: A survey of methods for explaining black box models. ACM Comput. Surv. (CSUR) **51**(5), 93 (2018)
8. Gunning, D.: Explainable artificial intelligence (XAI). Defense Advanced Research Projects Agency (DARPA) (2017)
9. Hitzler, P., Bianchi, F., Ebrahimi, M., Sarker, M.K.: Neural-symbolic integration and the semantic web. Semantic Web (2020). Accepted for publication
10. Holzinger, A., Biemann, C., Pattichis, C.S., Kell, D.B.: What do we need to build explainable AI systems for the medical domain? (2017)
11. Horridge, M., Bechhofer, S.: The OWL API: : A Java API for OWL ontologies. Semant. Web **2**(1), 11–21 (2011)
12. Lecue, F.: On the role of knowledge graphs in explainable AI. Semant. Web J. (2019). http://www.semantic-web-journal.net/system/files/swj2198.pdf. Accessed 26 July 2019
13. Levenshtein, V.I.: On the minimal redundancy of binary error-correcting codes. Inf. Control. **28**(4), 268–291 (1975). https://doi.org/10.1016/S0019-9958(75)90300-9
14. Muggleton, S., de Raedt, L.: Inductive logic programming: theory and methods. J. Logic Programm. **19–20**, 629–679 (1994). https://doi.org/10.1016/0743-1066(94)90035-3, http://www.sciencedirect.com/science/article/pii/0743106694900353. Special Issue: Ten Years of Logic Programming
15. Niles, I., Pease, A.: Towards a Standard Upper Ontology. In: Proceedings of the International Conference on Formal Ontology in Information Systems, vol. 2001, pp. 2–9 (2001)
16. Samek, W., Wiegand, T., Müller, K.: Explainable artificial intelligence: understanding, visualizing and interpreting deep learning models. CoRR abs/1708.08296 (2017). http://arxiv.org/abs/1708.08296
17. Sarker, M.K., Hitzler, P.: Efficient concept induction for description logics. In: Proceedings of the AAAI Conference on Artificial Intelligence, vol. 33, pp. 3036–3043 (2019)
18. Sarker, M.K., Xie, N., Doran, D., Raymer, M., Hitzler, P.: Explaining trained neural networks with semantic web technologies: first steps. In: Besold, T.R., d'Avila Garcez, A.S., Noble, I. (eds.) Proceedings of the Twelfth International Workshop on Neural-Symbolic Learning and Reasoning, NeSy 2017, London, UK, July 17–18, 2017. CEUR Workshop Proceedings, vol. 2003. CEUR-WS.org (2017)

19. Suchanek, F.M., Kasneci, G., Weikum, G.: YAGO: a core of semantic knowledge. In: Williamson, C.L., Zurko, M.E., Patel-Schneider, P.F., Shenoy, P.J. (eds.) Proceedings of the 16th International Conference on World Wide Web, WWW 2007, Banff, Alberta, Canada, May 8–12, 2007. ACM Press, New York (2007)
20. Zhou, B., Zhao, H., Puig, X., Fidler, S., Barriuso, A., Torralba, A.: Scene parsing through ADE20K dataset. In: IEEE Conference on Computer Vision and Pattern Recognition, CVPR 2017, Honolulu, HI, USA, 21–26 July 2017, pp. 5122–5130. IEEE (2017)

Characterizing the Diffusion of Knowledge in an Academic Community Through the Integration of Heterogeneous Data Sources and Graphs

Jared D. T. Guerrero-Sosa(ID) and Víctor Hugo Menéndez-Domínguez[(✉)](ID)

Facultad de Matemáticas, Universidad Autónoma de Yucatán, Mérida, Mexico
{jared.guerrero,mdoming}@correo.uady.mx

Abstract. The principle of open science is to spread the knowledge generated by institutions and individuals in order to promote the development of society. In this sense, knowing the impact of research is an important aspect for any scientist and institution. Characterizing the dissemination of knowledge has traditionally been carried out through the citation index of works published in journals and documentation repositories. This work presents a complementary aspect that may be relevant to identify the impact of a publication in an academic community. A case study is described in which, using a methodology and graphs to integrate different sources of heterogeneous data, an overview of the interest generated from production of a public university in the users of a specialized social network is provided. The different user groups are characterized by their academic profiles and countries of origin. In addition, the results allow identifying focus groups for possible collaborators or trends in research lines.

Keywords: Mendeley · Scopus · Graph theory · Diffusion of knowledge

1 Introduction

In recent years, the open science [29] movement has gained strength on the basis of the principle that information, data and scientific products are more accessible and more reliably leveraged with the active participation of all stakeholders. This is intended to promote innovation in the development of society based on the knowledge generated in institutions and research centers.

In the case of Mexico, the National Council for Science and Technology (CONACYT) has established a series of legal guidelines to ensure the accessibility of scientific research, financed by public resources, for all citizens through the dissemination of scientific, technological and innovation knowledge [7,8].

© Springer Nature Switzerland AG 2020
B. Villazón-Terrazas et al. (Eds.): KGSWC 2020, CCIS 1232, pp. 88–101, 2020.
https://doi.org/10.1007/978-3-030-65384-2_7

Thus, the democratization of knowledge will be possible to the extent that the dissemination of the results of research carried out by scientists around the world is maximized. The characterization of this diffusion plays a relevant role in measuring the impact of the production of an institution or an individual.

Usually, the impact of scientific production is made through some citation model, which tries to establish to what extent a product was relevant to generate a new one. That is, it measures the degree of knowledge contribution to generate new knowledge. However, these models are based on the products generated and not on the people or processes associated with the development of those products.

In this sense, repositories (such as SCOPUS, Web Of Science) and specialized social networks (such as Mendeley), being spaces for exchange and collaboration between their users, become a very rich source of the relationships between the products, users and the processes carried out.

This work presents the methodology used to characterize the dissemination of knowledge generated by an important public university in the southeast of Mexico in a specialized social network. For this, different data sources are used that, thanks to their APIs, allow their integration and thus obtain a general overview of the types of users that consume the generated knowledge as well as their knowledge areas of interest. Users are evaluated by academic profile and by geographical area. The visualization is done through graphs and tables.

The architecture proposed in this work allows to generate other graphs for the analysis of scientific collaboration in a specific institution [17,18].

2   State of the Art

A high-impact (or indexed) publication is one which can be located in a bibliographic database (or repository) whose publications comply with a series of quality indicators [4], such as the research impact, the relevance of the origin of the citations, the journal impact factor, among others. Scopus (owned by Elsevier) and Web of Science (owned by Clarivate) are considered the two most important bibliographic databases in the world.

Both Scopus and Web of Science allow access to data regarding their stored publications through various APIs. Some belonging to Scopus allow retrieving data related to affiliations [11], basic information [12] and more specific information [14] about scientific publications.

In addition to Scopus, Elsevier offers other products and solutions for students, researches and innovation professionals, such as Mendeley, which is a reference manager and academic social network for organizing research, establishing online collaborations and discovering new publications [14]. Mendeley offers a Software Development Kits for researchers, libraries, institutions and companies, which allows them to solve problems focused on knowledge areas, as well as benefits for researchers in the workplace [10].

The impact and relevance of scientific production based on bibliographic databases at the institutional level have been researched in various works.

In [19] it is stated that measuring the research impact is a complex task, but necessary due to the justification requested by governments regarding to the use of the economic resources allocated. However, another study [30] mainly exposed the existence of mechanisms for evaluating the research impact on the research process and not only on the results, in order to benefit not only the economic aspect.

In [5] the use of Altmetrics, a set of metrics different from the traditional ones, is studied for the measurement and evaluation of scientific production, using as data sources various conventional social networks and academic platforms. However, the study considers that Altmetrics allows only measuring the consumption of publications and suggests not overvaluing its indicators.

Mendeley has also been studied to measure the impact of the research. A study [15] ensures that the citation index considered to measure the effect of research funding delay scientific production by several years and as a consequence, the information is out of date. To avoid this, the work proposed a method for measurement of the research impact using the reader count based on Mendeley that can generate similar indicators to the citation index but requires further study.

[21] states that citation index is not able to measure the impact of new research, since it takes approximately three years for it to generate a significant number of citations; and to solve the problem, it was analyzed whether the number of Mendeley readers allows evaluating a research during the month of its publication. The results of the study show that the articles have attracted a number of readers in the month of their publication ten times more than the average number of citations in Scopus.

[1] identified that there is evidence of a high correlation between the Mendeley reader count and the citation index in scientific journal articles, but in the case of conference articles, the result is different. Journal and conference articles focused on Computer Science and Engineering were considered in the study. Moderate correlations were found between reader count and citation index in journal and in conference articles belonging to Computer Science, while correlations were lower in the same indicators for Engineering.

Platforms have also been developed for the analysis of the behavior of scientific research between individuals and institutions such as Semantic Scholar and the Semantic Repository of Researchers of Ecuador (REDI).

Semantic Scholar is a tool that, through machine learning techniques, allows researchers to understand the most relevant scientific works in their knowledge area [2].

REDI, through ontological models for the semantic network, focuses on the identification of Ecuadorian researchers and similar areas of knowledge to promote collaborations [6].

A useful tool to represent the relationships in the behavior of scientific production is the graph $G(V, E)$, which is a mathematical abstraction and is made up of V, which is a set of vertices and E, which is a set of edges [24]. There are various software tools that allow the creation and analysis of graphs, such as Gephi [16] and NodeXL [26].

The elements represented through the vertices and their relationships defined through the edges can be analyzed using the Graph Theory. The properties used in this work are the vertex degree, which is the total number of edges of a vertex [3]; the weight, which is a real value assigned to an edge and represents the value of the relationship of the vertices involved [27]; and the labeled graph, which is a graph with labels, either at the vertices, at the edges, or both [24].

3 Methodology

In this section, a methodology is presented for obtaining the data of the scientific production from Scopus of an institution and its respective statistics of Mendeley readers, in order to represent the characterization of the diffusion of knowledge through graphs. Based on the methodology of data mining for e-learning applications [23], the following steps, shown in Fig. 1 are proposed.

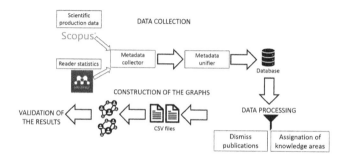

Fig. 1. Proposed methodology for the extraction of knowledge.

3.1 Data Collection

The architecture has a metadata collector in charge of using the Scopus and Mendeley web services. In the case of Scopus, the API allows the user to choose the response format (JSON, XML or ATOM + XML), while the Mendeley service used returns in JSON format.

In order to achieve uniformity of the data obtained by the different data sources, the architecture includes a metadata unifier, and for its optimal use, a series of rules has been implemented that map each metadata retrieved from Scopus and Mendeley for internal storage. This provides independence to the collector, allowing the incorporation of new data sources as they are declared in the mapping structure. Scopus metadata uses W3C CORS, Dublin Core and PRISM standards, while Mendeley returns the results in JSON objects.

Data from Scopus. In order to structure the information about affiliations, authors and publications, Scopus assigns an ID to each element. Each affiliation profile has a Scopus ID. Before data collection, it is necessary to consider that an specific institution might have more than one Scopus ID due to the different nomenclatures assigned by the authors at the time of publication. Therefore, to identify the different affiliation profiles of an institution, it is essential to use the Scopus Affiliation Search (Fig. 2a). For each profile, retrieve the Affiliation ID. An example of where to identify the Affiliation ID is shown in Fig. 2b.

a)   b)

Fig. 2. Scopus affiliation search and affiliation ID.

For retrieving the information of the scientific production from an specific institution, the next steps are followed:

- Since this project is framed in an academic context, the application makes use of an institutional token that has been provided by Scopus to the institution and thus has access to information that is restricted for public use.
- For the basic information about the scientific production, send a HTTP request to Scopus through the Scopus Search API using all the IDs of the affiliation associated with the institution as parameters. Each result has a metadata set and this must be stored in a database. The main identifier of the publications is the Scopus ID EID.
- For each retrieved information of a scientific publication, send a HTTP request to Scopus through the Scopus Abstract Retrieval API using its Scopus ID EID with the purpose of retrieve its subject areas. Each result has a metadata set and this must be stored in the database of the scientific production, updating the corresponding record.

Data from Mendeley. The information about each publication in Scopus can be obtained through Mendeley since both of them belong to Elsevier.

Mendeley Python SDK allows to search scientific publications by identifier, as ArXIV ID, DOI, ISBN, ISSN, Scopus ID EID, among others [20]. The only identifier in common for any type of publication (articles, books, book chapters, among others) is Scopus ID EID.

Therefore, for each publication, through Mendeley Python SDK, use the *by_identifier* method with the parameter *scopus* with the corresponding Scopus

ID EID, and the parameter *view* with the value *stats*, for retrieving the reader count and other specific statistics as reader count by academic status, reader count by subdiscipline and reader count by country. The response is a JSON file and the record of the publication in the database must be updated with this file.

It is important to mention that Mendeley considers that a user has accessed a scientific publication if they have consulted the basic information (authorship, abstract and keywords), regardless of whether it is open or restricted access.

3.2   Data Processing

Dismiss Publications. If a scientific publication has not been accessed through Mendeley, there will not be specific statistics about readers. It is necessary to omit those publications based on the retrieved information through Mendeley Python SDK in order to avoid building a graph with unnecessary information.

Assignation of Knowledge Areas. Scopus has 30 specific subject areas classified by four general subject areas [13]: Physical Sciences, Health Sciences, Social Sciences and Life Sciences.

We propose to analyze the subject areas using the knowledge areas established by the CONACYT [9], which is more specific than the Scopus classification: Area 1 - Physical Mathematics and Earth Science, Area 2 - Biology and Chemistry, Area 3 - Medical and Health Sciences, Area 4 - Humanities and Behavioral Sciences, Area 5 - Social Sciences, Area 6 - Agricultural Sciences and Biotechnology, and Area 7 - Engineering and Technology.

For each knowledge area of CONACYT, a list is created that includes all the specific subject areas of Scopus with which it is associated. Then, for each retrieved publication, in the list of subject areas, the main one is identified, which is in the first position. Subsequently, in the lists of knowledge areas of CONACYT, identify in which the main subject area of the publication is found.

3.3   Construction of the Graphs

It should be mentioned that using the information retrieved through Mendeley it is not possible to distinguish the different readers of scientific publications. Therefore, the graphs that are generated represent the access counts through different academic profiles and countries.

Access by Academic Profile. The scientific publications with at least one reader might include specific statistics about readers. This information is available in the JSON returned by Mendeley Python SDK. For each publication, it is required to identify if exists an object called *reader_count_by_academic_status*. The names in this object represent the academic profiles of the readers of the publication and their values show how many readers in each academic profile the publication has.

```
▼ reader_count_by_academic_status {4}
     Researcher : 3
     Student  > Master : 1
     Professor : 2
     Student  > Doctoral Student : 1
```

Fig. 3. Example of the reader count by academic profile of a scientific publication.

An example is shown in Fig. 3 where are 7 readers of a scientific publication classified in four academic profiles.

To build the graph, it is necessary to generate a CSV file that includes the table of edges of the graph. The steps to follow are described below:

1. Extract the different academic profiles from all the retrieved information through Mendeley Python SDK.
2. Using all the knowledge areas, all the retrieved types of publications, and all the academic profiles, create subsets of four elements, where each one will contain a knowledge area, a type of publication, an academic profile and the access count of the readers of the academic profile in question that have accessed to the type of publication of the knowledge area.
3. For each scientific publication, in the JSON returned by Mendeley Python SDK, identify the academic profiles in the "reader_count_by_academic_status" object.
4. Subsequently, for each academic profile in the publication, identify the subset whose elements coincide with the knowledge area of the publication, the type of publication and the academic profile in question.
5. In the identified subset, update the access count by adding the number of readers of the academic profile that have accessed to the publication.
6. After analyzing all the scientific production, build the CSV headers: *source*, *target* and *weight*.
7. Finally, identify the subsets whose access counts are greater than zero (to avoid adding unnecessary information to the graph) and construct the rows of the CSV file, where *source* includes the name of the knowledge area and the type of publication, *target* the name of the academic profile and *weight* the access count.

Access by Country. For each publication, it is required to identify if exists an object called *reader_count_by_country*. The names in this object represent the countries of the readers of the publication and their values show how many readers for each country the publication has.

The procedure for the construction of the CSV file with the table of edges of the graph follows the steps described below:

1. Extract the different countries from all the retrieved information through Mendeley Python SDK.

2. Using all the retrieved countries and all the knowledge areas, create subsets of three elements, where each subset includes a country, a knowledge area and the access count of the readers from the country in question that have accessed to the scientific production of the knowledge area.
3. For each scientific publication, in the JSON returned by Mendeley Python SDK, identify the countries in the *reader_count_by_country* object.
4. Subsequently, for each country, identify the subset whose elements coincide with the knowledge area and the country in question.
5. In the identified subset, update the access count by adding the number of readers from the country that have accessed to the publication.
6. After analyzing all the scientific production, build the CSV headers: *source, target* and *weight.*
7. Finally, identify the subsets whose access counts are greater than zero and construct the rows of the CSV file, where *source* includes the name of the knowledge area, *target* the name of the country and *weight* the access count.

3.4   Validation of the Results

The graphs visualization facilitates analyzing the diffussion of knowledge and its characteristics allow to carry out this task. Labeling all vertices makes it easy to identify the publication types retrieved and the countries or the academic profiles of the readers.

The thickness of each edge depends on its weight, where, the thicker it is, the greater the number of accesses from people of the academic profile, or from the country, depending on the graph.

The degree of each vertex that represents the academic profiles and the countries, indicates how many different types of publications have been accessed by Mendeley users belonging to these instances.

The weighted degree of each vertex that represents the different types of publications, indicates the total number of accesses obtained, considering, according to the graph, the academic profiles or the countries.

4   Case of Study

In order to evaluate the methodology proposed in this work, a case of study of the production registered in Scopus generated by the Universidad Autónoma de Yucatán (UADY), an important educational institution in the southeast of Mexico, was carried out. The UADY is made up of 15 faculties spread over five campuses, as well as a research center focused on two areas of study [28]. In 2019, the UADY had 26,182 in its total enrollment and 745 full-time professors, of which 259 belong to the National System of Researchers in Mexico [25].

A Python script was created using the Scopus Search API to retrieve the basic production information associated with the UADY. Subsequently, with the same script, the subject areas of each publication were retrieved using the Scopus Abstract Retrieval API.

The metadata for each publication were stored in a MongoDB database, a document database that facilitates storage in JSON format [22].

The recovered scientific production belongs to the full-time professors of the UADY, from 1979 until August 2020 which consists of 3,180 publications distributed as follows: 2,727 articles, 9 books, 84 book chapters, 16 letters to the editor, 243 conferences, 9 editorials and 92 reviews.

Using Mendeley Python SDK, the statistics of the readers of all UADY production were obtained. Of the 3,180 publications, 136 (4.27%) were discarded, which have not been accessed through Mendeley. The remaining 3,044 publications were considered to analyze access by academic profile and by country.

4.1   Access by Academic Profile

Of the 3,044 publications that have been accessed in Mendeley, 3,023 have statistics by academic profile. In Fig. 4 the graph obtained is presented. The vertices represent the different academic profiles of the readers and the types of publications belonging to the knowledge areas. The size of each vertex of the types of publications depends on their weight, whose value is the number of publications belonging to the knowledge area and type of publication, while the thickness of each edge depends on the number of accesses by the readers of the academic profile to the type of publication that belongs to the knowledge area.

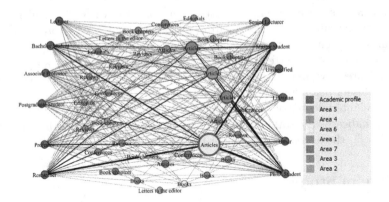

Fig. 4. Graph of access by academic profile.

The vertex with the greatest size belongs to the articles of Agricultural Sciences and Biotechnology and consists of 1,104 publications. The vertices with the smallest size belong to one book of Physical Mathematical Sciences and Earth Sciences, one conference article of Agricultural Sciences and Biotechnology, one editorial of Engineering and Technology, and one letter to the editor of Biology and Chemistry. Table 1 presents the 12 academic profiles that were identified in the readers of the scientific production of the UADY, their minimum and maximum number of accesses with the corresponding knowledge area and type of publication, their average access and their number of accessed types of publications. The values in the second, the third and the fourth columns where obtained based on the weights of the corresponding edges. The values in the fifth column are based on the degree of each vertex of the academic profiles.

Through the weight of the edges, the minimum and the maximum number of accesses by academic profile were identified and to which types of publications they belong. The average of accesses by academic profile in the different publications of the UADY are also shown. The degree vertices indicate how many types of publications the readers of the academic profile have accessed. Considering all types of publications and all knowledge areas, the vertices of the academic profiles can have a maximum degree of 33. Researchers have accessed most of the different types of scientific publications.

It has been identified that of the 12 academic profiles, 11 have accessed the articles belonging to the knowledge area of Agricultural Sciences and Biotechnology. People who did not specify their academic profiles in their Mendeley profile have mainly accessed articles from the area of Medicine and Health Sciences.

Table 2 shows, by knowledge area, the most consulted type of publication, the academic profile that has the majority of accesses to the publications and how many times the users of said academic profile have accessed. It was identified that in all knowledge areas, the most accessed products are articles, and most of the accesses come from doctoral students.

4.2   Access by Country

Of the 3,044 publications that have been accessed in Mendeley, 1,154 were identified with statistics by country.

In Fig. 5 the generated graph is presented. The vertices represent the countries that have accessed the UADY production and the knowledge areas of the publications (whose sizes depend on the total number of publications belonging to the knowledge area). The thickness of each edge depends on how many times the users of the country have accessed the publications of the knowledge area.

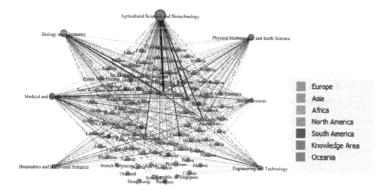

Fig. 5. Graph of access by country.

Table 1. Description of accesses by academic profile.

Academic profile	Minimum number of accesses	Maximum number of accesses	Average access	Degree vertex
Student/Bachelor	1 - Area 5 (books) and Area 4 (books)	3,175 - Area 6 (articles)	302.85	28
Student/Master	1 - Area 1 (books) and Area 5 (books)	4,547 - Area 6 (articles)	426.44	29
Student/Ph.D	1 - Area 6 (books) and Area 5 (editorial)	6,118 - Area 6 (articles)	551.23	30
Student/Postgraduate	1 - Area 6 (books), Area 1 (book chapters) and Area 4 (editorials and reviews)	1,272 - Area 6 (articles)	133	25
Librarian	1 - Area 2 (reviews)	397 - Area 6 (articles)	50.16	18
Lecturer	1 - Area 5 (reviews and conferences) and Area 4 (editorials and books)	403 - Area 6 (articles)	52.81	22
Senior Lecturer	1 - Area 1 (book chapters) and Area 3 (book chapters)	230 - Area 6 (articles)	35.22	18
Professor	1 - Area 2 (letters to the editor), Area 6 (conferences), Area 4 (editorials and book chapters)	2,037 - Area 6 (articles)	164.65	29
Associate Professor	1 - Area 7 (editorials), Area 4 (editorials), Area 5 (books and editorials) and Area 6 (books)	1,018 - Area 6 (Articles)	90.03	29
Researcher	1 - Area 4 (reviews y editorials), Area 5 (editorials and conferences) and Area 2 (letters to the editor)	4,552 - Area 6 (articles)	377	31
Other	1 - Area 4 (books and book chapters), Area 1 (books) and Area 6 (books)	1,328 - Area 6 (articles)	137	24
Unspecified	1 - Area 3 (book chapters), Area 7 (conferences and articles), Area 6 (reviews) and Area 2 (reviews)	76 - Area 3 (Articles)	19.92	14

Table 2. Most accessed types of publications by knowledge area.

Knowledge area	Most accessed type of publication	Access count
Physical Mathematics and Earth Science	Articles	2,011 (Ph.D. Student)
Biology and Chemistry	Articles	2,982 (Ph.D. Student)
Medical and Health Sciences	Articles	2,338 (Ph.D. Student)
Humanities and Behavioral Sciences	Articles	509 (Ph.D. Student)
Social Sciences	Articles	794 (Ph.D. Student)
Agricultural Sciences and Biotechnology	Articles	6,118 (Ph.D. Student)
Engineering and Technology	Articles	364 (Ph.D. Student)

Table 3 shows the users continents who have accessed the scientific production of the UADY, their minimum and maximum accesses with the corresponding country, and their average access. The values in the second, the third and the fourth columns where obtained based on the weight of the edges.

From the analyzed production, it was found that the accesses come mainly from North and Central America, with Mexico being the country with the most accesses, while the continent with the lowest number of accesses is Africa.

Table 4 shows, by knowledge area, the total number of scientific publications and the three countries with the highest numbers of accesses to its scientific production. The three countries with the highest number of accesses to publications are Mexico, the United States and Brazil, mainly in publications in the Agricultural Sciences and Biotechnology area.

Table 3. Description of accesses by continent.

Continent	Minimum number of accesses	Maximum number of accesses	Average access
North and Center America (12 countries)	1 (Panama)	728 Mexico	111.33
South America (10 countries)	2 (Paraguay)	495 (Brasil)	81.1
Europe (31 countries)	1 (Malta, Estonia, Reunion, Lithuania and Greece)	209 (United Kingdom)	29.58
Africa (18 countries)	1 (Ethiopia, Malawi, Mauritius, Namibia and Uganda)	27 (South Africa)	4.55
Asia (21 countries)	1 (Cyprus, Jordan, Hong Kong, Israel, Thailand and Bhutan)	75 (India)	13.23
Oceania (6 countries)	2 (New Caledonia and Papua New Guinea)	37 (Australia)	11.2

Table 4. Countries with the highest numbers of accesses to scientific publications of the knowledge areas.

Knowledge area	Top 3 - Countries with the highest number of accesses
Physical Mathematics and Earth Science (156 publications)	Mexico (85), United States (45) and Brazil (39)
Biology and Chemistry (220 publications)	Mexico (131), United States (93) and Brazil (72)
Medical and Health Sciences (162 publications)	Mexico (82), United States (71) and Brazil (60)
Humanities and Behavioral Sciences (30 publications)	United States (25), Mexico (15) and Canada (10)
Social Sciences (40 publications)	Mexico and United States (20), Canada, Germany and Brasil (6) and Argentina, Chile and Ghana (5)
Agricultural Sciences and Biotechnology (499 publications)	Mexico (381), Brazil (255) and United States (214)
Engineering and Technology (47 publications)	Brazil (21), Spain (16) and Mexico (14)

5   Conclusions

Characterizing the knowledge dissemination is relevant to the principles of Open Science. In this sense, analyzing the profiles and relationships of users in a community (whether a social network or repository) provides new perspectives that can complement traditional models of measuring the impact of a product on generating new research.

Such relationships between users and products are usually represented as graphs, facilitating their visualization and study. Thanks to these representations it is possible to infer the individual or group characteristics of users that are directly or indirectly related to their preferences, their behavior and their context in terms of the use they give to a product in the community.

In this work, a methodology has been presented to generate graphs that integrate information from different sources related to consumption and production of a higher education institution. The results allow characterizing the diffusion of knowledge in an academic community such as Mendeley.

To the extent that other social networks and repositories have services for external access to their data, it will be possible to generate a more accurate picture of the impact of dissemination on the development of knowledge. This requires mechanisms that guarantee the normalization and standardization of the information that is transferred. The heterogeneity in its subject matter and its structure generate considerable problems for its correct recovery: there are numerous formats, styles and languages used to represent the same information.

As future lines of research is the application of knowledge extraction techniques to identify related groups and related products as well as integrate new sources of information.

References

1. Aduku, K.J., Thelwall, M., Kousha, K.: Do Mendeley reader counts reflect the scholarly impact of conference papers? An investigation of computer science and engineering. Scientometrics **112**(1), 573–581 (2017). https://doi.org/10.1007/s11192-017-2367-1

2. AI2: Frequently Asked Questions (2020). https://www.semanticscholar.org/faq#open-data

3. Álvarez, M., Parra, J.: Teoría de grafos. Ph.D. thesis, Universidad del Bío-Bío (2013). http://repobib.ubiobio.cl/jspui/bitstream/123456789/1953/3/Alvarez_Nunez_Marcelino.pdf

4. Bar-Ilan, J.: Which h-index? - a comparison of WoS, scopus and Google scholar. Scientometrics **74**(2), 257–271 (2007). https://doi.org/10.1007/s11192-008-0216-y

5. Barnes, C.: The use of altmetrics as a tool for measuring research impact. Aust. Acad. Res. Libr. **46**(2), 121–134 (2015). https://doi.org/10.1080/00048623.2014.1003174

6. CEDIA: REDI-Nosotros (2020). https://redi.cedia.edu.ec/#/info/about

7. Conacyt: Lineamientos Generales de Ciencia Abierta (2017). https://www.repositorionacionalcti.mx/documentos

8. Conacyt: Lineamientos Jurídicos de Ciencia Abierta (2017). https://www.repositorionacionalcti.mx/documentos

9. Conacyt: Criterios SNI - Conacyt (2019). https://www.conacyt.gob.mx/index.php/sni/convocatorias-conacyt/convocatorias-sistema-nacional-de-investigadores-sni/marco-legal-sni/criterios-sni

10. Elsevier: How to use the API - Mendeley Developer Portal. https://dev.mendeley.com/overview/how_to_use_the_api.html

11. Elsevier: Affiliation Search API (2020). https://dev.elsevier.com/documentation/AffiliationSearchAPI.wadl

12. Elsevier: Scopus Search API (2020). https://dev.elsevier.com/documentation/ScopusSearchAPI.wadl

13. Elsevier: What are the most frequent Subject Area categories and classifications used in Scopus? (2020). https://service.elsevier.com/app/answers/detail/a_id/14882/supporthub/scopus/~/what-are-the-most-frequent-subject-area-categories-and-classifications-used-in/

14. Elsevier: Who uses - Mendeley — Elsevier (2020). https://www.elsevier.com/solutions/mendeley/who-uses
15. Fairclough, R., Thelwall, M.: National research impact indicators from Mendeley readers. J. Inform. **9**(4), 845–859 (2015). https://doi.org/10.1016/j.joi.2015.08.003
16. Gephi Consortium: Gephi - The Open Graph Viz Platform (2017). https://gephi.org/
17. Guerrero-Sosa, J.D.T., Menéndez-Domínguez, V.H., Castellanos-Bolaños, M.E., Curi-Quintal, L.F.: Analysis of internal and external academic collaboration in an institution through graph theory. Vietnam J. Comput. Sci. 1–25 (2020). https://doi.org/10.1142/S2196888820500220
18. Guerrero-Sosa, J.D.T., Menendez-Domínguez, V., Castellanos-Bolaños, M.-E., Curi-Quintal, L.F.: Use of graph theory for the representation of scientific collaboration. In: Nguyen, N.T., Chbeir, R., Exposito, E., Aniorté, P., Trawiński, B. (eds.) ICCCI 2019. LNCS (LNAI), vol. 11684, pp. 543–554. Springer, Cham (2019). https://doi.org/10.1007/978-3-030-28374-2_47
19. Khazragui, H., Hudson, J.: Measuring the benefits of university research: impact and the REF in the UK. Res. Eval. **24**(1), 51–62 (2015). https://doi.org/10.1093/reseval/rvu028
20. Mendeley: Models - Mendeley Python SDK 0.3.2 documentation (2014). https://mendeley-python.readthedocs.io/en/latest/models.html#mendeley.models.catalog.CatalogDocument
21. Mike, T.: Are Mendeley reader counts high enough for research evaluations when articles are published? Aslib J. Inf. Manage. **69**(2), 174–183 (2017). https://doi.org/10.1108/AJIM-01-2017-0028
22. MongoDB: Qué es MongoDB? (2020). https://www.mongodb.com/es/what-is-mongodb
23. Prieto, M.E., Zapata, A., Menendez, V.H.: Data mining learning objects. In: Romero, C., Ventura, S., Pechenizkly, M. (eds.) Handbook of Educational Data Mining, chap. 34, pp. 481–492. CRC Press (2011)
24. Sallán, J.M., Fonollosa, J.B., Fernández, V., Suñé, A.: Teoría de grafos. In: Sallán Leyes, J.M. (ed.) Métodos cuantitativos en organización Industrial I, chap. 7, pp. 137–172. Edicions UPC (2002)
25. SEP: En Transparencia — Rendición de cuentas (2020). https://sep.subsidioentransparencia.mx/2020/subsidio-ordinario/universidad/UADY
26. Social Media Research Foundation: NodeXL — Your Social Network Analysis Tool for Social Media (2016). https://www.smrfoundation.org/nodexl/
27. Trudeau, R.J.: Introduction to Graph Theory. Dover Books on Mathematics. Dover, Garden City (1993)
28. UADY: Universidad Autónoma de Yucatán (2019). https://www.uady.mx/nuestra-universidad
29. UNESCO: Open Science (2019). https://en.unesco.org/science-sustainable-future/open-science
30. Woolcott, G., Keast, R., Pickernell, D.: Deep impact: re-conceptualising university research impact using human cultural accumulation theory. Stud. High. Educ. **45**(6), 1197–1216 (2020). https://doi.org/10.1080/03075079.2019.1594179

Relation Classification: How Well Do Neural Network Approaches Work?

Sri Nath Dwivedi[1]([⊠]), Harish Karnick[2]([⊠]), and Renu Jain[3]([⊠])

[1] AITH, Kanpur, India
srinath.vedi@gmail.com
[2] IIT, Kanpur, India
hk@iitk.ac.in
[3] UIET, Kanpur, India
jainrenu@gmail.com

Abstract. Relation classification is a well known task in NLP. It classifies relations that occur between two entities in sentences by assigning a label from a pre-defined set of abstract relation labels. A benchmark data set for this task is the SemEval-2010 Task 8 data set. Neural network approaches are currently the methods that give state-of-art results on a wide range of NLP problems. There is also the claim that the models trained on one task carry over to other tasks with only a small amount of fine tuning. Our experience suggests that for the relation classification problem while a wide variety of neural network methods work reasonably well it is very hard to improve performance significantly by including different kinds of syntactic and semantic information that intuitively should be important in signalling the relation label. We think that improved performance will be hard to achieve without injecting controlled class specific semantic information into the classification process.

In our experimentation we have given many different kinds of syntactic and semantic information by tagging suitable words with relevant semantic/syntactic tags. We have also tried various embedding methods like Google embeddings, FastText, Word-to-vec and BERT. None of these make a substantial difference in the performance which hovers between 82% to 85%.

Surprisingly, when we looked at the top three classification performance it was above 96% that is 11 to 14% above the top one performance. This implies that it should be possible to boost the correct label from the second or third position to the first position by suitable semantic inputs and architectural innovations. We have experimented with an architecture that gives supplementary information about words in the sentence as well as the sentence itself in parallel with the main stream of information, namely the sentence itself. In one such case we are able to boost performance to state-of-art levels. A systematic investigation is ongoing.

© Springer Nature Switzerland AG 2020
B. Villazón-Terrazas et al. (Eds.): KGSWC 2020, CCIS 1232, pp. 102–112, 2020.
https://doi.org/10.1007/978-3-030-65384-2_8

1   Introduction

Relation classification identifies the type of relationship that exists between two given entities in a sentence - we consider only binary relationships. The type of this relationship depends on other words present in the sentence and more generally on the meaning that the sentence is trying to convey. Sentences usually have multiple entities and a single entity can be related to multiple other entities in the sentence. The type of this relation can be different in each case. So, in relation classification data sets it is necessary to mark the two entities whose relation is to be classified. The reason relation classification can be an interesting and challenging problem is the types of relation labels that are specified. The relation labels can be abstract, directed and there can be subtle differences between two or more labels that often depend on the meaning of the entire sentence. One such well known data set is the SEMEVAL-2010 Task 8 data set (henceforth Semeval data set). The Semeval data set has 9 bi-directional relations (giving 18 actual labels) and a nineteenth catch all label OTHER where none of the other eighteen labels are appropriate. The data set was labelled by human volunteers who were given detailed instructions for each label type.

From inspection of the Semeval data set it is clear that the relation type can often depend on linguistic markers like *is-x, x-of, in-x, from-x to-y, caused* (prepositions, verbs and nouns) that are proximate to the entities and/or the relation word(s). But in several cases the relation type is sensitive to the overall meaning of the sentence which implies that words distant from the entities and/or relation word influence the label type. We consider some examples below:

1. *The <e1> singer </e1>, who performed three of the nominated songs, also caused a <e2> commotion </e2> on the red carpet.* Relation label: Cause-Effect(e1, e2).
2. *The <e1> radiation </e1> from the atomic <e2> bomb explosion </e2> is a typical acute radiation.* Relation label: Cause-Effect(e2, e1). Clashes with Entity-Origin(e1, e2).
3. *A person infected with a <e1>flu</e1> <e2>virus</e2> strain develops antibodies against the virus.* Relation label: Cause-Effect(e2, e1).
4. A person infected with a <e1>Corona</e1> <e2>virus</e2> strain develops antibodies against it. Relation label: OTHER (Given by the authors based on labelling guidelines).
5. *A volunteer injected, during the phase-2 trials in India started by Oxford and AstraZeneca, with a <e1>flu</e1> <e2>vaccine</e2> developed antibodies against it.* Relation label: OTHER (Given by authors based on labelling guidelines).

The first three sentences are from the data set or guideline documents. The last two were created and labelled by the authors using the guidelines. It is clear that words like *caused* in Example 1 and *from* in Example 2 signal the type of the relation. However, note that due to the labelling guidelines Example 2 has been labelled Cause-Effect(e2, e1) because specifically radiation, light or heat is in the negative list for Entity-Origin. Otherwise the word *from* often signals an Entity-Origin relation. There are many such exceptions or subtleties in the labelling guidelines. Examples 3, 4 and 5 show why it can be hard to label correctly. One can argue that *flu* qualifies/ describes/ elaborates the word virus and vaccine in Examples 3 and 5 respectively much as the word *Corona* does in Example 4. While flu is caused by a virus in the context of the sentence the relation between *flu* and virus is better interpreted as one where *flu* is a qualifier or descriptor of the virus instead of virus being a cause of the flu. But the guidelines mean that Example 3 is classified as Cause-Effect while in an almost identical looking sentence, Example 4, the relation will be OTHER. The label set does not contain a label such as Entity-Descriptor or Entity-Qualifier. Example 5 shows how a very similar sentence (the relative clause is a garden path merely to increase the distance between *injected* and the entities) can never be classified as Cause-Effect in spite of being structurally similar and having significant overlap with Example 3. The point is that both the relation types and the guidelines that specify certain subtle semantic differences and exceptions that give a contra or pro indication for a label are at least slightly arbitrary.

The interesting question is whether task agnostic neural network approaches work well in such settings and if yes how well do they work and what do the results indicate.

For example, *New Delhi is the capital of India.* In this sentence *New Delhi* and *India* are the two entities that are related by *is-capital-of* giving the relation *is-capital-of(Delhi, India)*. There are many relational linguistic markers like *is-x, x-of, in-x, from-x to-y, caused* etc. that often signal the presence of a relation and also indicate the type of the relation.

We have seen that relation types are influenced by specific words that are proximate to the entities and relation words as well as by the overall meaning of the sentence that is sensitive to words that are distant. So, it is plausible that a neural network architecture with some kind of combination of a convolutional neural network and a recurrent neural network should be able to learn such relational dependencies between the two entities. Consequently, there is a reasonably large body of work that has used a wide variety of neural networks to do relation classification. A benchmark data set used for this is SemEval-2010 Task 8. Table 1 shows the top results from various such attempts since mid 2016 and we see that the F1 values have ranged between approximately 87% and 90%. The current best performance is 90.2%. The top performers include rather specialized networks and performance enhancing tweaks. We are more interested in seeing whether simple class specific semantic information can be encoded in these networks to enhance performance.

2   Related Work

In this section we briefly review the work on relation classification.

[31] proposed an RNN (Recurrent Neural Network) model and averaged model parameters to stabilize learning and improve generalization. They

achieved an F1 score of 79.40% . This work was based on earlier work in [18,27]. [4] used an LSTM network and shortest dependency paths to get an F1 of 83.7%. [5] used a combination of RNN, CNN and attention and got an F1 of 83.7%. [26] used attention in LSTMs to get an F1 of 84.0%. [25] classified relations via ranking and achieved an F1 of 84.10%. [2] used a CNN (Convolutional Neural Network), incorporated shortest dependency paths and used negative sampling for subjects and objects and achieved an F1 of 85.4%. [3] compared RNNs and CNNs and claimed RNNs work better than CNNs. What is evident from the above is that a wide variety of neural network architectures and addition of basic linguistic information like part-of-speech, dependencies, etc. do not substantially change performance.

We now review more recent work that tries to inject more specific 'semantic' information into the model learning process.

[6] used a GCN (Graphical CNN) along with extra information from a knowledge base. [24] claimed that entities participating in a relation influence its type more than the high-level linguistic information obtained through NLP tools. It used an end-to-end RNN incorporating an entity aware attention mechanism with a latent entity typing method. [23] [TRE] combined unsupervised and supervised learning to improve relation classification. A Transformer for relation extraction (TRE) makes use of pre-trained deep language representations instead of using explicit linguistic features of the language. It is combined with a self-attentive Transformer architecture to model long range dependencies between entities. [14] [Att-Pooling-CNN] uses a CNN with entity-specific and relation-specific attention helping the model to learn what is more relevant for a given classification. [22] [Entity-Aware BERT] was built on top of pre-trained self-attentive models to identify the positions of the entities and used Bidirectional Encoder Representations from Transformers (BERT) as the transformer-based encoder. [21] [KnowBert-W+W] incorporated contextual word knowledge from knowledge bases (KBs) consisting of high quality, human-curated knowledge rather than using unstructured, unlabeled text. They have presented a general method to insert multiple KBs into a large pre-trained model with a Knowledge Attention and Re contextualization (KAR) mechanism that is inserted between two layers of a pre-trained model like BERT. [20] [R-BERT] incorporated entity-level information like location of entities, marking the entities as first and second into a pre-trained BERT language model to improve relation classification. [19] [BERTEM+MTB] developed models that produced task agnostic relation representations using entity-linked text and learnt mappings from relation statements to relation representations. [29] [EP GNN] used an entity pair graph to represent the correlations between entity pairs and implemented an entity pair based CNN model. In the above methods, semantic guidance is being provided by emphasizing entities and/or relations in some way and also by incorporating extra knowledge via KBs or from unsurpervised corpora processed in specific ways. The results obtained are summarized in Table 1.

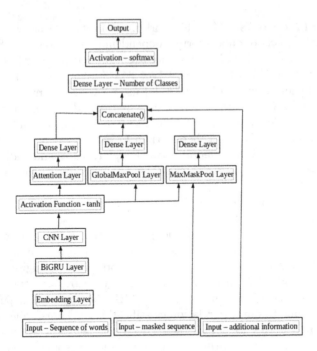

Fig. 1. Architecture diagram

3   Baseline

For our work we used the models described in [1] as the baseline. The basic model has two layers consisting of a CNN layer and a Bidirectional Gated Recurrent Unit (Bi-GRU) layer. GoogleNews-vectors-negative300 were used and three different models of the two layer architecture were constructed for the models that used fusion. These models were:

1. CBGRU-ME: contains a CNN layer, a Bi-GRU layer, max pooling and entity pooling.
2. CBGRU-A: is the same as the previous model except that instead of max pooling and entity pooling attention pooling is used.
3. CBGRU-MEA: is a combination of the previous two models that is CNN, Bi-GRU layers, max pooling, entity pooling and attention pooling. This is the model that has been used.

The architecture is shown in Fig. 1. Two methods were used for fusing the results from the three models: a) a voting scheme where the winning label had the highest number of votes and b) summing softmax probabilities of each classifier where the winning label had the highest summed probability. The performance details of the different individual models and the two models that use model fusion can be found in [1]. We use the voting model with a performance of 83.70% (F1) as our baseline. So, we have a strong baseline.

Table 1. Performance of recent models

Rank	Method	F1	Reference	Year
1	RESIDE	84.0	[6]	2018
2	Entity Attention Bi-LSTM	85.2	[24]	2019
3	TRE	87.1	[23]	2019
4	Att-Pooling-CNN	88.0	[14]	2016
5	Entity-Aware BERT	89.0	[22]	2019
6	KnowBert-W+W	89.1	[21]	2019
7	R-BERT	89.25	[20]	2019
8	BERTEM + MTB	89.5	[19]	2019
9	EP GNN	90.2	[29]	2019

4   Experiments

Our objective was to improve the accuracy of the baseline system used for relation classification by introducing simple class specific 'semantic' guidance in the form of extra information that can be easily computed from the learning set itself. A series of experiments were performed to examine the effects on the accuracy of a standard model of a CNN and Bi-GRU neural network by inserting different types of syntactic and semantic information. The process of experimentation involved 4 steps: 1. Identifying the types of linguistic information that plays an important role in relation classification 2. Extracting that information from the given dataset either by using available NLP tools or implementing statistical approaches. 3. Exploring different methods to insert the extracted linguistic information in the training and testing data 4. Running the model and compare the accuracy of models. To compare the performances of various experiments, a base experiment where only the entities were marked was taken and the accuracy of the this was 83.70%.

4.1   Experiments After the Inclusion of English Specific Linguistic Knowledge: First Experiment

Experience with the English language suggests that verbs, prepositions and nouns representing entities are strong indicators of the type of relation that exists between the entities in a sentence. To reconfirm this, a few sentences of each relation were examined manually and it appeared that prepositions and a few specific kind of main verbs play an important role in many relations and can be treated as a strong clue to the type of the relation. However, it was observed that prepositions either attached to the main verb of the sentence or attached to the second entity play a significant role in relation classification though many times this clue is ambiguous and indicate two or three relations instead of a single relation. We calculated different class specific statistics for words and created a list of the top N prepositions arranged in descending order of highest occurrence statistics for each relation class. Then for each sentence, in that relation class, the top ranked preposition word in the sentence was tagged with the semantic begin-end tags. These newly tagged sentences formed the learning set for training a standard CBGRU-MEA model. Relation based tagging was done in the training data set through an algorithm and in the test data, all prepositions were tagged. The accuracy achieved was only around 80%. A detailed analysis of miss-classified sentences showed that around 50% sentences of type OTHER were misclassified due to the occurrence of prepositions in these sentences making the system classify them into one of the more specific relation types.

4.2   Second Experiment

It is known that most of the time, the type and the action denoted by the main verb of any sentence defines the relationship of its subject and object entities present in the sentence. Hence, we experimented by putting emphasis on the verb relation in the sentence. To extract the relation verb, knowledge graph and NLTK tools were used and then the training as well as testing data were tagged by introducing special markers. The accuracy achieved was 84.37% which was a slight improvement over the base level but not significant.

Another similar experiment was done by finding the shortest dependency path (SDP) between the marked entities. We thought SDP contained enough information between the two entities to identify their relationship. We used SpaCy to find the SDP of a sentence. The SDP information was added in training and as well as during testing and the accuracy achieved was 82.84% which was again very close to base level.

4.3   Third Experiment: Adding Syntactical Category of Each Word

Each sentence of training data and testing data was parsed using NLTK tools to get the syntactic category of each word and then the part of speech of each word was attached with the word to check the effect of adding word level syntactical information. The accuracy achieved was 84.51% which was again slightly higher than the base model.

Fourth Experiment: After adding syntactic information, we also added some semantic information for entities and the main verb of the sentence. This was done with the help of Wordnet semantic tags representing a class of nouns and verbs. But, again there was no improvement.

In addition to this, many other experiments were performed like marking higher frequency verbs and nouns, increasing the training data set by adding more sentences by using the hyponyms of each entity word and the main verb, etc. but the accuracy did not improve as expected.

4.4   Using Different Word Embeddings

For the base line models, Google embeddings of size 300 were used. However, it was observed that there are many words for which Google embeddings are not available and so the Google average embedding had to be used for all such words. To avoid the average embedding, we generated embeddings using FastText and WordtoVec but found that the accuracy of the model went down slightly instead of improving. We also used the BERT word vector representation (of 768 size) and the results obtained were comparable to those from the Google embeddings. Hence, we concluded that Google embeddings could be used in future experiments.

4.5   Experiments by Taking Top 3 Choices

We tried tagging some sentences manually using the Semeval Task 8 guidelines and found that in many instances, it was very difficult even for us to distinguish between two similar types of relations. For example, Content-Container or Component-Whole and several other pairs like Entity-Origin, Cause-Effect. This has been elaborated in the introduction. Therefore, we set the system to output top 3 choices identified by the system and then checked whether the top 3 choices contained the correct label or not. To our surprise the accuracy was 96.55% which was very encouraging. This meant that the system had to learn to distinguish the right type from a very limited set of possible types.

5   Data Set, Experiments and Results

The SemEval-2010 Task 8 data set has 9 categories and an *OTHER* category for relations that do not belong to any of the nine (giving a total of 10 categories). Since each relation is a binary relation the entity order matters, so if R is the relation and e_1, e_2 are entities $R(e_1, e_2)$ and $R(e_2, e_1)$ are different relations unless R is symmetric. None of the SemEval-2010 Task 8 relations, not including *OTHER*, is symmetric. So, there are $9 \times 2 + 1 = 19$ class labels (Table 2).

Only 9 classes (order agnostic) were used to calculate the statistic for words that were semantically tagged.

There are 8000 sentences for training and 2717 sentences for testing. Each sentence has two entities marked by entity start and end tags. It also has a relation label indicating the type of relation between the tagged entities.

Experimentation is still in its early stages. We report results on eight experiments in the form of table below. Our best result which matches the state-of-art is obtained using a two stage network by giving the top 3 labels obtained from the standard CNN-BiGRU classifier as additional input while training a second stage classifier. This has given us an F1 score of 90.64%. These are early results and need to be confirmed with more extensive experimentation on the Semeval and other data sets.

Table 2. Table: experiment results

Expt. No.	Semantic input	Tagging status	F1 score
a)	None	Entities	83.70%
b)	Class based prepositions	Entities and prepositions	80.38%
c)	Relation verb	Entities and Relation verb	84.37%
d)	Shortest dependency path	Entities and relation word	82.84%
e)	Part of Speech	Entities and POS of every word	84.89%
f)	Hyponyms	Entities	82.21%
g)	Semantic Information of entities and verb	Entities and semantic tags	82.78%
h)	Top 3 tags	Entities	90.64%

6   Discussion and Conclusions

We saw that vanilla neural network methods work reasonably well reaching an F1 score close to the mid eighties. However, adding various kinds of specific syntactic and/or semantic information to the neural network does not significantly change performance. At the same time the top-3 performance is significantly better - almost 12% better - reaching 96.55% using just the baseline architecture. We hypothesized that it should be possible to teach the network to distinguish the top label when it is present in the top-3. Our initial attempt did this by training a two stage network where in the second stage the network is trained with the top 3 labels as input and we got a state-of-art performance of 90.64%. We think a systematic and controlled way to add very specific semantic information in parallel should be able to help improve classification performance. We saw that a two stage model that first learns to predict the top three labels and then separately learns to choose the correct label from the top 3 performs surprisingly well.

Acknowledgement. I would like to express my gratitude to Sahitya Patel, M.Tech, IIT Kanpur and Pawan Kumar, Ph.D student of IIT Kanpur. They were very helpful and provided me technical support required for the experiments.

References

1. Patel, S.: Multi-Way Classification of Relations Between Pairs of Entities, IIT Kanpur M.Tech. thesis (2018)
2. Xu, K., Feng, Y., Huang, S., Zhao, D: Semantic relation classification via convolutional neural networks with simple negative sampling. arXiv preprint(2015). arXiv:1506.07650

3. Zhang, D., Wang, D.: Relation classification via recurrent neural network arXiv preprint (2015). arXiv:1508.01006

4. Yan, X., Mou, L., Li, G., Chen, Y., Peng, H., Jin, Z.: Classifying relations via long short term memory networks along shortest dependency path. arXiv preprint (2015). arXiv:1508.03720

5. Zhang, X., Chen, F., Huang, R.: A combination of RNN and CNN for attention-based relation classification. J. Procedia Comput. Sci. **131**, 911–917 (2018). Elsevier

6. Vashishth, S., Joshi, R., Prayaga, S.S., Bhattacharyya, C., Talukdar, P.: Reside: improving distantly-supervised neural relation extraction using side information. journal: arXiv preprint arXiv:1812.04361 (2018)

7. Cho, K., et al.: Learning phrase representations using RNN encoder-decoder for statistical machine translation. journal: arXiv preprint arXiv:1406.1078 (2014)

8. Kim, J., Lee, J.-H.: Multiple range-restricted bidirectional gated recurrent units with attention for relation classification. journal: arXiv preprint arXiv:1707.01265 (2017)

9. Liu, Y., Wei, F., Li, S., Ji, H., Zhou, M., Wang, H.g: A dependency-based neural network for relation classification. journal: arXiv preprint arXiv:1507.04646 (2015)

10. Miwa, M., Bansal, M.: End-to-end relation extraction using lstms on sequences and tree structures. journal: arXiv preprint arXiv:1601.00770 (2016)

11. Nguyen, T.H., Grishman, R.: Combining neural networks and log-linear models to improve relation extraction. journal: arXiv preprint arXiv:1511.05926 (2015)

12. Qin, P., Xu, W., Guo, J.: An empirical convolutional neural network approach for semantic relation classification. Neurocomputing **190**, 1–9 (2016). Elsevier

13. Vu, N.T., Adel, H., Gupta, P., Schütze, H.: Combining recurrent and convolutional neural networks for relation classification. journal: arXiv preprint arXiv:1605.07333 (2016)

14. Wang, L., Cao, Z., De Melo, G., Liu, Z.: Relation Classification via Multi-level Attention CNNs. Tsinghua University, Beijing (2016)

15. Xu, K., Feng, Y., Huang, S., Zhao, D.: Semantic relation classification via convolutional neural networks with simple negative sampling. journal: arXiv preprint arXiv:1506.07650 (2015)

16. Xu, Y., et al.: Improved relation classification by deep recurrent neural networks with data augmentation. journal: arXiv preprint arXiv:1601.03651 (2016)

17. Yan, X., Mou, L., Li, G., Chen, Y., Peng, H., Jin, Z.: Classifying relations via long short term memory networks along shortest dependency path. journal: arXiv preprint arXiv:1508.03720 (2015)

18. Blunsom, P., Hermann, K.M.: The Role of Syntax in Vector Space Models of Compositional Semantics (2013)

19. Soares, L.B., FitzGerald, N., Ling, J., Kwiatkowski, T.: Matching the Blanks: Distributional Similarity for Relation Learning. journal: arXiv preprint arXiv:1906.03158 (2019)

20. Wu, S., He, Y.: Enriching Pre-trained Language Model with Entity Information for Relation Classification. journal: arXiv preprint arXiv:1905.08284 (2019)

21. Peters, M.E., et al.: Knowledge Enhanced Contextual Word Representations. journal: arXiv preprint arXiv:1909.04164 (2019)

22. Wang, H., et al.: Extracting Multiple-Relations in One-Pass with Pre-Trained Transformers. journal: arXiv preprint arXiv:1902.01030 (2019)

23. Alt, C., Hübner, M., Hennig, L.: Improving relation extraction by pre-trained language representations. journal: arXiv preprint arXiv:1906.03088 (2019)

24. Lee, J., Seo, S., Choi, Y.S.: Semantic Semantic relation classification via bidirectional LSTM networks with entity-aware attention using latent entity typing. Symmetry **11**(6), 785 (2019). Multidisciplinary Digital Publishing Institute
25. Dos Santos, C.N., Xiang, B., Zhou, B.: Classifying relations by ranking with convolutional neural networks. arXiv preprint (2015). arXiv:1504.06580
26. Zhou, P., et al.: Attention-based bidirectional long short-term memory networks for relation classification. In: 54th Annual Meeting. on Proceedings, (Volume 2: Short Papers), pp. 207–212. Association for Computational Linguistics (2016)
27. Socher, R., Huval, B., Manning, C.D., Ng, A.Y: Semantic compositionality through recursive matrix-vector spaces. In: Proceedings of the 2012 Joint Conference on Empirical Methods in Language Processing Natural and Computational Natural Language Learning on Proceedings, Organization. Association for Computational Linguistics (2012)
28. Socher, R., Bauer, J., Manning, C.D., Ng, A.Y.: Parsing with compositional vector grammars. In: 51st Annual Meeting on Proceedings, Association for Computational Linguistics (Volume 1: Long Papers), pp. 455–465 (2013)
29. Zhao, Y., Wan, H., Gao, J., Lin, Y.: Improving relation classification by entity pair graph. In: Asian Conference on Machine Learning, pp. 1156–1171 (2019)
30. Wang, L., Cao, Z., De Melo, G., Liu, Z.: Relation classification via multi-level attention CNNs. In: 54th Annual Meeting on Proceedings, Association for Computational Linguistics (Volume 1: Long Papers), pp. 1298–1307 (2016)
31. Hashimoto, K., Miwa, M., Tsuruoka, Y., Chikayama, T.: Simple customization of recursive neural networks for semantic relation classification. In: Conference on Proceedings, Empirical Methods in Natural Language Processing, pp. 1372-1376 (2013)
32. Cai, R., Zhang, X., Wang, H.: Bidirectional recurrent convolutional neural network for relation classification. In: the 54th Annual Meeting on Proceedings, the Association for Computational Linguistics (Volume 1: Long Papers) pp. 756–765 (2016)
33. Qin, P., Xu, W., Guo, J.: Designing an adaptive attention mechanism for relation classification. In: 2017 International Joint Conference on Neural Networks (IJCNN), pp. 4356–4362. IEEE (2017)
34. Manning, C., Surdeanu, M., Bauer, J., Finkel, J., Bethard, S., McClosky, D.: The stanford CoreNLP natural language processing toolkit. In: 52nd Annual Meeting on Proceedings, the Association for Computational Linguistics: System Demonstrations, pp. 55–60 (2014)
35. Yu, M., Gormley, M., Dredze, M.: Factor-based compositional embedding models. In: NIPS Workshop on Learning Semantics, on Proceedings, pp. 95–101 (2014)
36. Patel, S.: http://172.28.64.70:8080/jspui/handle/123456789/17624

Standards Conformance Metrics for Geospatial Linked Data

Beyza Yaman[1](✉), Kevin Thompson[2], and Rob Brennan[1]

[1] ADAPT Centre, Dublin City University, Dublin, Ireland
{beyza.yaman,rob.brennan}@adaptcentre.ie
[2] Ordnance Survey Ireland, Dublin, Ireland
kevin.thompson@osi.ie

Abstract. This paper describes a set of new Geospatial Linked Data (GLD) quality metrics based on ISO and W3C spatial standards for monitoring geospatial data production. The Luzzu quality assessment framework was employed to implement the metrics and evaluate a set of five public geospatial datasets. Despite the availability of metrics-based quality assessment tools for Linked Data, there is a lack of dedicated quality metrics for GLD, as well as, no metrics were found based on geospatial data standards and best practices. This paper provides nine new metrics and a first assessment of public datasets for geospatial standards compliance. Our approach also demonstrates the effectiveness of developing new quality metrics through analysis of the requirements defined in relevant standards.

1 Introduction

Geospatial data has long been considered a high value resource. Geospatial Linked Data (GLD) is ideally positioned to provide an open, web-based mechanism to exchange and interlink the geospatial entities for emerging national geospatial data infrastructures. As societal dependence on accurate real time geopositioning and contextualisation of data increases, so do the quality demands on geospatial data. All geospatial data is subject to a degree of measurement error. Further issues can occur during the data lifecycle: digitalization, curation, transformation and integration of geospatial measurements and metadata all have risks. Typically, spatial measurements must be integrated into a digital twin of an entity which can include or interlink topographical, political, historical, environmental and other factors. Thus, producing and updating geospatial data is expensive [10]. In the past, quantifying positional accuracy was sufficient, but now geospatial data must also comply with broader usage requirements such as the FAIR data principles [15].

There are a number of relevant standards and best practices for publishing high quality geospatial data and Linked Data. This includes ISO standards, Open Geospatial Consortium (OGC) standards, and W3C Spatial Data on the Web Best Practices (SDOTW). However, data publishers are not always able to assure

© Springer Nature Switzerland AG 2020
B. Villazón-Terrazas et al. (Eds.): KGSWC 2020, CCIS 1232, pp. 113–129, 2020.
https://doi.org/10.1007/978-3-030-65384-2_9

that they produce data conforming to these standards. Thus, it is important for publishers to have quality assessment processes and tools to provide assurance and enable improvement of these complex data life-cycles. Unfortunately, no existing tools directly address standards compliance for GLD.

Several quality assessments of GLD have previously been conducted [9,10, 12] but one of them relies on crowdsourced evaluations rather than automated metrics [9], another one provides a generic Linked Data quality assessments of the data that is not specific to geospatial concerns [10] and the other is tied to a custom ontology predating GLD standardisation [12]. In contrast, our starting point was to examine the relevant standards for geospatial data and to develop new quality metrics targeted at the GLD domain.

The research question investigated in this work is: To what extent can quality metrics derived from geospatial data standards be used to assess the standards compliance and quality of GLD. Thus, we reviewed the applicable standards for GLD from the ISO, OGC and W3C to identify a set of compliance points for each standard and a set of testable recommended best practices. Then a new set of metrics were developed to evaluate each compliance point. The metrics were implemented in the Luzzu open source quality assessment framework. A set of existing open GLD datasets were then evaluated for standards compliance quality by performing metric computation. All metrics developed here are described in the daQ vocabulary and published as an open resource for the community[1]. This paper is an extension of the previous work accepted from ISWC2020 poster&demo session [17] where an initial 3 metrics were proposed. In this work we describe 6 additional metrics which are developed as a part of LinkedDataOps project [16].

Our contributions are: *i)* Identification of standards conformance points for GLD across ISO, OGC and W3C standards; *ii)* Design and open source implementation of 9 new standards-based geospatial quality metrics in the Luzzu framework and providing a set of daQ ontology [3] describing the metrics; *iii)* providing a first comparative quality survey of public GLD datasets in terms of standards compliance.

The remainder of this paper is organized as follows: Sect. 2 describes the motivational OSi use case, Sect. 3 summarizes related works and background including GLD infrastructure and Luzzu framework. Section 4 discusses our approach including standardization proposals and defines the new metrics. We present the evaluation, our experiments and analysis of the results in Sect. 5. Conclusions and future work are discussed in Sect. 6.

2   Use Case

National mapping agencies such as Ordnance Survey Ireland (OSi) are now geospatial data publishers more than cartographic institutions. OSi's national geospatial digital infrastructure (Fig. 1) encompasses surveying and data capture, image processing, translation to the Prime2 object-oriented spatial model

---

[1] https://github.com/beyzayaman/standard-quality-metrics.

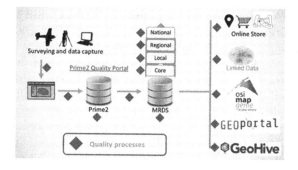

Fig. 1. OSi geospatial information publishing pipeline with quality control points

of over 50 million spatial objects tracked in time and provenance, conversion to the multi-resolution data source (MRDS) database for printing as cartographic products or data sales and distribution at data.geohive.ie [5]. These services run on a state of the art Oracle Spatial and Graph installation supporting both relational and RDF models. Managing data quality throughout the data pipeline and lifecycle is key to OSi (Fig. 1) and there are already quality checks on the data quality dimensions of positional accuracy, logical consistency, completeness, representational conciseness, syntactic validity, positional validity and semantic accuracy. Current data quality assessment within OSi depends on *i)* two automated tools: the rules-based 1Spatial 1Integrate and Luzzu for Linked Data [4] and *ii)* manual or semi-automated techniques by domain experts.

Moreover, the United Nations Global Geospatial Information Management (UN-GGIM) framework highlights the importance of standards conformance of data for quality. Thus there is a need for monitoring and reporting on the standards conformance of OSi GLD. For example, to provide continuous upward reporting to the Irish government, European Commission, UN; and provide feedback to managers within OSi for engineering team. Through a year-long series of internal workshops with stakeholders across the organisation the following requirements were addressed: *i)* **Req 1:** Identification of the relevant standards conformance points for GLD. *ii)* **Req 2:** Metrics for assessment of GLD for geospatial standards conformance. *iii)* **Req 3:** Quality assessment tools and processes for geospatial standards conformance. *iv)* **Req 4:** Fusion with existing quality metrics for visualization, analysis and reporting. Requirement showed a necessity for a new GLD standards conformance quality monitoring approach as for the first time quality is being measured in terms of standards compliance and specifically for the geospatial domain.

3   Related Work

This section discusses traditional and Linked Data solutions for geospatial data quality and standards conformance assessment.

Non-semantic Approaches to Geospatial Data Quality Assessment.
Rules-based quality assessment, as implemented in the 1Integrate tool suite for
spatial systems such as Oracle Spatial and Graph, is flexible and often used
for implementing data cleansing as well as quality assessment. In practice, rules
definitions are expensive to develop and maintain. Luzzu framework is useful
as it generates self-describing plug and play metrics and quality observations
metadata. Scalability is another area in which rules-based assessment can fail.
Execution of the explicit rules over 50 million spatial objects can take days,
even on custom high end hardware, like an Oracle exadata platform. Especially when large-scale data transformations must be carried out (for example
for schema updates or to fix systematic errors identified in older releases) then
the time required is unsustainable. Using probabilistic (sampling-based) metrics,
as deployed in Luzzu, for computationally expensive metrics is an advantage.

GLD Quality Assessment. The LinkedGeoData [2] and GeoLinkedData [11]
projects study spatial features in their datasets, however, the quality assessment
step is not addressed in their work. The most notable project is GeoKnow [10]
which assesses spatial data quality using standard quality metrics i.e. no metrics
addressing the specific requirements or models of GLD were used. However, most
of the implemented metrics provide statistical summaries for the data by looking
at the coverage of the data instead of specific geospatial measures.

Semantic approaches have significant advantages as interpretative frameworks for quality results. Quality assessments are published using the W3C data
quality vocabulary [14] or dataset quality vocabulary [3]. The results are cat-
egorised into specific quality dimensions (e.g. consistency) using the taxonomy
(e.g. Zaveri et al. [18]) into hierarchies when analysing geospatial data quality [6].
Another advantage is the ability of semantic models to encompass multiple data
quality models through R2RML mappings or data quality observations. They
allow observations easily consumed in tool chains (e.g. analysis dashboards) compared to the non-standard outputs of proprietary tools, such as 1Integrate, that
require domain expert knowledge to develop extraction rules.

The Luzzu framework is employed in this study to take advantage of the
advantages of a semantic data quality approach. Luzzu [4] is an open-source,
Java based, Linked Data quality assessment framework which allows users to
create custom quality metrics to produce a time series of quality observations
about datasets. This is an interoperable tool allowing ontology driven backend
to produce machine readable quality reports and metadata about the assessment results. The quality metadata is represented by domain independent daQ
ontology based on W3C RDF Data Cube and PROV-O vocabularies.

4   A New Assessment Method for Standards Conformance of Geospatial Linked Datasets

This section addresses the process of creating the new geospatial metrics and
introduce the new metrics. The followed process was to *i)* identify a list of
geospatial data standards conformance points or best practice recommendations

and *ii)* prioritise the list (Sect. 4.1); *iii)* devise a set of new quality metrics for automated dataset assessment in a quality framework (Sect. 4.2). Each metric was then assigned to an appropriate quality dimension as defined by Zaveri *et al.* [18] and a set of semantic metric descriptions created using the daQ ontology (Sect. 4.3). The descriptions facilitated collection of rich dataset quality observations as W3C data cubes for further analysis, integration and visualisation.

4.1   Identifying Geospatial Data Quality Standards Conformance Points

In this section we identify, evaluate and compare a set of relevant standards and recommendations for GLD quality proposed by the OGC, ISO and W3C. The ISO/TC 211 Geographic information/Geomatics committee defines geographic technology standards in the ISO 19000 series [1] as well as the OGC creates open geospatial standards. The both organizations have close connections such that some documents prepared by OGC are adopted by ISO or implemented by the collaboration of both parties. We evaluate the standards in 3 main groups:

Geospatial Datasets: ISO 19103, 19107, 19108, 19109, 19112, 19123, 19156 [1] are published to describe the data, in particular the schema, spatial referencing by geospatial data, and methods for representing geographical data and measurements. OGC equivalence of the documents can be seen on the right hand side of the table. Old ISO 19113/19114/19138 are combined to 19157 data quality standards. Thus, while ISO 8000 defines data quality concepts and processes for generic information systems, ISO 19157 and ISO 19158 provide more detailed guidance on data quality practices for geospatial data. ISO 19158 specifies metrics and measurements for evaluation of data quality elements at different stages of the geospatial data lifecycle. It also defines quality metric evaluation by using aggregation methods and thresholds. ISO 19157 defines a set of data quality measures when evaluating and reporting data quality of geospatial data.

Geospatial Metadata: ISO 19111 and 19115 describe the metadata standards for geospatial data. While ISO 19115 focuses on metadata for cataloging and profiling purposes with the extensions for imagery and gridded data; ISO 19111 describes appropriate metadata for a Coordinate Reference System.

Geospatial Linked Data: There are three relevant types of documents for data quality. *i)* ISO 19150 which guides high level ontology schema appropriate for geospatial data and rules for using OWL-DL. *ii)* OGC's GeoSPARQL standard that define a set of SPARQL extension functions for geospatial data, a set of RIF rules and a core RDF/OWL vocabulary for geographic information based on the General Feature Model, Simple Features, Feature Geometry and SQL MM [13]. *iii)* W3C has two documents, first the Data on the Web Best Practices recommendation for improving the consistency of data management and secondly the SDOTW working group note which complements the earlier recommendation but is specialized for geospatial data.

In total OGC's GeoSPARQL defines 30 requirements for geospatial data and there are 14 best practices identified for geospatial data by W3C (Table 1). Each

Table 1. OSi priority standards compliance points identified

Origin	Req.	Description
OGC	R1	Implementations shall allow the RDF property geo:asWKT or geo:asGML to be used in SPARQL graph patterns
OGC	R2	All RDFS Literals of type geo:wktLiteral shall obey a specified syntax and ISO 19125-1
OGC	R3, R4	Implementations shall allow the RDFS class geo:Geometry with geo:hasGeometry property to be used in SPARQL graph patterns
OGC	R5	Implementations shall allow the RDFS class geo:Geometry with geo:hasDefaultGeometry property used in SPARQL graph patterns
W3C	R6	Use spatial data encodings that match your target audience
W3C	R7	Use appropriate relation types to link Spatial Things where source and target of the hyperlink are Spatial Things
ISO	R8	Polygons and multipolygons shall form a closed circuit
ISO	R9	Provide information on the changing nature of spatial things

of these may be used to construct standards compliance quality metrics. A possible set of metrics was proposed and discussed in a series of workshops with OSi staff drawn from the Geospatial Services, Data Governance & Quality department. First of all, OSi data quality system requirements and background discovered in meetings and workshops. It served as a basis for further development of OSi data quality governance in project. We first described the background in the form of the existing OSi data publishing pipeline and the available quality assessment points.

Following, the concepts and architecture of the end to end data quality portal initiative are described and both existing metrics and new sources of metrics for the OSi end to end quality monitoring framework are discussed. We evaluated the quality of the existing data in OSi with Luzzu framework. We used a set of generic quality metrics and appointed a threshold to ensure the conformance of the datasets to the given indicators. However, due to generic structure of the metrics it was not possible to evaluate the datasets according to the geospatial dimensions. Also the legislations, regulations and standardization requirements by organizations such as OECD, UN, and EC are needed to comply to ensure the reliant governance of the data in the public agencies. The aim is efficiency in the provision of public services. The requirements and best practices in Table 1 were identified as high priority for the initial deployment.

Table 2. New geospatial standards conformance quality metrics

Req.	ID	Metric name	Dimension
R1	CS-M1	Geometry Extension Property Check	Completeness
R2	CS-M2	Geometry Extension Object Consistency Check	Completeness
R3, R4	CS-M3, CS-M4	Geometry Classes and Properties Check	Completeness
R5	CS-M5	Spatial Dimensions Existence Check	Completeness
R6	I-M6	Links to Spatial Things (internal & external)	Interlinking
R7	I-M7	Links to Spatial Things from popular repositories	Interlinking
R8	CY-M8	Polygon and Multipolygon Check	Consistency
R9	T-M9	Freshness Check	Timeliness

A major focus of developing an end to end quality governance system for OSi is to establish a set of new metrics that will give OSi the ability to monitor and report on quality in a way that can satisfy their customers and unique requirements of the geospatial domain. Thus, initial candidate standards which are discussed in Sect. 4.2 were considered as a set of standards for OSi to measure its compliance with. It was seen most crucial to enable publication of the associated data in-line with agreed standards. In accordance with OSi staff, most essential metrics were chosen *i)* to check the usage of chosen standards to reduce the heterogeneity in representing data, *ii)* to measure the discoverability and freshness of the data to see the impact on the usage by the LOD cloud users *iii)* to measure the consistency of the data to provide high uniformity *iv)* to measure the completeness of the data to provide high coverage to the users. Thus, the metrics in Table 2 are chosen representing each dimension with the feedback of the OSi staff. We have chosen to implement different standardization metrics to demonstrate the potential of developing any metrics *w.r.t.* the required standards. Furthermore, we collaborated with OSi using different means of communications such as "basecamp" and "gogs" for the efficient development. In the following section we will introduce the implemented metrics.

4.2   New Geospatial Data Quality Metrics

Nine new metrics are defined here for the nine priority conformance points identified in the last section. Design principles were used for effective data quality metrics for both decision making under uncertainty and economically oriented data quality management [8]. Together these metrics enable the assessment of a dataset in terms of standards conformance including metadata, spatial reference systems and geometry classes. Each metric is identified by their quality dimension, summarised in Table 2 and discussed below in detail.

Geometry Extension Property Check (CS-M1): This metric addresses requirement R1 "Implementations shall allow the RDF property geo:asWKT or geo:asGML to be used in SPARQL graph patterns". Thus, conformant GLD datasets must have at least one geometry property associated with individuals which are geospatial features. Two properties are allowed by the GeoSPARQL standard, well known text (WKT) or geography markup language (GML). Both OGC and ISO standards rely on WKT geometries and GML serialization.

Metric Computation: If the entity in the dataset is a member of class geo:Geometry then this metric checks the rate of employed geo:asWKT or geo:asGML properties in the dataset. This is evaluated using functions as *hasWKT(e)* or *hasGML(e)* which return a boolean value. The metric is computed as a rate over the whole dataset as follows (Note that the following metrics also compute their rate over the whole dataset and thus Eq. 1 will not be repeated in each metric definition):

$$\sum_{i=1}^{e} \frac{\overline{e}(i)}{size(e)} \tag{1}$$

$$\overline{e} := \{e | \forall e \in class(geo : Geometry) \cdot hasWKT(e) \vee hasGML(e)\}$$

Geometry Extension Object Consistency Check (CS-M2): This metric addresses requirement R2 "All RDFS Literals of type geo:wktLiteral shall obey a specified syntax and ISO 19125-1". According to the OGC GeoSPARQL requirements, WKT serialization regulates geometry types with ISO 19125 Simple Features [ISO 19125-1], and GML serialization regulates them with ISO 19107 Spatial Schema.

Metric Computation: This metric checks the conformance of the dataset to the serialization requirement of OGC GeoSPARQL by checking the conformance of objects in terms of the order of use of coordinate system URI, spatial dimension and literal URI. Geometry data should consist of an optional URI identifying the coordinate reference system (e.g., CRS84, WGS 84) followed by WKT describing a geometric value. Spatial dimension may include polygon, multipolygon, line, point, or multilinestring shapes. Finally, the syntax should include the geo:wktLiteral URI declaring the object is a literal.

$$\overline{e} := \{e | \forall e \in class(geo : Geometry) \cdot hasCRSURI(e) \wedge$$
$$hasSpatialDimension(e) \wedge hasWKTLiteral(e))\}$$

Geometry Classes and Properties Check (CS-M3, CS-M4): These metrics address requirements R3 and R4 "Implementations shall allow the RDFS class geo:Geometry with geo:hasGeometry and geo:hasDefaultGeometry properties to be used in SPARQL graph patterns". OGC requires that each geometry object is an individual of the root geometry class geo:Geometry. In addition, a geo:Feature should be related to a geometry describing its spatial extent via the geo:hasGeometry property. The geo:hasDefaultGeometry property is also required to link a feature with its default geometry.

Metric Computation: This metric checks the rate of declaration of geometry classes and properties in the datasets. The *hasGeometry(e)* and *hasDefaultGeometry(e)* functions check each entity and return a boolean value for property existence. The metric checks each entity which is an individual of the geo:Geometry class.

$$\overline{e} := \{e | \forall e \in class(geo : Geometry) \cdot hasGeometry(e))\}$$

$$\overline{e} := \{e | \forall e \in class(geo : Geometry) \cdot hasDefaultGeometry(e))\}$$

Spatial Dimension Existence Check(CS-M5): This metric addresses requirement R5 "Use spatial data encodings that match your target audience". W3C SDOTW suggests encoding in a useful way such that machines can decode and process the encoded data using *Spatial Dimension* which is the measure of spatial extent, especially width, height, or length.

Metric Computation: This metric assesses the rate of spatial dimension properties related to each entity in the dataset. It compares the total number of spatial dimensions (multipolygon, polygon, line, point, multilinestring) described for each entity in the dataset to the overall number of entities.

$$\overline{e} := \{e | \forall e \in class(geo : Geometry) \cdot (isMultipolygon(e) \vee$$
$$isPolygon(e) \vee isLine(e) \vee isPoint(e) \vee isMultilinestring(e))\}$$

Links to Spatial Things Check (I-M6, I-M7): This metric addresses requirement R6 "Use appropriate relation types to link Spatial Things where source and target of the hyperlink are Spatial Things". Thus, W3C SDOTW suggests using appropriate relation types to link *Spatial Things* which is any object with spatial extent, (i.e. size, shape, or position) such as people, places [14]. W3C SDOTW suggests two types of links for Spatial things: i) links to other spatial things using an object with its own URI within dataset or to other datasets decreasing the computational complexity and enriching the data semantically ii) links to spatial things from popular repositories which increases the discoverability of the dataset. However, the challenge in this metric is that it is not possible to understand if a link has spatial extent without visiting the other resource. Thus, first a set of different pay-level-domains are detected manually and according to the used schema, the rate of the links are computed as an efficient approximation.

Metric Computation: First the metric detects the rate of entities having links to external spatial things in other datasets and internal spatial links within dataset. In I-M6, the *hasST(e)* function checks the entities with these links and later this number is divided into the overall number of entities.

$$\bar{e} := \{e | \forall e \in class(geo : Geometry) \cdot hasST(e))\}$$

Metric Computation: This metric detects the rate of entities having links to external spatial links in popular and highly referenced datasets. In this work, we specifically looked at the usage of DBpedia, Wikidata and Geonames datasets. We counted the entities with these links and divided to the overall entity number.

$$\bar{e} := \{e | \forall e \in class(geo : Geometry) \cdot (isDBpedia(e) \vee isWikidata(e) \vee isGeonames(e)))\}$$

Consistent Polygon and Multipolygon Usage Check(CY-M8): This metric addresses requirement R7 "Polygons and multipolygons shall form a closed circuit". Polygons are topologically closed structures, thus, the starting point and end point of a polygon should be equal to provide a consistent geometric shape.

Metric Computation: This metric checks the equality of the starting and end points of polygons. Each polygon in a multipolygon must be checked. We measure the rate of correctly described polygons and multipolygons in a dataset. In metric CY-M8 the function `hasClosedPolygon(e)` detects the correct usage for each entity in the dataset.

$$\bar{e} := \{e | \forall e \in class(geo : Geometry) \cdot (hasClosedPolygon(e))\}$$

Freshness Check (T-M9): This metric addresses requirement R8 "Provide information on the changing nature of spatial things". According to ISO and W3C it is crucial to provide the provenance information about when data has changed during their lifecycle.

Metric Computation: This metric checks the age of the data (f) by looking at the creation time and when it was last updated to the recent version. This metric was used as an updated version from [4]. In this formula, Volatility (v) is "the length of time the data remains valid" which is analogous to the shelf life of perishable products; Currency (c) is "the age of the data when it is delivered to the user" [7]. This metric is computed at the dataset and not instance level due to lack of information in the entity level.

$$f = (max(1 - c/v, 0))$$

4.3   Semantic Metric Models

Semantic metric models were created for all of the metrics described above as follows. The daQ ontology was extended with the new metrics by inheriting upper daQ concepts. Then each metric was classified under Linked Data quality dimensions and categories as presented in Zaveri *et al.* and descriptive metadata added. This allowed us to produce and publish daQ machine readable metadata as Linked Data for further processing such as metric fusion or visualisation or root cause analysis.

5   Evaluation

This section describes a first study showing our new metrics in operation with experimental set-up in Sect. 5.1 followed by results in Sect. 5.2, and the lessons learned in Sect. 5.3.

5.1   Experimental Setup

Experiments were executed to measure the metrics' ability to detect the standards compliance of GLD and the extent of standards compliance of published open GLD to meet OSi's requirements. Investigation was performed by implementing new metrics as Luzzu plug-ins in Java and assessing open GLD datasets. We used a computer with Intel i7 8th generation processor and 8 GB memory.

Datasets: Major open topographical geospatial datasets describing political or administrative boundaries were chosen to ensure geometrical features were represented in each dataset. Despite this selection, there is considerable variation in the datasets in number of triples, size, languages and used coordinate reference systems (CRS) as depicted in Table 3. Ordnance Survey Ireland (OSi) is the national mapping agency of Ireland and they publish a subset of their data as Linked Open Data. The OSi boundaries dataset describes political and administrative boundaries in Ireland. Ordnance Survey UK is the national mapping agency of the United Kingdom and they also publish their data partially as Linked Data. LinkedGeoData is provided by the University of Leipzig by converting OpenStreetMap data to Linked Data. Greece LD is provided by the University of Athens as part of the TELEIOS project.

Table 3. Dataset summary

Dataset	#Triple	Size	Languages	CRS
OSi	1936763	274M	EN, GA	IRENET95/ITM
OS UK	64641	224.1M	EN	WGS 84
LinkedGeoData	464193	1.5G	EN, Various	WGS 84
Greece LD	24583	183M	EN, GR	WGS 84

Method: Assessments were performed on each dataset using the Luzzu framework. In addition to assessing the full datasets, subset were also assessed to provide a common baseline for comparison between datasets. Observations for the nine metrics presented in Sect. 4.2 were collected as quality metadata using the daQ vocabulary as mentioned in Sect. 4.3.

5.2   Results and Discussion

This section discusses the performance of each dataset w.r.t. the given metrics. The metric values shown are the average value of the metric for all GLD resources in the dataset (Table 4). The table also shows the mean observed values of each metric across all datasets (last column) and the mean of all metrics for each dataset as simple aggregated quality indicator (last row).

In general we see that most datasets either conform or do not conform to specific standards and hence individual metrics score 1 or 0. Nonetheless the aggregated metric value gives an insight into the overall level of standards compliance for a specific dataset. However these relative scores should not be interpreted as an absolute statement of quality. Choice of which metrics are relevant for a specific application or dataset is always a key quality management decision. It can be said that OSi have selected these metrics as important for their datasets and thus these metrics help OSi monitor quality. Note that standards compliance is not the same as functional capability, thus using a non-standard ontology to express GLD may grant the same or better capabilities but from the user's perspective it may be more difficult to use (requiring mappings, query-re-writing etc.) and thus having a lower quality from the perspectives of "fitness for use" or "adherence to standards" [18].

It is interesting to note that sub-datasets such as the OSi parishes sample can have quite different standards compliance metrics scores than their parent datasets. This partially due to the scale and complexity of national spatial data collection which is an ongoing task with evolving requirements, methods and teams contributing to maintaining an overall dataset composed of many contributions over time. Specific results for each metric are discussed below.

Geometry Extension Property Check (CS-M1): The Greek LGD and OS UK score zero (non compliant). The Greek LGD doesn't use required properties (geo:asWKT[2] and geo:asGML) and OS UK uses a property from their specialized ontology instead. OSi and LinkedGeoData use the standard properties. A drawback of this metric is that it requires a specific vocabulary, but that reflects what the standards require for conformance. Adding support for inference like property inheritance is useful in theory but given the practicalities of closed world data quality assessment and Linked Data publishing practices it is not necessary for a useful implementation.

Geometry Extension Object Consistency Check (CS-M2): Again OS UK and Greek LGD does not conform to the standards due to the use of

---

[2] Prefix for geo: http://www.opengis.net/ont/geosparql#.

Table 4. Quality assessment results for datasets

Metric name	OSi full	OSi parishes	OS UK parishes	LinkedGeoData boundaries	Greek GLD coastlines	Greek GLD water bodies	Mean
CS-M1	1	1	0	1	0	1	0.66
CS-M2	1	1	0	1	0	0	0.5
CS-M3	1	1	0	0	0	1	0.5
CS-M4	0	0	0	0	0	0	0
CS-M5	1	1	1	1	1	1	1
I-M6	0.36	0.94	0.84	1	0	0	0.52
I-M7	0.142	0	0	0.0004	0	0	0.024
CY-M8	1*	1	1	–	1	–	1
T-M9	0	0	1	*	0	0	0.33
Agg. metric	0.50	0.66	0.52	0.57	0 0.22	0.33	

non-standard, specialized ontologies in the dataset (e.g., `strdf:WKT`[3] instead of `geo:wktLiterals`). OSi and LinkedGeoData conform to the standards for every geospatial entity in the dataset.

Geometry Classes and Properties Check (geo:hasGeometry Property (CS-M3) and geo:hasDefaultGeometry Property (CS-M4): OS UK entities do not have any geometry property or class, Greek LGD use a property from their own ontology, and LinkedGeoData have used NeoGeo geometry ontology[4] all of which are different from the OGC standard. OSi is the only dataset that used OGC features but it is not complete as well because `geo:hasDefaultGeometry` was not used by any of the datasets. Even though using open standards is a requirement for 5-star Linked Data publishing, this doesn't seem to be followed by most of the publishers.

Spatial Dimensions Existence Check (CS-M5): All the datasets performed well as all the entities in the datasets have spatial dimensions provided as points, polygons, multipolygons and waterlinestrings.

Links to Spatial Things (Internal & External) (I-M6): It was seen that while the LinkedGeoData dataset has links to the GADM dataset[5], the OSi full dataset has links to Logainm dataset[6], but for the parishes it doesn't have any external links. OS UK provides two different granularities in county and Europe within the dataset.

Interlinking & Links to Spatial Things from Popular Repositories (I-M7): DBpedia, Wikidata and Geonames were considered as popular knowledge graphs [14] and we have discovered that OSi has links to DBpedia, LinkedGeoData has links to Wikidata with the rates given in Table 4. Considering

---

[3] Prefix for strdf: http://strdf.di.uoa.gr/ontology#.
[4] http://geovocab.org/geometry.
[5] http://gadm.geovocab.org/.
[6] https://www.logainm.ie/en/inf/proj-machines.

LinkedGeoData provides a wide range of properties it would have been expected to see links to DBpedia or higher ratio of links for Wikidata. Thus publishers can consider using interlinking tools such as Silk[7] or LIMES[8] to enrich their data and increase the discoverability on the web.

Aggregated Results for Interlinking: This metric is very similar to the Debattista et al. [4] external link data providers metric which calculates all the datasets in the LOD cloud where LOD cloud has average 27% external links to other datasets [4]. Our results show that compared to the LOD cloud, these datasets have a higher rate of external spatial links but a much lower rate of links to popular datasets. If we consider the aggregated result for the Interlinking dimension, the rate is similar to LOD cloud rate with a mean of 27%.

Polygon and Multipolygon Check (CY-M8): As can be seen from the Table 4 all the datasets conform to this standard (note that full OSi was computed with sampling so it is estimated and denoted with *). In particular, it was seen that OSi, OS UK, Greek GLD have polygons and multipolygons included in their dataset, whereas entities are only represented by points in LinkedGeoData, and waterlinestring by Greek GLD thus, we kept them outside of the computation (denoted with -). This indicates there is currently too little geospatial polygon data on the web whereas it is very important for GIS applications e.g. historians working on historic roads and boundaries[9].

Freshness Check (T-M9): OS UK provides both creation and modification metadata for the dataset with the date of November 2019 which makes the dataset quite fresh. LinkedGeoData provides a modification date but no creation date. Hence freshness was not computed as it is based on creation time. No creation time was available in the OSi boundaries dataset but this has been fixed for the newer release of buildings data. This result confirms that provenance information is not given a high importance when publishing datasets [4].

In summary, the last row of Table 4 shows the mean aggregated GLD standards quality metric for each dataset. This could be considered as an estimate for the overall quality dimension of standards compliance for each dataset. Also it can be seen from Table 4 that different subsets of the datasets result in different scores even in the same dataset such as OSi or Greek GLD. Adoption of non-standard vocabularies decreases the scores. Overall the aggregated metric values are in the mid-range for most datasets, showing that usage of GLD standards and best practices are not widely applied by the publishers yet. A lack of standardisation has increased the heterogeneity of GLD and this makes it more difficult to use the datasets or to compare them with standardized metrics.

5.3   Lessons Learned from OSi Deployment

The adoption of semantic technology for quality metric specification and assessment in OSi has shown the following: *i)* Initially we believed that Linked Data

---

[7] https://github.com/silk-framework/silk.
[8] https://github.com/dice-group/LIMES.
[9] https://github.com/silknow.

quality assessment techniques were far advanced of the mainstream state of the art due to the obvious enhancements of the work by Zaveri et al. [18] compared to generic data quality standards like ISO 8000. However geospatial data quality has a long tradition, and this reflected in the relative maturity of the ISO 19157 standard which has an extensive taxonomy of quality dimensions that go beyond the Linked Data work. We are currently working to reconcile and map between all of these standards. *ii)* The flexibility and self-describing nature of Linked Data for expressing data quality assessment results is very useful and this is an area in which semantic technology facilitates the unification of quality assessments from many different tools across the data production pipeline assessing diverse technologies. *iii)* In addition to the standard data quality dimensions it would be useful to have the ability in tools to assign metrics to custom dimensions, for example on a per standard or standards organisation basis, to enable more fine-grained, deployment-specific reporting. *iv)* The current dominant approach of Linked Data assessment tools addressing the entire dataset with a single set of observations is limiting when it comes to further analysis and it would be useful to have standard ways to assign metric observations to sub-sets of a dataset.

6 Conclusion and Future Work

This paper investigated to what extent quality metrics derived from geospatial data standards can be used to assess the standards compliance and quality of GLD. Nine new metrics have been defined and implemented in the Luzzu quality assessment framework. The metrics have been used to assess four open GLD datasets. This has shown that, despite the availability of best practice advice and standards for GLD, there is still little standards conformance in the GLD Linked Data cloud. The ability to make this standards compliance assessment of GLD in an objective, quantitative, automated way is an advance in the state of the art. Standards conformance was not viewed equally important by all publishers of the test datasets. However, it is hoped that this study is still informative for publishers who wish their data to conform to the requirements and best practices published by standardization organisations. It should be noted that the Greek LGD and OS UK datasets were largely created before the standardization efforts we check for and thus conformance is not expected.

Ordnance Survey Ireland has seen the utility of this approach and started to roll out this new standards-based assessment for its own datasets. This work could have a longer term impact through exposure at the Eurogeographics consortium of European national mapping agencies with consequent potential impact on EU INSPIRE data collection practices. In future work we intend to develop additional standards conformance metrics and integrate them into our end to end quality dashboard for the OSi data publishing pipeline.

Acknowledgement. This research received funding from the European Union's Horizon 2020 research and innovation programme under Marie Sklodowska-Curie grant agreement No. 801522, by Science Foundation Ireland and co-funded by the European

Regional Development Fund through the ADAPT Centre for Digital Content Technology [grant number 13/RC/2106] and Ordnance Survey Ireland.

References

1. International standardization organization. https://ec.europa.eu/eip/ageing/standards/ict-and-communication/data/iso-19000-series_en. Accessed 15 Sept 2020
2. Auer, S., Lehmann, J., Hellmann, S.: LinkedGeoData: adding a spatial dimension to the web of data. In: Bernstein, A., et al. (eds.) ISWC 2009. LNCS, vol. 5823, pp. 731–746. Springer, Heidelberg (2009). https://doi.org/10.1007/978-3-642-04930-9_46
3. Debattista, J., Lange, C., Auer, S.: daQ, an ontology for dataset quality information. In: Proceedings of the Workshop on Linked Data on the Web co-located withthe 23rd International World Wide Web Conference (WWW 2014), Seoul, Korea, 8 April 2014, CEUR Workshop Proceedings, vol. 1184, CEUR-WS.org (2014). http://ceur-ws.org/Vol-1184/ldow2014_paper_09.pdf
4. Debattista, J., Lange, C., Auer, S., Cortis, D.: Evaluating the quality of the LOD cloud: An empirical investigation. Semant. Web **9**(6), 859–901 (2018). https://doi.org/10.3233/SW-180306
5. Debruyne, C., et al.: Ireland?s authoritative geospatial linked data. In: d'Amato, C., et al. (eds.) ISWC 2017. LNCS, vol. 10588, pp. 66–74. Springer, Cham (2017). https://doi.org/10.1007/978-3-319-68204-4_6
6. Devillers, R., Bédard, Y., Jeansoulin, R.: Multidimensional management of geospatial data quality information for its dynamic use within GIS. Photogram. Eng. Remote Sens. **71**(2), 205–215 (2005)
7. Hartig, O., Zhao, J.: Using web data provenance for quality assessment. In: Proceedings of the First International Workshop on the role of Semantic Web in Provenance Management (SWPM 2009), Collocated with the 8th International Semantic Web Conference (ISWC-2009), Washington DC, USA, 25 October 2009, CEUR Workshop Proceedings, vol. 526, CEUR-WS.org (2009). http://ceur-ws.org/Vol-526/paper_1.pdf
8. Heinrich, B., Hristova, D., Klier, M., Schiller, A., Szubartowicz, M.: Requirements for data quality metrics. J. Data Inf. Qual. (JDIQ) **9**(2), 1–32 (2018)
9. Karam, R., Melchiori, M.: Improving geo-spatial linked data with the wisdom of the crowds. In: Proceedings of the Joint EDBT/ICDT 2013 Workshops, pp. 68–74. ACM (2013)
10. Lehmann, J., et al.: Managing geospatial linked data in the GeoKnow project. In: The Semantic Web in Earth and Space Science. Current Status and Future Directions, Studies on the Semantic Web, vol. 20, pp. 51–78. IOS Press (2015). https://doi.org/10.3233/978-1-61499-501-2-51
11. Moellering, H.: A draft proposed standard for digital cartographic data, national committee for digital cartographic standards. In: American Congress on Surveying and Mapping Report, vol. 8 (1987)
12. Mostafavi, M.-A., Edwards, G., Jeansoulin, R.: An ontology-based method for quality assessment of spatial data bases. In: Frank, A.U., Grum E. (eds.) Third International Symposium on Spatial Data Quality, Geoinfo series, vol. 1/28a, no. 28a, pp. 49–66. Department for Geoinformation and Cartography, Vienna University of Technology, Bruck an der Leitha (2004). https://hal.inria.fr/inria-00000447/file/Mostafavi_ISSDQ04.pdf

13. Perry, M., Herring, J.: OGC GEOSPARQL-a geographic query language for RDF data. OGC implementation standard, 40 (2012)
14. Tandy, J., van den Brink, L., Barnaghi, P.: Spatial data on the web best practices. W3C Working Group Note (2017)
15. Wilkinson, M.D., et al.: The fair guiding principles for scientific data management and stewardship. Sci. Data **3**, 1–9 (2016)
16. Yaman, B., Brennan, R.: LinkedDataOps: linked data operations based on quality process cycle. In: EKAW Posters & Demonstrations (2020, in press)
17. Yaman, B., Thompson, K., Brennan, R.: Quality metrics to measure the standards conformance of geospatial linked data. In: Taylor, K.L., Gonçalves, R., Lécué, F., Yan, J. (eds.) Proceedings of the ISWC 2020 Demos and Industry Tracks: From Novel Ideas to Industrial Practice co-located with 19th International Semantic Web Conference (ISWC 2020), Globally online, 1-6 November 2020(UTC), CEUR Workshop Proceedings, vol. 2721, pp. 109–114. CEUR-WS.org (2020). http://ceur-ws.org/Vol-2721/paper526.pdf
18. Zaveri, A., Rula, A., Maurino, A., Pietrobon, R., Lehmann, J., Auer, S.: Quality assessment for linked data: a survey. Semant. Web **7**(1), 63–93 (2016)

An Ontological Model for the Failure Detection in Power Electric Systems

Amed Leiva Mederos[1], Doymer García-Duarte[2], Daniel Galvez Lio[1],
Yusniel Hidalgo-Delgado[3]([⊠]), and José Antonio Senso Ruíz[4]

[1] Centro de Investigaciones en Informática, Facultad de Matemática Física y
Computación, Universidad Central "Marta Abreu" de Las Villa, Santa Clara, Cuba
{amed,dgalvez}@uclv.edu.cu

[2] Facultad de Ingeniería Eléctrica, Universidad Central "Marta Abreu" de Las Villa,
Santa Clara, Cuba
dgduarte@uclv.cu

[3] Departamento de Informática, Universidad de las Ciencias Informáticas,
Habana, Cuba
yhdelgado@uci.cu

[4] Facultad de Comunicación, Universidad de Granada, Granada, Spain
jsenso@ugr.es

Abstract. Several ontologies have been developed for the detection of
failures in electric power systems. However, these ontologies have been
developed for specific aspects of the electricity grid and do not consider
the necessary elements for the representation of a fault detection system
based on Smart Grid trends. In this paper, we describe the development
process of EPFDO, an ontology composed of a network of ontologies
that allow the representation of intelligent system elements. EPFDO
includes Sensors cases, Electrical Demand Management, Geographical
Location, Operations, among other aspects that make EPFDO a more
useful system for researchers who may have a standard for fault detection
according to domain requirements.

Keywords: Ontologies · Power electric systems · Smart Grid · Failure
detection

1 Introduction

Although there is no consensus, the SmartGrid concept is aimed at improving
current electric power systems that generally work by distributing the energy
from some power plants to millions of users. SmartGrid makes a more opti-
mized distribution of this energy, allowing better response to situations where
distribution plants are stressed by high consumption [19].

The design of an ontology for the detection of failures in electric systems
under the conditions of Smart Grid is a complex task. The changes that occur in
an electric power system demand models of ontologies that allow the controllers
of the electric stations to perform an efficient job. The potential of the semantic

© Springer Nature Switzerland AG 2020
B. Villazón-Terrazas et al. (Eds.): KGSWC 2020, CCIS 1232, pp. 130–146, 2020.
https://doi.org/10.1007/978-3-030-65384-2_10

web and knowledge-based systems are valuable tools to develop new energy control systems, however, the conditions in which each electric system is developed are very diverse in terms of topology, components, and objectives which is a challenge when it is necessary to design ontologies for this field of knowledge. The electric power systems (EPS) or electric power networks, are intended to provide consumers with the necessary electrical energy for their activities in the quantity, time, and place required and with adequate quality and accounting, at the lowest possible cost, preserving primary resources and the environment [7]. These systems are faced with new challenges that somehow violate the maintenance and decision-making in power networks. Some of these challenges are:

1. Management and calculation of new variables, impossible to handle with current systems, which cause undescribed failures,
2. System Control in a more distributed way,
3. Need for high levels of prevention, stability and security of the power supply in case of failures,
4. Control decisions and decision making demand autonomy and decentralization,
4. Renewable Energy Prediction and climatological phenomena,
5. Users are increasingly aligned within the system and connected from their mobile phones to services,
6. Occurrence of various failures due to the expansion and diversity of the network.

The models of ontologies that detect failures in electric systems have been solving many of these problems in isolation and more specific contexts, so the development of an ontological solution that integrates all the necessary elements in an electric system is still pending to facilitate a design standard. It causes that those systems that today use ontologies and semantic web mechanisms for the management of electric power systems do not fully guarantee decision making quickly and efficiently. In this paper, we describe the development process of Electric Power Fault Detection Ontology (EPFDO), an ontology composed of a network of ontologies that allow the representation of intelligent system elements. EPFDO includes Sensors cases, Electrical Demand Management, Geographical Location, Operations, among other aspects that make EPFDO a more useful system for researchers who may have a standard for fault detection according to domain requirements.

2   Related Work

The first works that appeared in the literature related to the issue of fault detection in electric power systems using ontologies date from 1996 and have been directed towards the power grid in general, to transformers, to the quality of energy and, the power systems, renewable energy. These ontologies describe the essential concepts that relate to an electrical network [2,5]. They have classes where all the electrical components are grouped: breakers, circuits, switches, lines, substations, and another class called components of the structure where all the elements that the system must measure and manage automatically (like the voltage, among other) are joined together. The classes of ontologies [2,5] described above focus more on energy analysis and management processes and do not explicitly define the elements of intelligent control. However, there are other ontologies that we believe have a better conceptual definition and allow greater reuse of their structures [19]. These models [19] manage to generalize the control and network structure patterns clearly, aspects that are very mixed in the previous systems [2,5].

Articles have been published about ontology designs that can be used to detect failures in specific aspects of the power system. Within the ontologies specialized in the electrical network, PQData [26] can be observed, an ontology that describes the measures of energy quality from a definition of classes where the power, frequency, voltage, Harmonics, Inter harmonics, flickering, and the events associated with the occurrence of problems with energy quality are calculated.

There are other specialized ontologies on this subject. Among them, those that model the knowledge of transformers and their failures [15,24,25,31] are distinguished. These ontologies have few design values for the design of a network-level fault detection system. Its importance is that it has been used for the use of artificial intelligence methods to detect faults. Its classes are aimed at the detection of physical and mechanical problems in key elements of the electric system, such as transformers. Following the idea of the application of artificial intelligence techniques in the ontology designed by Lin [15], the Bayesian network method is used to classify faults in an electric system. In this work, the diagnosis of failures is carried out using a transformer ontology based on semantics and a Bayesian Network. In this way, system failures and their features are related to the causes, symptoms, and diagnostic methods related to the problem detected.

Big Data techniques have been combined with ontologies and used in the development of electric power systems [11]. The conception of ontologies in electric systems uses Big Data techniques to describe the structure, constituent elements, and basic calculations of an electric power system based on the multidimensional reasoning method. In the work related to Big Data, there is no reference to the detection of system failures, however, it provides class structures for ontological design in this field. The most abundant works in the field of artificial intelligence and ontologies for electric power systems have been dedicated to the use of software agents that perform operations on electric power systems [24,26,27] using very small ontologies whose conceptual value is sometimes minimal. These applications have generalization limitations to other tools and systems. They are very specific solutions and depend on the context and the network where they are applied, so they cannot be used as ontological design patterns.

Although most of the referred ontologies perform control and measurement of magnitudes [2,5,11,14,25,31] there are no formal references in their classes to actuators, data hosting systems, platforms, and methods to perform observations. These elements that refer to system control and decision-making have been replaced by classic inference rules developed in SWRL or some cases by the use of fuzzy logic-based rules [25]. The SWRL rules facilitate the construction of totally true axioms and the fuzzy rules have the advantage of being able to process the disjunction as an axiom. The fuzzy rules also allow to study the data sets in a blurred way and to handle very precise behaviors of the electricity grid, aspects that have been analyzed with the inclusion of classes with sensors from the appearance of the SSN and SOSA vocabulary respectively [18] that they provide better management of control variables and constitute a standard suggested by the W3C. The sensors constitute basic tools in the electric systems oriented to the Smart philosophy. They capture the stimuli of the environment and send data that allow describing states of the electricity grid and making decisions [7]. Only the work of Das, Bhowmik, and Giri [7] and that of Santos [28] refers to sensors and SCADA systems. Das, Bhowmik, and Giri [7] present an algorithm for a sensor to extract data from an electrical network. The main problem of the use of sensors is that in most of the works they do not address a data management model at the ontology level that allows the use of Synchrophasors [19]. This would allow handling complex variables correctly synchronized to the ontology to calculate powers, flows, and detect faults. The control tasks are solved with the design of multi-agent systems that work on ontologies [16,19,20,24,26] that execute the operations carried out by human beings in-network dispatch environments and the management of renewable and conventional energies.

Another aspect that has not been referred to for ontologies is the geolocation elements necessary in geographically distributed power electric systems. Intelligent electric systems are not only made up of the power generation and transmission system, they also have associated user systems that collaborate in the detection of failures by sending telephone reports and receive the service using Smart technologies through cellphones in their homes. For this part of the System, 5 ontologies are reported in the literature: ThinkHome ontology [12], SAREF4EE ontology [6], BOnSAI ontology [29], ProSGV3 ontology [9] and OEMA Ontology Network [4]. These ontologies differ greatly in their organization and structure. The most complete is OEMA that integrates all the benefits of others and has become a reference option for the integration of Smart Grid systems in the field of energy. Below we can find a table with the ontologies studied. The authors include those that are oriented to the detection of faults and others that by their design also allow detecting disturbances within the electric system.

The analysis of the related approaches shows great diversity in the domain due to high semantic heterogeneity and specialization that generates an interoperability problem that leads to rendering these ontologies in practice. Also, specialization and generalization in ontologies leave many conceptual problems that do not allow knowing the regularity of the domain. Therefore, there is a need to create a unified ontology that represents all fault detection domains in electric power systems. This ontology can be a standard knowledge base for the management of electrical failures in Smart Grid environments and will be composed of a group of interconnected ontologies that will facilitate the classification of fault data in electric systems by establishing high-level relationships between the concepts that describe this topic.

3 Ontology Generation Process for Fault Detection in Power Electric Systems

This section explains the development process of the EPFDO ontology network with phases for the definition of requirements, selection of vocabularies for reuse, implementation, and integration of ontology, and evaluation of ontology, documentation, and maintenance. The ontology construction process has followed the regularities for the development of ontologies [2,10] and the Neon specifications [30] through an application that corresponds to an ontology of fault detection in electric power systems.

3.1 Non-functional Requirements

The fault detection domain must be represented with specialized ontologies that facilitate the classification of electrical failures. This structure will favor the use of its classes for the construction of Smart Grid systems that allow faults to be detected. One of the goals of the EPFDO ontology is to provide a common representation of data for the detection of electrical failures. As in OEMA, each element of the ontology (class, property) must be named using only one term to avoid semantic heterogeneity. The language of the Ontology will be OWL-2, and the elements of the ontology will use as annotation of the positions of Camel Case (CamelCase).

Reach of the Ontology. One of the ways to determine the scope of the ontology is to outline a list of questions that such a system should answer [4]. In the thematic area of Electrical Engineering, the following are the possible questions to be answered by the ontology:

1. What type fails causes event X?
2. Where did fault X occur?
3. What is the fault that occurs in X?
4. What are the causes of fault X?
5. Which sensors detect fault X?
6. On which line did fault X occur?
7. What should be done if fault X occurs?
8. What magnitude describes fault X?
9. Does the quality of energy X cause the fault x?

Judging by this list of questions, the ontology must include information on the various types of faults, lines, and their geographical location, as well as the protections and actions necessary for the management of the systems.

3.2   Specification of Vocabulary and Reuse of Ontologies and Concepts

The development of the EPFDO ontology is based on different vocabularies that allow having and reusing classes and properties of other ontologies. In the domain of fault detection in electrical engineering, there are many applications made on ontologies with few design values. That is why languages have been chosen that provide clues for the formalization of ontologies and are listed below:

- FOAF [3]. It describes the characteristics of people and social groups that are independent of time and technology. FOAF defines the classes for Project, Organization, and Group as another type of agent. It is related to metadata formats among which are: Dublin Core, SKOS, DOAP, SIOC, vocabulary Org. In addition to the basic terms of FOAF, there are a number of terms that are used such as Internet accounts, address books, and other web-based activities.
- Geoposition [1]: Specified vocabulary for the construction of geographical ontologies and geospatial data.

We also reuse several ontology systems developed for the domain whose conceptual quality is sufficient for developing other ontological schemes. The ontologies that best described the domain and the most complete, were used for this design. The ontologies that have been selected for reuse are:

- PQont [14]: It is an ontology with all energy measurements and their power quantities.
- SSN [18]: It is an ontology to define a semantic sensors network (SSN) and their observations, the procedures involved in the observation, the observed properties, as well as the actuators. SSN follows horizontal and vertical modularization architecture by including a simple central ontology, but with a high level of autonomy called SOSA (Sensor, Observation, Sample, and Actuator) for its elementary classes and properties.
- OEMA Energy and equipment ontology [4]: Ontology that describes the necessary equipment in the power grid in homes.
- Dalianis F. and Persson [5]: describes the elements of an electrical network and correctly declares the energy distribution system and its components.
- Santiago [19] successfully declares the operations of a system, control tasks and the elements and magnitudes of electricity.
- Kolozaly [13] provides temporary concepts such as StreamData, Segment, StreamAnalysis in addition to the concepts TimeLine, PROV-O, SSN and Event Ontology.

Timeline Ontology Represents OWL-Time with several timelines, temporal concepts, and interval relations. The concepts of ODS ontology are in line with the principles of PROV-O ontology from which it adopts the concepts, Agent, Entity, Activity. In terms of the event description, it uses the concept of the event ontology and provides a definition that incorporates the StreamEvent concept to express an artificial classification of a time region, corresponding to a particular data flow. ODS also expands the observations of the sensors described in SSN Ontology through the concept, StreamData, which allows describing a Segment or Point linked to time intervals.

The concepts that we have declared in this section were selected through the use of the AgreementMaker software tool, software that allows mapping ontologies, and determining if there is a similarity of terms and equality in the order of the hierarchical structure of the classes. AgreementMaker has helped to find not only similar classes but also properties related to certain concepts that appear in an ontology. This tool allowed us to identify univocal terms not polysemic or homonyms. The choice of the terminological conceptual base of the ontology has started from the following criteria:

1. Select the class whose hierarchy best describes each concept associated with the detection of faults in electrical networks.
2. Select classes that have annotations and definitions accepted by the IEEE.
3. The terms of other ontologies associated with the domain serve to build relations of synonymy within the ontology.
4. A base ontology is taken to integrate ontologies to it and thus build the domain.

This approach to the organization of ontologies uses a mixed solution: Symmetric and Asymmetric. The Symmetric [17] initially integrates all the selected ontologies with their most complete concepts. The ontologies that are integrated are PQont [14], Dalianis [5], Santiago [19] and Bernaras [2] and the asymmetric one, where an input ontology is taken as the objective to join the other input ontologies into one [23] giving preference to the objective ontology which in this case is EPFD (Electric Power Fault Detection) [8] which contains all non-renewable energy elements, weather event classes and fault calculation rules.

3.3   Implementation

The EPFDO ontology implementation process consists of creating new generic classes to include the concepts extracted from the other ontologies. For example: the Class electrical network was constituted by Line, Positions, and Circuits. A class was created to represent faults (i.e., overvoltages, low voltages, short circuits) in addition to the identification of the causes. This process was followed by all classes of the system. The higher-level classes of the ontology are Sensors, Actuators, Lines, Data, Alarms, Geospatial, Infrastructure, Renewable Energies, Energy Quality, Failures, Climatological Events, among others. This process has generated the first EPFDO domain ontologies: infrastructure ontology, sensor ontology, fault ontology, event ontology, organization ontology, geospatial data ontology, Non-Renewable Energy ontology, and operations ontology, control tasks ontology, state ontology, people ontology, energy quality ontology, and demand management ontology. The Fig. 1, shows the top-level classes of the EPFDO.

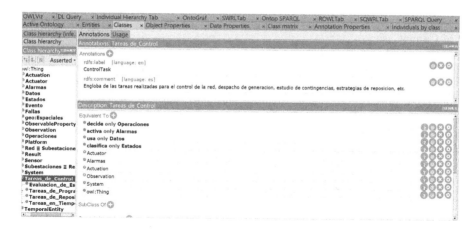

Fig. 1. EPFDO ontology classes

During the reuse process of ontologies, the following techniques have been applied: generalization, specification, and subdivision. Through generalization classes, subclasses and properties in the ontology have been unified. For example, the Reused Physical Entities classes have been added as a subclass to the infrastructure class in EPFDO. The generalization technique has allowed the addition of reused classes and properties of ontology as main classes and super-properties. For example, the Control Tasks class has become the main class that groups the Fault Locator class. The use of subdivision and redefinition has allowed classes that constituted a single concept to be divided into more specific and better-described classes; such is the case of the Event Class that has been subdivided into 2: Temporary Entities and External Events. In the Temporary Entities class, all the climatological phenomena that can affect the operation of the network are shown; and in the External Events class all the events that not only influence the electrical network and its failures but also the demand, are grouped, such is the case of a party or social or religious activity. In addition, the following ontology engineering activities have been carried out:

- Knowledge Extension: From the integration of the ontologies, new classes and properties are created that confer greater semantic coverage on the concepts and generate new conceptual relationships between the classes of the ontologies used in the study. For example, the infrastructure class is subdivided into infrastructure_technology and Domus_infrastructure (houses, institutions, power plant workplaces, commercial premises, etc.) and joins the Space Objects class through the network property: located_in.
- Rename the concepts and properties of ontology: In this case, only the names and properties of the concepts that are created after the ontological merger are changed. The new concepts will have the EPFDO identifier. Concepts that are inherited from other systems maintain their URI and their class name and property as long as their domain and rank relationship remains unchanged.

All reused ontological resource names are in accordance with the provisions of CamelCase.

- Make modifications and combinations in domains and ranges of properties: This task consists of modifying and adding new qualities to the domains, ranges, and properties of reused ontologies. The class Transformer in the ontology uses the properties *high voltage* and *temperature rise* to detect a winding failure. For example, Transformer (? P) high voltage (? P,? S) ôil temperature rise (? s) -¿ Winding failure (? p,? s). With this change, the ontology affirms that other infrastructures may have problems due to deficiencies in the quality of energy, which causes failures. The classes that join this scheme come from the specialized ontologies in the domain PQOnt [14], Dalianis F. and Persson [5], Santiago [19], Bernaras [2] and other vocabularies and ontologies [1,3,4,18] that then they integrate into EPFDO.
- Creation of new ontologies: To develop EPFDO, new domain ontologies with a high level of specialization are needed. An ontology-based on geo-positioning classes was developed since the benefits of DBpedia and other resources would not be sufficient for the maintenance of the ontology. We adopt a solution to generate the geographical classes in the ontology automatically implemented and defined by Puebla Martínez [22] where the generation of an extended ontology is appreciated, which by means of rules extracts from a database of individuals, axioms, and concepts. This ontology draws on the OSM database and creates special relations automatically.

Units of measure and magnitudes are included in the PQOnt ontology [14], and it is not necessary to generate a new ontology for these purposes.

- Knowledge Distribution: To perform this engineering task we have applied the ODP N-ary design pattern [14] that facilitates the restructuring of reused concepts. Some of the ontologies we present [5,14,19] have semantically distributed and unconnected concepts. Example: The transformer class that comes from the Bernaras ontology [2] appeared as a separate concept from the power grid since these are not only used within it and the system components are all in the infrastructure ontology so it was decided to place the transformers within the infrastructure ontology of OEMA [4] that has more detail in its classes to place these concepts.
- Design data ranges: They allow to determine faults in the systems and components of the electrical network. In this way, synchrophasors can be placed in the network. The Fig. 2 shows the temperature values for a transformer.
- Generate restrictions: Multiple class restrictions are created that facilitate the inference in the EPFDO ontology. The restrictions facilitate detailed reasoning of the ontology and the links between reused classes, data properties and objects. Example: in the control task class there are restrictions for data and alarms. With this, the ontology is saying that control tasks involve the states of the electricity grid, real-time and historical data and operations, which has a start and end time.

Axioms have been built to serve as a basis for the management of the system in general, they are the following:

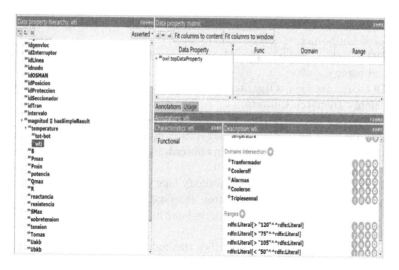

Fig. 2. Temperature range data of a transformer

Axioms have been developed which allow inferring the problems that occur in the electricity grid from the TBox and the ABox. The example presents a TBox where, for example, the overvoltage (1) denotes the concept that there is at least one line in a state of overvoltage in the electrical network and this implies a disconnection action.

TBox (Failure ≡ Failure ⊓ (∃ triggered by Event) ⊓ (∃ occurs.Electrical Network) ⊓ (∀ demand.Operation)

ABox Failure (Overvoltage), caused by (lightning strike), occurs (Line1), demand (Disconnection)

Generate Annotations: All classes of the resulting Ontology have annotations that specify their concepts and classes.

Eliminate: The last step in the development of ontology is to eliminate all duplicate concepts. It also eliminates those concepts that are outdated and do not correspond to the domain.

4 EPFDO Ontology Network

The EPFDO ontology network is constituted by different ontologies and specialized classes that allow the organization of knowledge in this domain and make EPFDO a network of ontologies that represent the domains of fault detection in electric power systems.

The ontologies that make up the system are shown below:

- EPFDO infrastructure: Contains all the necessary infrastructure for the detection of electrical failures, equipment and buildings.
- EFPD sensors: Contains all classes that come from the ssn vocabulary with variations in name changes and control process settings.

– EPFDO failures: Contains all possible failures in the electric system and those that occur in homes.
– EPFDO events: Declares the physical, weather and social activities that demand energy.
– EPFDO Organization: Organizations; Thermoelectric Power Plants, Offices and Energy Dispatch Centers
– EPFDO geospatial data: Provides classes to facilitate the geolocation of elements in the electric system, infrastructure, entities, faults and network users
– EPFDO Non-Renewable Energy: in this ontology are all the data and systems of wind, hydraulic, solar panels, etc.
– EPFDO operations: It is a task ontology that records all the operations that controllers must do to detect failures, manage demand
– EPFDO control tasks: Activities carried out in the management of the electric system.
– EPFD states: Ontology that describes the concepts related to the states that the power grid can have. They are: Alert, Emergency, Replacement and Insurance.
– EPFDO Person: Organizes users that can be people or entities. The ontology has the email addresses, the names and the address.
– EPFDO energy quality: Contains all the electrical quantities and associates the faults associated with the network disturbances, also includes calculation rules to determine system failures. It also includes payments and fees of customers of the electricity grid
– EPFDO demand management: Allows managing the demand. Estimate in advance the request for the generation of the network in a certain period of time, with the uncertainty associated with any estimate. To predict demand, historical demand data are needed, weather data, important events, etc.
– EFPD: Stream Annotation Ontolog. It has all the annotations that facilitate the use of Streams in the domain and the visualization of the data.

5   Evaluation

The OOPS online software tool [21] was used in the ontology evaluation. To evaluate the ontology, it was populated to be able to test it with electricity data that are in Excel files distributed in European Union databases as shown in Fig. 3. The data recorded by these files are: Substations, Location of the Equipment, Transmission Circuits and their Changes, Circuit Type, Mega Watts Consumption in various stations, Stations, Lines, Generators, Protections, Positions, Transformers, Location of Electrical and Physical Elements and Magnitudes. Extracting the information from these files forced to develop a parser that would facilitate the extraction of data from the ontology and to locate a tool capable of connecting with OWL to load the data. People data, failures and data reports were selected from Excel files containing name, address, age, consumption in kv, managed by the Electrical Company. The test was performed with 7895 instances. After populating the ontology with the instances, an analysis is carried out

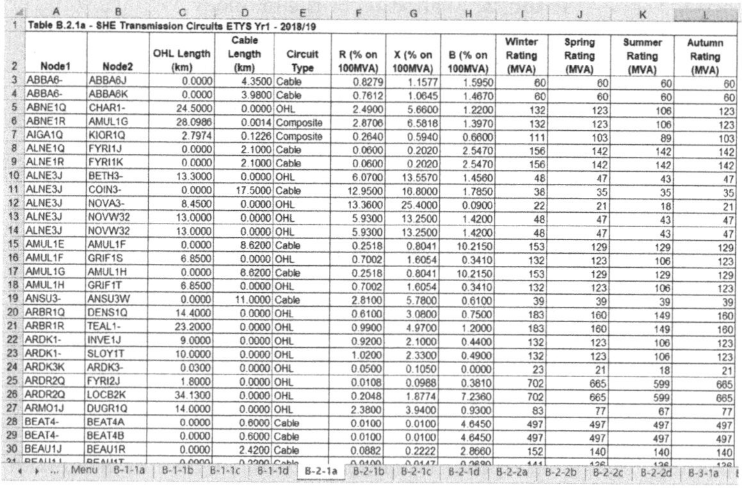

	A	B	C	D	E	F	G	H	I	J	K	L
1	Table B.2.1a - SHE Transmission Circuits ETYS Yr1 - 2018/19											
2	Node1	Node2	OHL Length (km)	Cable Length (km)	Circuit Type	R (% on 100MVA)	X (% on 100MVA)	B (% on 100MVA)	Winter Rating (MVA)	Spring Rating (MVA)	Summer Rating (MVA)	Autumn Rating (MVA)
3	ABBA6-	ABBA6J	0.0000	4.3500	Cable	0.8279	1.1577	1.5950	60	60	60	60
4	ABBA6-	ABBA6K	0.0000	3.9800	Cable	0.7612	1.0645	1.4670	60	60	60	60
5	ABNE1Q	CHAR1-	24.5000	0.0000	OHL	2.4900	5.6600	1.2200	132	123	106	123
6	ABNE1R	AMUL1G	28.0986	0.0014	Composite	2.8706	6.5818	1.3970	132	123	106	123
7	AIGA1Q	KIOR1Q	2.7974	0.1226	Composite	0.2640	0.5940	0.6600	111	103	89	103
8	ALNE1Q	FYRI1J	0.0000	2.1000	Cable	0.0600	0.2020	2.5470	156	142	142	142
9	ALNE1R	FYRI1K	0.0000	2.1000	Cable	0.0600	0.2020	2.5470	156	142	142	142
10	ALNE3J	BETH3-	13.3000	0.0000	OHL	6.0700	13.5570	1.4560	48	47	43	47
11	ALNE3J	COIN3-	0.0000	17.5000	Cable	12.9500	16.8000	1.7850	38	35	35	35
12	ALNE3J	NOVA3-	8.4500	0.0000	OHL	13.3600	25.4000	0.0900	22	21	18	21
13	ALNE3J	NOVW32	13.0000	0.0000	OHL	5.9300	13.2500	1.4200	48	47	43	47
14	ALNE3J	NOVW32	13.0000	0.0000	OHL	5.9300	13.2500	1.4200	48	47	43	47
15	AMUL1E	AMUL1F	0.0000	8.6200	Cable	0.2518	0.8041	10.2150	153	129	129	129
16	AMUL1F	GRIF1S	6.8500	0.0000	OHL	0.7002	1.6054	0.3410	132	123	106	123
17	AMUL1G	AMUL1H	0.0000	8.6200	Cable	0.2518	0.8041	10.2150	153	129	129	129
18	AMUL1H	GRIF1T	6.8500	0.0000	OHL	0.7002	1.6054	0.3410	132	123	106	123
19	ANSU3-	ANSU3W	0.0000	11.0000	Cable	2.8100	5.7800	0.6100	39	39	39	39
20	ARBR1Q	DENS1Q	14.4000	0.0000	OHL	0.6100	3.0800	0.7500	183	160	149	160
21	ARBR1R	TEAL1-	23.2000	0.0000	OHL	0.9900	4.9700	1.2000	183	160	149	160
22	ARDK1-	INVE1J	9.0000	0.0000	OHL	0.9200	2.1000	0.4400	132	123	106	123
23	ARDK1-	SLOY1T	10.0000	0.0000	OHL	1.0200	2.3300	0.4900	132	123	106	123
24	ARDK3K	ARDK3-	0.0300	0.0000	OHL	0.0500	0.1050	0.0000	23	21	18	21
25	ARDR2Q	FYRI2J	1.8000	0.0000	OHL	0.0108	0.0988	0.3810	702	665	599	665
26	ARDR2Q	LOCB2K	34.1300	0.0000	OHL	0.2048	1.8774	7.2360	702	665	599	665
27	ARMO1J	DUGR1Q	14.0000	0.0000	OHL	2.3800	3.9400	0.9300	83	77	67	77
28	BEAT4-	BEAT4A	0.0000	0.6000	Cable	0.0100	0.0100	4.6450	497	497	497	497
29	BEAT4-	BEAT4B	0.0000	0.6000	Cable	0.0100	0.0100	4.6450	497	497	497	497
30	BEAU1J	BEAU1R	0.0000	2.4200	Cable	0.0882	0.2222	2.8660	152	140	140	140

Menu | B-1-1a | B-1-1b | B-1-1c | B-1-1d | B-2-1a | B-2-1b | B-2-1c | B-2-1d | B-2-2a | B-2-2b | B-2-2c | B-2-2d | B-3-1a

Fig. 3. Excel with data

Table 1. Evaluation of the ontology

Dimension	Result
Concision	Error P02 y P03. Established Classes like synonyms and Classes without annotations; classified as minor errors
Structural Dimension	Error P07 the classes do not present union and interception specified in OWL language. It is a minor error
Usability Profile Dimension	Error P01 Problems of equivalence among the ontology toponyms and the non-authorized terms described in the location

taking into account the following variables: Consistency, Concision, Structural Dimension, and Usability Profile Dimension (Table 1).

The completeness of the ontology was also evaluated by making a comparison of the new ontology with the ontological models referenced in the literature [2,5,14,19], and the use of the Protegé tool. The quality of completeness lies in the management of new elements that allow managing the fault, such as geolocation, energy quality, the use of classes with sensors and a great culmination of annotations that describe the equipment that exists in the network (Table 2).

Finally, we demonstrate how the ontology is capable of using SWRL and DL Query rules for the detection of system failures. In Fig. 4, there is a case in which the system is able to determine an event that occurs in a transformer located on a line of the electrical network to which a fault occurs. By intercepting the classes associated with an event that occurs in a power line, it is possible to detect a

Table 2. Evaluation of the ontology

Object	Previous models	EPFDO
Classes	108	204
Equivalence of Classes	89	302
Subclasses Relations	87	254
Instances	Not described	7895
Asertions of Objects Properties	154	632
Assertions of Data Properties	1230	3654
Similar Instances	142	637
Annotations	451	965

fault accurately. The result of the consultation is that lightning has fallen on the power lines, an act that involves the data classes, Generators, Switches, Lines, Nodes, Observations, Positions, Protections, Network, Disconnectors, Sensors, Substations, System, Transformers and Spatial Data.

Finally, we demonstrate how the ontology is capable of using SWRL and DL Query rules for the detection of system failures. Below there is a case in which the system can determine an event that occurs in a transformer located on a line of the electrical network to which a fault occurs. By intercepting the classes associated with an event that occurs in a power line, it is possible to detect a fault accurately. The result of the consultation is that lightning has fallen on the power lines, an act that involves the data classes, Generators, Switches, Lines, Nodes, Observations, Positions, Protections, Network, Disconnectors, Sensors, Substations, System, Transformers and Spatial Data.

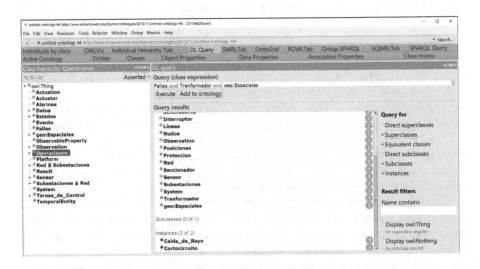

Fig. 4. Query in DL

The response of the Ontological network discovers the event, the failure caused in this case an overvoltage and identifies the line where the event occurs and the transformer that is associated with the line and is also affected. Also, line control data is obtained.

6   Documentation

The ontology is published at http://uclv.edu.cu/ontology. In this address the files that support the maintenance of the ontology can be found:

- Ontology XML File
- Archive in RDF of the Ontology
- IEEE Normative Documents that support the classes and systems
- Ontology descriptive data model
- Diagram of UML Classes of Ontology
- A package with axiomatizations and inference rules
- A set with class query elements
- Data sets for implementation.

7   Sustainability and Challenges

To ensure that this ontology can be used and reused in various designs, it focuses on the principles of (Open-World Assumption, OWA), which requires that ontologies must be corrected and extended to last as knowledge organization systems, since its ultimate goal is to support the work of scientists to classify individuals. This design also observes the rules of objectivity and represents the objective reality of the domain.

Even the ontological design in this domain must face challenges so that these systems are totally intelligent. The ontologies must resolve the representation of the commutations or the external impacts that are unpredictable for the systems to work in the Smart environment; for this purpose, new proposals and data models must be designed, inference rules must also be generated to model the over-surges and the voltage in the electrical networks. The ontologies that are designed for this domain must integrate the following elements:

- The recording and automatic analysis of characteristics of fast electromagnetic processes, surges, over currents and non-stationary disturbances;
- Phase-to-ground fault detection after insulation damage in the distribution network with an isolated or compensated neutral;
- Location of the phase-to-ground fault point according to the transient initial current process in the distribution network with cable and overhead lines;
- The control of the equipment isolation resource.

8   Conclusions

Much has been written on the design of ontologies for fault detection in electric power systems; however, most of the works that refer to this topic have ontologies aimed at specific plots of the electrical network, such as transformers and quality of the energy, where solutions based on artificial intelligence techniques are applied. The best-developed ontologies for the detection of faults in the fault detection domain in electric power systems have among them high conceptual and structural diversity, which implies high levels of semantic heterogeneity and specialization that creates an interoperability problem that leads to them not being able to be implemented in real systems that embrace the Smart Grid philosophy.

Regulating the conceptual diversity and specialization of ontologies has been one of the most complex tasks of EPFDO, a time-consuming and expensive process. Among the five ontologies used for integration, there is much conceptual heterogeneity and timeless definitions. In our opinion, the challenge of the greater cost was to create a class to standardize the electrical network and its components, an aspect that always has differences in design, since it depends on the network environment.

EPFDO is an ontology made up of the necessary elements for the intelligent ontological design of the detection of failures in electric power systems. Its main attributes are the observation of trends in the development of power systems and respect for the proceeds of the IEEE consortium. In addition, it includes Sensors cases, Electrical Demand Management, Geographical Location, Operations, etc., aspects that make EPFDO a more useful system for researchers who may have a standard for fault detection according to domain requirements.

The EPFDO network of ontologies is composed of 14 main concepts: Sensors, Failures, Events, Organization, Geospatial Data, Non-Renewable Energy, Operations, Control Tasks, States, Person, Energy Quality, Demand Management, Stream Annotation Ontology. A test was performed for the automated population of the Ontology with a dataset of 7895 instances to perform the evaluation. The result of the population and the consultations with DlQ shows that the network can locate faults with a high level of precision through the concepts referred to previously.

There are still many elements of the electrical network that are capable of generating failures and must be represented at the ontology level to give a greater level of intelligence to the fault detection systems of the future.

References

1. WGS84 Geo Positioning: an RDF vocabulary (2007)
2. Bernaras, A., Laresgoiti, I., Bartolome, N., Corera, J.: An ontology for fault diagnosis in electrical networks. In: Proceedings of International Conference on Intelligent System Application to Power Systems, pp. 199–203 (1996). https://doi.org/10.1109/ISAP.1996.501068
3. Brickley, D., Miller, L.: FOAF Vocabulary Specification 99 (2014)

4. Cuenca, J., Larrinaga, F., Curry, E.: A unified semantic ontology for energy management applications, vol. 1936, pp. 86–97 (2017)

5. Dalianis, H., Persson, F.: Reuse of an ontology in an electrical distribution network domain. In: Proceedings of the AAAI 1997 Spring Symposium Series, Ontological Engineering, pp. 25–32 (1997)

6. Daniele, L., Solanki, M., den Hartog, F., Roes, J.: Interoperability for smart appliances in the IoT world. In: Groth, P., et al. (eds.) ISWC 2016. LNCS, vol. 9982, pp. 21–29. Springer, Cham (2016). https://doi.org/10.1007/978-3-319-46547-0_3

7. Das, S., Bhowmik, S., Giri, C.: End device energy optimization in ASPL for semantic sensor network, pp. 1–6. IEEE, India (2017). https://doi.org/10.1109/ANTS. 2017.8384148. https://ieeexplore.ieee.org/document/8384148

8. García-Duarte, D., Leiva-Mederos, A., Galvez-Lio, D.: Electric power fault detection: ontolgy (2019). www.semanticweb.org/doymer/ontologies/2019/11/red

9. Gillani, S., Laforest, F., Picard, G.: A generic ontology for prosumer-oriented smart grid. In: 3rd Workshop on Energy Data Management at 17th International Conference on Extending Database Technology, Greece (2014). https://hal-emse.ccsd. cnrs.fr/emse-00948316

10. Haase, P., et al.: The NeOn ontology engineering toolkit. In: WWW 2008 Developers Track (2008). https://www.aifb.kit.edu/web/Inproceedings1757

11. Huang, Y., Zhou, X.: Knowledge model for electric power big data based on ontology and semantic web. CSEE J. Power Energy Syst. **1**(1), 19–27 (2015). https://doi.org/10.17775/CSEEJPES.2015.00003. Conference Name: CSEE Journal of Power and Energy Systems

12. Kofler, M.J., Reinisch, C., Kastner, W.: A semantic representation of energy-related information in future smart homes. Energy Build. **47**, 169–179 (2012). https://doi.org/10.1016/j.enbuild.2011.11.044. http://www.sciencedirect. com/science/article/pii/S0378778811005901

13. Kolozali, S., Bermudez, M., Barnaghi, P.: Stream Annotation Ontology (2016)

14. Kucuk, D., Salor, O., İnan, T., Cadirci, I., Ermis, M.: PQONT: a domain ontology for electrical power quality. Adv. Eng. Inform. **24**(1), 84–95 (2010)

15. Lin, H., Tang, W.H., Ji, T.Y., Wu, Q.H.: A novel approach to power transformer fault diagnosis based on ontology and Bayesian network, pp. 1–6. IEEE (2014)

16. Liu, L., Zu, X., Xu, R.: Multi-agent system coordination architecture and its use in electric power decision support system, pp. 731–736. IEEE (2008)

17. Noy, N.F., Musen, M.A.: Algorithm and tool for automated ontology merging and alignment. In: Proceedings of the 17th National Conference on Artificial Intelligence (AAAI 2000). Available as SMI technical report SMI-2000-0831, vol. 115. AAAI (2000)

18. OCG, W.: Semantic Sensor Network Ontology (2017)

19. Padron Hernández, S.: Inteligencia artificial en la operación de redes eléctricas. Aplicación a sistemas aislados. Ph.D. thesis, Universidad de Las Palmas de Gran Canaria (2015)

20. Pezeshki, H., Wolfs, P., Johnson, M.: Multi-agent systems for modeling high penetration photovoltaic system impacts in distribution networks. In: 2011 IEEE PES Innovative Smart Grid Technologies, pp. 1–8, November 2011. https://doi.org/10. 1109/ISGT-Asia.2011.6167149

21. Poveda Villalon, M.: Ontology evaluation: a pitfall-based approach to ontology diagnosis. Ph.D. thesis, Universidad Politecnica de Madrid, Escuela Tecnica Superior de Ingenieros Informaticos (2016)

22. Puebla-Martínez, M.E., Perea-Ortega, J.M., Simón-Cuevas, A., Romero, F.P.: Automatic expansion of spatial ontologies for geographic information retrieval. In: Medina, J., et al. (eds.) IPMU 2018. CCIS, vol. 854, pp. 659–670. Springer, Cham (2018). https://doi.org/10.1007/978-3-319-91476-3_54

23. Radulovic, F., Poveda-Villalón, M., Vila-Suero, D., Rodríguez-Doncel, V., García-Castro, R., Gómez-Pérez, A.: Guidelines for Linked Data generation and publication: an example in building energy consumption. Autom. Constr. **57**, 178–187 (2015)

24. Samirmi, F.D., Tang, W., Wu, H.: Power transformer condition monitoring and fault diagnosis with multi-agent system based on ontology reasoning. In: 2013 IEEE PES Asia-Pacific Power and Energy Engineering Conference (APPEEC), pp. 1-6 (2013). ISSN: 2157-4847

25. Samirmi, F.D., Tang, W., Wu, Q.: Fuzzy ontology reasoning for power transformer fault diagnosis. Adv. Electr. Comput. Eng. **15**(4), 107–114 (2015). https://doi.org/10.4316/AECE.2015.04015

26. Santofimia, M.J., del Toro, X., Roncero-Sánchez, P., Moya, F., Martinez, M.A., Lopez, J.C.: A qualitative agent-based approach to power quality monitoring and diagnosis. Integr. Comput. Aided Eng. **17**(4), 305–319 (2010)

27. Santos, G.J.L.d.: Ontologies for the interoperability of multiagent electricity markets simulation platforms. Ph.D. thesis (2015)

28. Santos, J., Braga, L., Cohn, A.G.: Engineering time in an ontology for power systems through the assembling of modular ontologies, pp. 255–258 (2010)

29. Stavropoulos, T.G., Vrakas, D., Vlachava, D., Bassiliades, N.: BOnSAI: a smart building ontology for ambient intelligence. In: Proceedings of the 2nd International Conference on Web Intelligence, Mining and Semantics, WIMS 2012, pp. 1–12. Association for Computing Machinery, New York, June 2012. https://doi.org/10.1145/2254129.2254166

30. Suárez-Figueroa, M.C.: NeOn Methodology for building ontology networks: specification, scheduling and reuse. Ph.D. thesis, Informatica (2010)

31. Wang, D., Tang, W.H., Wu, Q.H.: Ontology-based fault diagnosis for power transformers. In: IEEE PES General Meeting, pp. 1–8, July 2010. https://doi.org/10.1109/PES.2010.5589575. iSSN 1944-9925

A Spatiotemporal Knowledge Bank from Rape News Articles for Decision Support

P. U. Usip$^{(\boxtimes)}$, F. F. Ijebu, and E. A. Dan

Computer Science Department, University of Uyo, Uyo, Nigeria
{patienceusip,ijebufrancis,emmanueldan}@uniuyo.edu.ng

Abstract. Rape cases have been on the increase during the COVID'19 pandemic. All News media including the online Newsfeed report these cases around our communities. It is important for intending visitors or residents to be properly informed of specific locations and the times these occurrences are predominant. Our proposed model is aimed at providing a spatiotemporal knowledge bank useful for personal, governmental and/or organizational decision support on occurrences like rape and armed robbery. This model uses a hybrid of preposition enabled natural language processing (PeNLP) parser and ontology-based approach for spatiotemporal data extraction from online news publications to create the knowledge bank for decision support systems (DSS). Protégé is used in the development of the ontology and the resulting graph shows the knowledge bank entities. The result from the PeNLP parser stored in the knowledge bank follows the domain categorization modeled in the graph. The Precision, Recall and F-measure in spatial feature extraction were 100%, 88.89% and 94.12% respectively. The average Precision, Recall and F-measure of our model in temporal feature extraction is 100%. These results represent a successful extraction of spatiotemporal features from online news reports necessary for reasoning in any DSS.

Keywords: Location-based · Spatiotemporal · Ontology · PeNLP Parser · Knowledge graph

1 Introduction

Every activity of man today generates some kind of data; some of which the generators do not know the usefulness at the point of generation. Most successful and widely accepted governmental policies and organizational decisions are based on useful and effective data gathered over a period of time. Previously, public opinions were sort and gathered manually, but today, the web and internet are far reaching medium for opinion sampling towards decision support. The volume of information on the web increases with improvement in web technology [1]. A general user of the internet frequently turns to the web to solicit knowledge on varied topics of interest. The unstructured nature of most web based information sometimes makes it difficult to acquire useful knowledge automatically.

© Springer Nature Switzerland AG 2020
B. Villazón-Terrazas et al. (Eds.): KGSWC 2020, CCIS 1232, pp. 147–157, 2020.
https://doi.org/10.1007/978-3-030-65384-2_11

There are innumerable online reporters and webpages posting information about incidences and agents involved in occurrences. Hence, it is extremely difficult to validate the authenticity of some online news publications. With the uncertain nature of web articles, researching the safety or crime rate of an environment through online newspapers and blogs can be misleading, very tedious, time consuming, and error prone. However, reading an online crime report; one is likely to find a location (spatial data) and time or duration of occurrence (temporal data), a combination of which defines spatiotemporal information.

It is possible for an individual to use a combination of online newspaper articles to discover certain occurrence frequency of an event of interest in a geographical area. For instance, cases of rape have been on the increase in recent times, especially during the COVID'19 pandemic. Advocacy against rape also became more pronounced; such that more information about rape cases is made available online. For a human agent to know the rape prone geographical areas in a city for necessary action, several publications would need to be read. That of course is time consuming compared to a computer based solution that reads and retrieves relevant information from text automatically.

However, there is no cyberinfrastructure to help concerned agencies and the general web user access such structured spatiotemporal data for decision support. To this end, we observe that if published news articles about rape cases and other crimes within a city are subjected to a spatiotemporal data extraction tool, a knowledge bank of events and time can be automatically created.

Therefore, this paper presents a method that mines spatiotemporal data from plain news text to form a knowledge bank that will be useful to decision sup-port systems (DSS). The knowledge bank would be beneficial to Government, NGOs and the general public. The government can use the spatiotemporal information in deciding the provision of basic amenities and security. NGOs can intensify sensitization and provide help to residents of certain event prone areas, while the general public can use spatiotemporal information to make decisions on prevention and personal safety.

The remainder of this work is organized as follows; Sect. 2 presents related works. In Sect. 3, the proposed methodology and its implementation are described. Section 4 presents the results of our submission and discussed their relevance; this is followed by a conclusion in Sect. 5.

2   Literature Review

Intuitively, the human brain is able to identify, connect and make meaning out of related spatial information within a plain text, irrespective of how dynamic the presentation might have been. However, to computationally retrieve, process, and correctly interpret spatiotemporal information is a complicated task because the data might consist of different locations at various times in different formats [2]. Spatiotemporal data consist of the state of an object, an event or a position in space over a period of time. For example, incidences like fire outbreak, road accident, rainfall, traffic jams, rape, robbery etc. are spatiotemporal because the event happens at location L at time T.

The complexity of English language expressions and the dynamism of some scenario description among different speakers make spatiotemporal data extraction from natural text very challenging. For the present case, news reports by different media houses usually follow some standards. Though these standards are not the concern of this work; understanding them could make the mining process easier. Temporal data mining places greater attention on the temporal element of data, spatial extraction techniques focus on useful patterns from spatial dataset, while spatiotemporal extraction is either an extension of the temporal or spatial mining methods, or is based on evaluation rule, spatiotemporal pattern and spatiotemporal moving pattern [3]

In [4], a system to create, execute and visualize scientific questions consisting of spatiotemporal expression was proposed. The terms of spatial and event or theme extraction is related to our proposed solution. However, their consideration of temporal data is abstracted and oversimplified as considerations of time intervals and date-time instants are ignored. Time has been broadly classified as relative or absolute. Where relative time is described as being dependent on an inertial frame of reference; consisting of successions, simultaneities and duration, absolute time does not depend on any inertial frame of reference [5]. Natural language research on time has evolved from temporal expression extraction and annotation to temporal reasoning and understanding [6]. The Stanford Core NLP is one software package that has been useful in pushing the edge in the new direction.

Within the Stanford Core NLP lies the SUTime library, an open source Java coded tool which has been identified as useful for recognition, extraction and normalization of temporal expressions from plain text in natural language. The work by Li et al. [4] successfully used the SUTime library in their intelligent cyberinfrastructure; this supports the usability of the SUTime library on temporal extraction and normalization for spatiotemporal knowledge bank creation. After a review of time ontologies and models, Ermolayev et al. [7] concludes that features such as density, relaxed linearity scale factors, proper and periodic sub-intervals and temporal measures and clock are not satisfactorily covered and incorporated in the SUTime library. Other temporal data ex-traction libraries like PrettyTime and Apache OpenNLP have also been made available as open source libraries for time feature extraction.

There is currently a vast amount of spatiotemporal data available on the open web. With this increased data availability; comes new big data management and data mining techniques. Almost in every area of society, data mining tools and techniques for information extraction and normalization are being developed. Structured data is derived from unstructured data and organized in such a way that they can be stored [8,9]. The stored data forms a repository that holds reference knowledge, hence referred to as Knowledge Based Systems. Automated systems access stored knowledge and analyzes segments; from which predictions can be made. Such predictions could help shape management decisions like in the medical domain as reported in [10–12] hence, systems with this capability are known as Decision Support System (DSS).

In the agricultural sector, spatial data aid effective decision about crops and farm management, in the sense that a spatial DSS can provide strategic web based operational tools for forest resources management and multi-purpose planning [13]. Thus, Terribile et al. [14] proposed a geospatial cyberinfrastructure based tool for viticulture decision support and landscaping. With a 20,000 hectare landmass in southern Italy as case study, their tool was able to acquire, process and manage climatic and pedological data, visualize spatial data of vineyards and provide data in appropriate format for computer simulation and modeling of farming space. Though the authors did not generate any knowledge bank in their work, they utilized geospatial tools and data to provide a platform for enhanced decisions in viticulture.

The need for better decision support system (DSS) to help individuals and groups is still a major concern to many researchers. However, there are a number of models and functional DSS that have been developed and/or pro-posed in literature. One of such submission is in [15]; a clinical DSS is presented while advocating increased performance and efficiency of clinical DSS for better health care management among physicians and patients. Knowledge based systems useful for decision making are Knowledge Based Decision Support Systems (KBDSS). KBDSS are designed to ensure precise decision making aided by timely valid data, information and knowledge. With improving cyberinfrastructure support, most contemporary KBDSS are web based.

A systematic review of technologies and application domains of KBDSS was conducted by [16]. The report highlighted the medical domain as a major beneficiary of decision support systems and ontology as an efficient knowledge modeling technique associated with decision support systems. Ontologies being formal representation of knowledge form the foundation of knowledge graph development [17,18]. Knowledge graphs are created to add smartness to a system and aid machine understanding of data content and context of a geoprocessing function.

The general form ontology (GFO) and the web ontology language (OWL) have been used for time and knowledge modeling in literature. In Cox and Little [19], the OWL time ontology is described, identifying different classes for time and calendar vocabulary formalization. The OWL ontology has capability to capture temporal intervals, day, month, year and general date-time descriptions from natural text. Baumann et al. [20] on the other hand described the GFO time ontology and identified the continuants (material endurants), material presentials and material processes as classes for entities associated with time. Our comparative observation shows OWL time ontology is more robust than the GFO ontology.

The use of ontologies for time and decision support system modeling dates back several decades. In [21], Protégé II was used for implementation of protocol-based DSS. Protégé is a renowned integrated development environment for OWL ontology development. Similarly, Sherimon and Krishnan in [22], proposed OntoDiabetic, ontology based decision support system to assess risk factors and provide appropriate treatment suggestions for diabetic patients. The model implementation used OWL2 rules and reasoning. Security and crime related spatiotemporal data have also been widely modeled with ontologies.

Accessible knowledge banks for computer aided decision making are a scare commodity in literature. However, Jung and Chung [23] proposed an obesity control system through recommendations drawn from a dietary nutrition knowledge bank. They submit that with an effective nutritional knowledge bank; appropriate recommendations can be made to individuals and personalized diet menus could also be generated. This they suggest will help socioeconomic losses arising from increased obesity cases in the society. In [24], an open access knowledge bank was developed to help in clinical diagnostic decision support. While acknowledging the robust nature of machine learning algorithms underlying clinical decision support systems; they argue that DSS based on knowledge banks should not be phased out as they are highly complementary to the available machine learning algorithms.

Crime based analysis from spatiotemporal data was the concern of the work in [25]. Sham et al. [26] investigated factors that contribute to women's travelling safety issues and identified insecurity, misinformation and punctuality as major factors that contribute to safety issues. Gupta et al. [27] in their study proposed the use of data mining techniques for data extraction, analysis, and visualization to identify crime patterns and hotspots within selected locality. Decision making in a forensic unit can be facilitated by calculating the probability hypothesis of cause of a crime through the evidences, which could be spatiotemporal [28]. This further highlights the importance of spatiotemporal data in criminal investigation and military support [29].

3   Methodology

Any new framework for spatiotemporal data mining should define the discovery problem more formally and utilize useful available spatiotemporal operations and topological relationships [3]. In accordance with Lee and Lee's position, our model uses ontology to formally represent spatiotemporal characteristics and features of interest while the PeNLP Parser [29] which is part of an ongoing work performs spatial features extraction. The identification of spatial, agent and events in plain text is aided by the PeNLP while temporal feature identification is achieved with rule based methodology.

3.1   System Architecture

From the architecture in Fig. 1 unstructured web-based newspaper publication is supplied to the spatiotemporal extractor as input.

The spatiotemporal extractor consists of the PeNLP parser responsible for sentence-by-sentence evaluation of given news text for any spatial, temporal and agent or event occurrence. The knowledge bank is not fed with information until the spatiotemporal extractor validates the formality of the extracted temporal

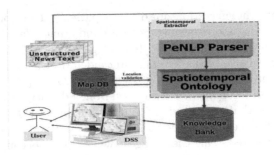

Fig. 1. Ontology-based knowledge extraction architecture

elements with the spatiotemporal ontology, the second module in the architecture. After spatial elements are validated with the ontology for formality, the locational names are further passed to the Map database to determine the availability of corresponding coordinates for visualization upon user request.

The knowledge bank holds the structured spatiotemporal information which it makes available to decision support system where analysis and recommendation or prediction can be done. The graph showing the ontology clearly shows the structure of the spatiotemporal knowledge bank. The output from any DSS is expected to help the user make informed decision.

3.2   The PeNLP Parser

The novel human intelligent Preposition-enabled Natural Language Processing (PeNLP) approach is a sentence based parser where grammatical prepositions are used to identify the spatial and temporal concepts in any given unstructured text. The approach is further described in [30]. In the present work, the Parser also deploys the temporal features in Apache openNLP.

The spatiotemporal extractor is developed with java programming language within which the Apache OpenNLP library was integrated to perform natural language processing and preposition enabled location identification. The adapted OpenNLP library is inefficient in temporal identification and extraction from plain text, hence, the need for a rule-based method for temporal feature extraction based on the ontological formalization.

The Parser is fed with manually curated news articles from verified newspapers publisher's official websites. Articles of interest are those on rape and armed robbery. The as-is report on the newspaper portal is converted to plain text and saved with file name which is supplied to the PeNLP extractor for further analysis.

A sentence by sentence analysis for spatiotemporal element identification is implemented. The work envisages that the richness of the English language vocabulary and differences in speakers' expression will suffice in the reporting news, such that a sentence may speak of an event or agent without reference to the location or time of occurrence or activity. As such, preceding sentences and succeeding sentences are considered for spatial and temporal element if current sentence containing the event or agent does not specify the location or time associated with the event or agent's action.

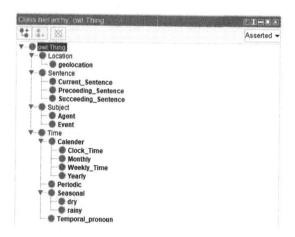

Fig. 2. Knowledge extractor class hierarchy

3.3 The Spatiotemporal Ontology

The ontology for the proposed spatiotemporal extractor is designed following the OWL principles and implemented in the Protégé with its class hierarchy and OntoGraf shown in Fig. 2 and Fig. 3 respectively.

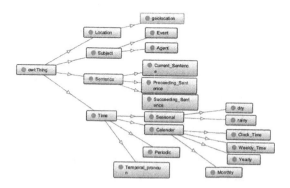

Fig. 3. Graph showing knowledge extractor ontology

The formalisms are explicitly expressed using First Order Logic (FOL) with Location, L, implying a Geolocation ($\mathbf{L_G}$) identified and visualized on the Google map being the result from the PeNLP parser. Though time, T, has a complex expression vocabulary, we simplify it here using temporal pronoun ($\mathbf{T_P}$), seasonal (**S**), periodic (**P**) and calendar time (C_A). Seasonal time is ei-ther dry, D, or rainy, R. On the other hand, Calendar time can be clock time (C_L), weekly (W), monthly (MM) and yearly (YY) time. The FOL expressions include the following expressions:

$$L \Rightarrow L_G$$
$$L_G <=> L_{\text{Google\_Map}}$$
$$T \Rightarrow S \wedge C_A \wedge P \wedge T_P$$
$$S \Rightarrow D \wedge R$$
$$C_A \Rightarrow C_L \wedge W \wedge MM \wedge YY$$
$$C_L \Rightarrow (am \wedge pm) \vee (AM \wedge PM)$$

The choice of the OWL ontology is dependent on the robustness of the formalization technique. The Map database is Google Map integrated via its API for Java environment. The decision support system is not given much attention at this stage because its design and development is out of the scope of this paper. It is worthy of note that the DSS, spatiotemporal extractor and knowledge bank are all designed to be web based.

4   Results and Discussion

In the work of Li et al. [4], attention was on the development of a web based model to support intelligent question answering using available online data. The main components targeted are space, time and event or occurrence, as the questions of interest in their research was spatiotemporal queries. Similar to the work in this paper because geospatial data are extracted; however, our submission is different because our extracted geospatial data is further structured and added to a corpus forming the knowledge bank.

From the sample input on the News publication, the model is able to identify times of the year that amount to a season. For instance, rainy and dry seasons or the months corresponding to these seasonal periods of the year are effectively identified and extracted. Temporal pronouns like today, yesterday, to-morrow, next Tuesday etc. are also identifiable.

The sample News article was parsed using the PeNLP parser and the structured results in the knowledge bank is based on the knowledge extractor ontology. The results show a total of 16 sentences were parsed with 8 Spatial components identified and extracted, 4 categories of the temporal entities were also identified and extracted with 6 under Year, 3 under Month, 1 under Week and 1 under Clock. The actual number of sentences was 10. The actual spatiotemporal entities were 9 Spatial, 6 year, 3 month, 1 week and 1 Clock. The obtained results from PeNLP parser were evaluated using the primary metric precision, recall, and F-measure in equations (1) to (3) and computed as given for spatial and temporal components. Given the metrics as:

$$\text{Precision, P} = l_2/l_1 \tag{1}$$

$$\text{Recall, R} = l_2/l \tag{2}$$

$$\text{F-measure} = \text{Fm} = 2 * (\text{P} * \text{R}/\text{P} + \text{R}) \tag{3}$$

where l = actual number of Entities in news article
l_1 = identified entities by PeNLP Parser
l_2 = number of correctly identified entities
On substituting the resulting values of extracted spatial components of 9 actual and 8 extracted, the precision, recall and F-measure were computed as follows:
$P = 8/8 = 1$;
$R = 8/9 = 0.8889$
$\text{Fm} = 2 * (1 * 0.8889)/(1 + 0.8889) = 0.9412$

From the computation of average Precision, Recall and F-measure, 100% success is attained for spatial feature extraction in our method. More specifically, in temporal feature extraction in Table 1; our method achieved a 94.12% success rate with F-measure evaluation. The Precision is 100%, while the Recall is 88.89%.

Table 1. Temporal results from news articles reporting rape cases in Akwa Ibom

Sentence	Actual Temporal entities, l	Temporal Entities identified by PeNLP Parser, l1	Temporal Entities correctly identified, l2	Precision	Recall	F-measure
Yearly	6	6	6	1	1	1
Monthly	3	3	3	1	1	1
Weekly	1	1	1	1	1	1
Clock Time	1	1	1	1	1	1
Average				1	1	1

The resulting knowledge bank has recorded huge success but for the few identified variations between the extracted results and the actual results, which were due to inappropriate punctuations by the reporters which resulted to 6 additional sentences adding up to 16 instead of 10 sentences.

5   Conclusion

Researching the safety or crime rate of an environment through online newspapers and blogs can be very tedious, time consuming and error prone. Advocacy against the increasing rape cases has also become more successful due to the availability of information on the web. For instance, cases of rape have been on the increase even during this COVID'19 pandemic. Advocacy against rape has also become more pronounced, such that more information about rapes is now available. The need for residents and commuters around reported locations to be aware and more cautious of times and seasons to avoid those locations become very necessary. This called for the development of the knowledge bank that can support any DSS in analysis.

The resulting knowledge bank adopted the PeNLP parser in the extraction of locational and temporal terms. The implementation of the architecture adapted OpenNLP library. The inefficiency of the OpenNLP in temporal identification and extraction from text was overcome by the introduction of the knowledge ontology where rules for temporal feature extraction were axiomatized. Though time has a complex expression vocabulary, it was simplified here using temporal pronoun, seasonal, periodic and calendar time. One limiting factor of the parser is inappropriate punctuation and poorly constructed grammar by reporters. Further work will consider integration of the knowledge bank with any DSS and evaluation of its ability to use extracted spatiotemporal features to aid actual decision supports by giving recommendations.

References

1. Arulanandam, R., Savarimuthu, B.T.R., Purvis, M.A.: Extracting crime information from online newspaper articles. In: Proceedings of the Second Australasian Web Conference, vol. 155, pp. 31–38 (2014)
2. Rao, K.V., Govardhan, A., Rao, K.C.: Spatiotemporal data mining: issues, tasks and applications. Int. J. Comput. Sci. Eng. Surv. 3(1), 39 (2012)
3. Lee, J.-W., Lee, Y.-J.: A knowledge discovery framework for spatiotemporal data mining. JIPS 2(2), 124–129 (2006)
4. Li, W., Song, M., Tian, Y.: An ontology-driven cyberinfrastructure for intelligent spatiotemporal question answering and open knowledge discovery. ISPRS Int. J. Geo-Inf. 8(11), 496 (2019)
5. Gill, T.L.: Relative and absolute time. In: Journal of Physics: Conference Series, IOP Publishing, vol. 1239, p. 012–013 (2019)
6. Wong, K.-F., Xia, Y., Li, W., Yuan, C.: An overview of temporal information extraction. Int. J. Comput. Process. Oriental Lang. 18(02), 137–152 (2005)
7. Ermolayev, V., Batsakis, S., Keberle, N., Tatarintseva, O., Antoniou, G.: Ontologies of time review and trends. Int. J. Comput. Sci. Appl. 11(3), 57–115 (2014)
8. Han, X., Wang, J.: Using social media to mine and analyze public sentiment during a disaster: a case study of the 2018 Shouguang city flood in china. ISPRS Int. J. Geo-Inf. 8(4), 185 (2019)
9. Madkour, A., Aref, W.G., Prabhakar, S., Ali, M., Bykau, S.: TrueWeb: a proposal for scalable semantically-guided data management and truth finding in heterogeneous web sources. In: Proceedings of the International Workshop on Semantic Big Data, pp. 1–6 (2018)
10. Wang, Y., Kung, L., Byrd, T.A.: Big data analytics: understanding its capabilities and potential benefits for healthcare organizations. Technol. Forecast. Soc. Change 126, 3–13 (2018)
11. Lin, C., et al.: Automatic prediction of rheumatoid arthritis disease activity from the electronic medical records. PloS One 8(8), e69932 (2013)

12. Wu, G., et al.: Development of a clinical decision support system for severity risk prediction and triage of covid-19 patients at hospital admission: an international multicentre study. Eur. Respir. J. **56**(2), 1–26 (2020). https://doi.org/10.1183/13993003.01104-2020

13. Marano, G., et al.: A geospatial decision support system tool for supporting integrated forest knowledge at the landscape scale. Forests **10**(8), 690 (2019)

14. Terribile, F., et al.: A geospatial decision support system for supporting quality viticulture at the landscape scale. Comput. Electron. Agric. **140**, 88–102 (2017)

15. Yang, J., Kang, U., Lee, Y.: Clinical decision support system in medical knowledge literature review. Inf. Tech. Manage. **17**(1), 5–14 (2015). https://doi.org/10.1007/s10799-015-0216-6

16. Zaraté, P., Liu, S.: A new trend for knowledge-based decision support systems design. Int. J. Inf. Decis. Sci. **8**(3), 305–324 (2016)

17. Tiwari, S., Abraham, A.: Semantic assessment of smart healthcare ontology. Int. J. Web Inf. Syst., 1–17 (2020). https://doi.org/10.1108/IJWIS-05-2020-0027

18. Mishra, S., Jain, S.: Ontologies as a semantic model in IoT. Int. J. Comput. Appl. **42**(3), 233–243 (2020)

19. Cox, S., Little, C., Hobbs, J., Pan, F.: Time ontology in OWL. W3C recommendation, vol. 19 (2017)

20. Baumann, R., Loebe, F., Herre, H.: Axiomatic theories of the ontology of time in GFO. Appl. Ontol. **9**(3–4), 171–215 (2014)

21. Tu, S.W., Eriksson, H., Gennari, J.H., Shahar, Y., Musen, M.A.: Ontology-based configuration of problem-solving methods and generation of knowledge-acquisition tools: application of PROTEGE-II to protocol-based decision support. Artif. Intell. Med. **7**(3), 257–289 (1995)

22. Sherimon, P., Krishnan, R.: Ontodiabetic: an ontology-based clinical decision support system for diabetic patients. Arab. J. Sci. Eng. **41**(3), 1145–1160 (2016)

23. Jung, H., Chung, K.: PHR based life health index mobile service using decision support model. Wirel. Pers. Commun. **86**(1), 315–332 (2016)

24. Mueller, M.M., et al.: Patient blood management: recommendations from the 2018 Frankfurt consensus conference. JAMA **321**(10), 983–997 (2019)

25. Ghazali Noor, R.: Saman: Development of a decision support system with risk: supporting police and government in crime prevention. J. Appl. Sci. **11**(6), 340–344 (2016)

26. Sham, R., Omar, N., Amat, D.W.: Hot spot urban crime area for woman travellers. Procedia-Soc. Behav. Sci. **68**, 417–426 (2012)

27. Gupta, M., Chandra, B., Gupta, M.: A framework of intelligent decision support system for Indian police. J. Enterp. Inf. Manage. **27**(5), 512–540 (2014)

28. Saman, M., Hitam, S.: Probabilistic knowledge base system for forensic evidence analysis. J. Theoret. Appl. Inf. Technol. **59**(3), 708–716 (2014)

29. Mishra, S., Jain, S.: An intelligent knowledge treasure for military decision support. Int. J. Web-Based Learn. Teach. Tech. (IJWLTT) **14**(3), 55–75 (2019)

30. Usip, P.U., Ekpenyong, M.E., Nwachukwu, J.: A secured preposition-enabled natural language parser for extracting spatial context from unstructured data. In: Odumuyiwa, V., Adegboyega, O., Uwadia, C. (eds.) AFRICOMM 2017. LNICST, vol. 250, pp. 163–168. Springer, Cham (2018). https://doi.org/10.1007/978-3-319-98827-6_14

Exploring Sequence-to-Sequence Models for SPARQL Pattern Composition

Anand Panchbhai[3], Tommaso Soru[1,3(✉)], and Edgard Marx[1,2,3]

[1] AKSW, University of Leipzig, Leipzig, Germany
tom@tommaso-soru.it
[2] Leipzig University of Applied Sciences, Leipzig, Germany
[3] Liber AI Research, London, UK

Abstract. A booming amount of information is continuously added to the Internet as structured and unstructured data, feeding knowledge bases such as DBpedia and Wikidata with billions of statements describing millions of entities. The aim of Question Answering systems is to allow lay users to access such data using natural language without needing to write formal queries. However, users often submit questions that are complex and require a certain level of abstraction and reasoning to decompose them into basic graph patterns. In this short paper, we explore the use of architectures based on Neural Machine Translation called *Neural SPARQL Machines* to learn pattern compositions. We show that sequence-to-sequence models are a viable and promising option to transform long utterances into complex SPARQL queries.

Keywords: Linked data · SPARQL · Question Answering · Deep learning on knowledge graphs · Compositionality

1 Introduction

Knowledge graphs have recently become a mainstream method for organising data on the Internet. With a great amount of information being added every day, it becomes very important to store them properly and make them accessible to the masses. Languages like SPARQL have made querying complex information from these large graphs possible. Unfortunately, the knowledge of query languages such as SPARQL is still a barrier that makes it difficult for lay users to access this data readily. A number of attempts have been made to increase the accessibility of knowledge graphs. Prominent among them is the active application of various paradigms of computer science ranging from heuristic-based parsing methodologies to machine learning.

Recent advances in Natural Language Processing have shown promising results in the task of machine translation from one language to another. Eminent among them are neural architectures for sequence-to-sequence (Seq2Seq) learning [15] in Neural Machine Translation (NMT). Considering SPARQL as another language for such a conversion, attempts have been made to convert

© Springer Nature Switzerland AG 2020
B. Villazón-Terrazas et al. (Eds.): KGSWC 2020, CCIS 1232, pp. 158–165, 2020.
https://doi.org/10.1007/978-3-030-65384-2_12

natural language questions to SPARQL queries by proposing Neural SPARQL Machines [13,14] (NSpM). Rather than using language heuristics, statistical or handcrafted models, NSpM completely rely on the ability of the NMT models. The architecture majorly comprises of 3 components (i.e., generator, learner, and interpreter), and its modular nature allows the use of different NMT models [13].

This paper tries to answer the problem of Knowledge Graph Question Answering (KGQA) from a fundamental perspective. We build upon the NSpM architecture to tackle 2 main research questions:

(RQ1) Can we employ Seq2Seq models to learn SPARQL pattern compositions?
(RQ2) Targeting compositionality, what is the best configuration for a NSpM to maximise the translation accuracy?

To address the first question, we start by augmenting the template generation methodology proposed for the NSpM model in [14]. This is followed up with an analysis of compositional questions. This analysis will help gauge the competence of NMT models to learn SPARQL pattern compositions. In the later sections, we will lay out the best configuration for NSpM to maximise its translation performance. We released all code and data used in the experiments.[1]

2   Related Work

Many approaches have tried to tackle the challenge of KGQA. In a number of these approaches, an attempt is made to retrieve the answers in the form of triple stores [5,11,17]. Questions can be asked in a variety of forms. Work has been done specific to simple questions pertaining to facts [9], basic graph patterns (BGP) [11,20] and complex questions [5,17]. The advent of QA datasets like QALD [18,19], LC-QuAD [16], and DBNQA [6] has accelerated the use of deep learning based techniques for the purpose of KGQA. KQA Pro [12] is a relatively new dataset that tries to tackle the problems present in previous QA datasets by using recursive templates and crowd-sourced paraphrasing methods, incorporating compositional reasoning capability in complex KGQA. Some of the entries of challenges like QALD comprise the state of the art in KGQA. The approaches range from a ad-hoc rule-based implementations to end-to-end deep learning pipelines.

WDAqua [4] is a rule-based combinatorial system to engender SPARQL queries form natural-language questions. The system is not based on machine learning and does not require any training. *ganswer2* [23] uses a semantic query graph-based approach to generate SPARQL queries from natural language questions and redefines the problem of conversion of natural language queries to SPARQL as a sub-graph matching problem. It constitutes of 2 stages, where the first stage focuses on understanding the questions and the second stage deals with query evaluation. The approach won the QALD-9 challenge [18]. Other Seq2Seq architectures have been proposed to target structured QA, however to the best of our knowledge, none of them has tackled the SPARQL compositionality problem in neural approaches [8,21,22].

---

[1] https://github.com/LiberAI/NSpM/wiki/Compositionality.

3 Methodology

3.1 Problem Statement

We define the problem of SPARQL compositionality from a machine-learning point of view. Given two questions a = *"When was Barack Obama born?"* and b = *"Who was the 44th President of the USA?"*, their composition $a \circ b$ is the composite question *"When was the 44th President of the USA born?"*.

Let us introduce a set X of questions

$$X = \{a_1, b_1, a_1 \circ b_1, \ldots, a_{n-1}, b_{n-1}, a_{n-1} \circ b_{n-1}, a_n, b_n\} \tag{1}$$

mapped to its respective set of queries Y. The basic problem of compositionality is to be able to predict $f(a_n \circ b_n)$ by learning $f : X \to Y$. In other words, we expect the learning model to generalise on the seen examples (X, Y) and learn to compose on the unseen example $a_n \circ b_n$.

3.2 Template Generation

The generator is the first part of the NSpM architecture. The training data outputted by the generator is heavily dependent on the structure of the input templates. Manual curation of templates has been carried out in a number of works [14,17,18]. Part automated and part manual methods powered by crowd sourcing have been used in various versions of the QALD benchmarks, LC-QuAD, and KQA Pro.

This work proposes a completely automated way of generating templates, as it follows a bottom-up approach. A ranking-based method is proposed to ensure that the templates used are natural and germane to the questions asked by general users. The template generation methodology proposed here is for the DBpedia knowledge graph [7].

The first step deals with iterating over all the properties of a given class. For each class of the DBpedia ontology, we retrieve metadata such as label, domain, range, and comments.[2] Based on the properties, questions can be constructed. For instance, *date of birth* is the property of an individual and is represented by dbo:birthDate in DBpedia. Information about all entities having a dbo:birthDate value are fetched using SPARQL queries of the form: SELECT DISTINCT(?a) WHERE { ?a dbo:birthDate [] }. As individual dbr: Barack_Obama is one of those entities having a dbo:birthDate value, questions can be framed as *What is the date of birth of Barack Obama?* with corresponding SPARQL query: SELECT ?x WHERE { dbr:BarackObama dbo:birthDate ?x }. The current question is a very primitive one and has a specific form: *What is the ⟨Property name⟩ of ⟨Entity name⟩?*. More often than not, users ask more involved questions. Given the structural form of the SPARQL language, a bottom up approach was again adopted to build questions of varying types.

---

[2] The metadata can be fetched from http://mappings.dbpedia.org/server/ontology/ classes/.

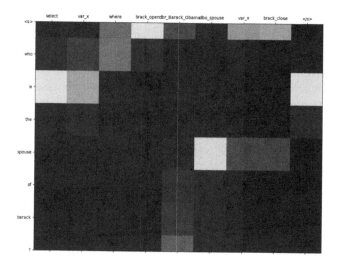

Fig. 1. Attention heat-map of a Neural SPARQL Machines at work. The x-axis contains the natural language question while the y-axis contains the sequence encoding of the corresponding SPARQL query.

Types of Questions. SPARQL supports answering conditional questions using conditional operators. Comparative questions are one of the basic types of questions asked as queries. Similarly, other functionalities provided by SPARQL such as LIMIT and OFFSET could be used for creating more complex questions pertaining to aggregational queries and questions containing superlatives. Questions with boolean answers can be answered using the ASK query form. Intuitively, increasingly complex compositional questions can be generated by recursively running the same steps above.

Ranking. On close inspection, we noticed that a number of templates generated felt unnatural. To tackle this issue, we assigned a rank to each template based on a page ranking mechanism on the basis of the hypothesis that the relevance of a template can be determined by the popularity of the corresponding answers. The ranking mechanism used here is SubjectiveEye3D[3], which is similar to PageRank [10].

The ranking step takes place after the generation and checking of the compatible entities. For example, in the question *"What is the date of birth of spouse of <A>?"*, the placeholder <A> can be replaced by entity labels (e.g., "Barack Obama"). Here, dbr:Barack_Obama and the required date of birth are the two directly useful entities, whereas the intermediate entity is dbr:Michelle_Obama. A damping factor was introduced as the depth of question increased to take the route of getting the answer into consideration. In the previous example, the route is: dbr:Barack_Obama → dbr:Michelle_Obama → dbo:birthDate. 0.85

---

[3] https://github.com/paulhoule/telepath/wiki/SubjectiveEye3D.

was selected as a damping factor empirically, following the probability arrived in a similar research done in [1]. The accumulated scores for a given templates were averaged to get the final rank. The decision to consider a given template is based on a threshold mechanism. The threshold should be decided class-wise and a single general threshold should not be used for all classes, since the pages related to certain classes (e.g., eukaryotes) are viewed less than pages related to others (e.g., celebrities). The relative number of views within eukaryotes-related pages is however useful for the ranking of templates.

4   Results and Discussion

We employed a parameter search where we varied various parameters of the NSpM architecture. The results obtained are shown in Table 1. Due to the sheer size of DBpedia, we selected the subset of entities belonging to the eukaryotes class to carry out our compositionality experiments. Eukaryotes is a large class of DBpedia with 302,686 entities and 2,043 relations.[4] 169 unique templates were generated by the automatic template generation pipeline, these templates yielded 21,637 unique natural language question-query pairs. The best results for the given dataset were obtained for the configuration of NMT with 2 layers, 128 units, 0.7 dropout, scaled Luong attention and with pre-trained embeddings. Ensuring that the entities were present in the training set for a predetermined number of times also helped boost the translation performance, as previously found in [13]. Use of attention in the NMT architecture helped the model in it's translation capabilities as is evident from the results present in Table 1. Figure 1 depicts the attention weights for a translation of a natural-language question into a sequence encoding a SPARQL query in the form of a heat-map.

For answering the question related to compositionality and the ability of the Seq2Seq NMT model, experiment #1.1 was carried out. As previously introduced, by compositionality here we mean that a and b were introduced in the training phase, we test for $a \circ b$ or $b \circ a$. a and b represent the properties or entities. On randomly splitting the dataset thus generated into 80% train, 10% validation and 10% test, we were able to achieve 97.69% BLEU score and 89.75% accuracy on 40,000 iterations of training. Perfect accuracy was not achieved due to (1) entity mismatch and (2) certain instances where the training set did not contain the entities that were present in the test set. These issues can be tackled by increasing the number of examples per entity in the training set, however it is unrealistic to expect an algorithm to disambiguate all entities, as they may be challenging even for humans.

Though the model produced favourable results, a more challenging task was created to assess the ability of Seq2Seq NMT model towards learning pattern compositions. A special pair of training and test set (experiment #1.2) was created while putting a restriction on the entities present in the training set. In this regard, the training set could contain templates $a, b, a \circ c, d \circ b$, whereas the test set contained $a \circ b, a, b, c, d$. A property once introduced in given depth

---

[4] Retrieved on 19/10/2020 from https://dbpedia.org/sparql.

Table 1. Parameter search results. Each model configuration was run for at least 40,000 epochs. All options of the type column have the following meaning: (a) random splitting into 80% training, 10% validation, and 10% test sets; (b) ensuring same vocabulary of training and test sets; (c) frequency threshold ensured that the training set had a predetermined number of iterations of a given word to give the model ample opportunity to learn the word to be tested; (d) the restrictions of experiment #1.2 were followed. Best BLEU and accuracy are given in percentage.

#	Type	#Layers	#Units	Dropout	Attention	Emb.	BestBLEU	BestAcc.
Attention or no attention								
1.1	a	2	128	0.2	No	No	**97.7**	**89.8**
1.2	a	2	128	0.2	Scaled Luong	No	97.5	88.0
1.3	b, c, d	2	128	0.2	No	No	66.4	5.7
1.4	b, c, d	2	128	0.2	Scaled Luong	No	85.2	34.3
Dropout								
2.1	b, c, d	2	128	0.05	Luong	No	58.0	0.0
2.2	b, c, d	2	128	0.5	Luong	No	86.0	40.9
2.3	b, c, d	2	128	0.7	Luong	No	85.0	45.1
2.4	b, c, d	2	128	0.9	Luong	No	59.6	2.3
Attention type								
3.1	b, c, d	2	128	0.5	Luong	No	76.7	9.1
3.2	b, c, d	2	128	0.5	Bahdanau	No	62.5	0.0
3.3	b, c, d	2	128	0.5	Scaled Luong	No	86.0	40.9
Number of units								
4.1	b, c, d	2	256	0.5	Scaled Luong	No	82.9	25.0
4.2	b, c, d	2	512	0.5	Scaled Luong	No	55.8	0.0
Number of layers								
5.1	b, c, d	1	128	0.7	Scaled Luong	No	1.0	0.0
5.2	b, c, d	3	128	0.5	Scaled Luong	No	58.7	0.0
5.3	b, c, d	2	128	0.5	Scaled Luong	No	86.0	40.9
5.4	b, c, d	4	128	0.5	Scaled Luong	No	63.0	0.0
Pre-trained embeddings								
6.1	b, c, d	2	128	0.7	Scaled Luong	Yes	93.0	63.0

was not introduced there again in the training set; instead, it was added to the test set. These results are represented in the last row in Table 1. As can be seen, we obtained a BLEU score of 93% and accuracy of 63%. The results thus obtained tell us few very important things about the ability of the NMT model, as even with less amount of data per entity the NMT model was able to learn the structure of SPARQL query that needed to be generated. This shows the ability of Seq2Seq to adapt to complex language structure whenever necessary. On analysing the result, it was discovered that the low accuracy and high BLEU was again due to the entity mismatch that took place despite the model predicted the right structure of the queries. The model in the previous experiment was able to produce high accuracy merely because it had more opportunity to learn the given word and structure when compared to experiment 1.2.

While conducting these experiments, we were able to gauge the importance of various parameters which are an essential part of template generation and the NSpM model. The study carried out here and the results stated are limited to the particular ontology class of Eukaryotes. Although the generated system is not potent to answer questions beyond this class, later studies can train on more number of classes to address this problem. The ability of the model to handle more complex questions with varying template structure also needs to be explored.

5   Conclusion

This study suggested a way to generate templates automatically for the NSpM pipeline. An optimal configuration was also suggested based on the experiments conducted as part of the study. The results suggest that Seq2Seq NMT model holds the potential to learn pattern compositions. We plan on making the generated templates sound more human by integrating NLP paraphrasers and pre-trained language models such as GPT [2] and BERT [3].

This work was partly carried out at the DBpedia Association and supported by Google through the Google Summer of Code 2019 programme.

References

1. Brin, S., Page, L.: The anatomy of a large-scale hypertextual web search engine. Comput. Network. ISDN Syst. **30**(1), 107–117 (1998). Proceedings of the Seventh International World Wide Web Conference
2. Brown, T.B., et al.: Language models are few-shot learners (2020)
3. Devlin, J., Chang, M.W., Lee, K., Toutanova, K.: BERT: pre-training of deep bidirectional transformers for language understanding. arXiv (2018)
4. Diefenbach, D., Singh, K., Maret, P.: WDAqua-core0: a question answering component for the research community. In: Dragoni, M., Solanki, M., Blomqvist, E. (eds.) SemWebEval 2017. CCIS, vol. 769, pp. 84–89. Springer, Cham (2017). https://doi.org/10.1007/978-3-319-69146-6_8
5. Dubey, M., Dasgupta, S., Sharma, A., Höffner, K., Lehmann, J.: AskNow: a framework for natural language query formalization in SPARQL. In: Sack, H., Blomqvist, E., d'Aquin, M., Ghidini, C., Ponzetto, S.P., Lange, C. (eds.) ESWC 2016. LNCS, vol. 9678, pp. 300–316. Springer, Cham (2016). https://doi.org/10.1007/978-3-319-34129-3_19
6. Hartmann, A.K., Marx, E., Soru, T.: Generating a large dataset for neural question answering over the DBpedia knowledge base. In: Workshop on Linked Data Management, co-located with the W3C WEBBR 2018 (2018)
7. Lehmann, J., et al.: DBpedia - a large-scale, multilingual knowledge base extracted from Wikipedia. Semant. Web **6**(2), 167–195 (2015)
8. Liang, C., Berant, J., Le, Q., Forbus, K.D., Lao, N.: Neural symbolic machines: learning semantic parsers on freebase with weak supervision. arXiv preprint arXiv:1611.00020 (2016)
9. Lukovnikov, D., Fischer, A., Lehmann, J., Auer, S.: Neural network-based question answering over knowledge graphs on word and character level. In: Proceedings of the 26th International Conference on World Wide Web, pp. 1211–1220 (2017)

10. Page, L., Brin, S., Motwani, R., Winograd, T.: The PageRank citation ranking: bringing order to the web. Technical report, Stanford InfoLab (1999)
11. Shekarpour, S., Marx, E., Ngomo, A., Sina, S.: Semantic interpretation of user queries for question answering on interlinked data. Elsevier-Web Semantics (2015)
12. Shi, J., Cao, S., et al.: KQA pro: a large diagnostic dataset for complex question answering over knowledge base (2020)
13. Soru, T., et al.: SPARQL as a foreign language. In: 13th International Conference on Semantic Systems (SEMANTiCS 2017) - Posters and Demos (2017)
14. Soru, T., Marx, E., Valdestilhas, A., Esteves, D., Moussallem, D., Publio, G.: Neural machine translation for query construction and composition. In: 2nd ICML Workshop on Neural Abstract Machines & Program Induction (2018)
15. Sutskever, I., Vinyals, O., Le, Q.V.: Sequence to sequence learning with neural networks. In: Advances in Neural Information Processing Systems (2014)
16. Trivedi, P., Maheshwari, G., Dubey, M., Lehmann, J.: LC-QuAD: a corpus for complex question answering over knowledge graphs. In: d'Amato, C., et al. (eds.) ISWC 2017. LNCS, vol. 10588, pp. 210–218. Springer, Cham (2017). https://doi.org/10.1007/978-3-319-68204-4_22
17. Unger, C., Bühmann, L., Lehmann, J., Ngonga Ngomo, A.C., Gerber, D., Cimiano, P.: Template-based question answering over RDF data. In: Proceedings of the 21st International Conference on World Wide Web, pp. 639–648 (2012)
18. Usbeck, R., Gusmita, R.H., Saleem, M., Ngonga Ngomo, A.C.: 9th challenge on question answering over linked data (QALD-9). Question Answering over Linked Data 7(1) (2018)
19. Usbeck, R., Ngomo, A.C.N., Conrads, F., Röder, M., Napolitano, G.: 8th challenge on question answering over linked data (QALD-8). Language 7, 1 (2018)
20. Zhang, Y., He, S., Liu, K., Zhao, J., et al.: A joint model for question answering over multiple knowledge bases. In: 30th AAAI Conference (2016)
21. Zheng, W., Yu, J.X., Zou, L., Cheng, H.: Question answering over knowledge graphs: question understanding via template decomposition. Proc. VLDB Endow. 11(11), 1373–1386 (2018)
22. Zhong, V., Xiong, C., Socher, R.: Seq2SQL: generating structured queries from natural language using reinforcement learning. arXiv preprint arXiv:1709.00103 (2017)
23. Zou, L., Huang, R., Wang, H., Yu, J.X., He, W., Zhao, D.: Natural language question answering over RDF: a graph data driven approach. In: Proceedings of the 2014 ACM SIGMOD International Conference on Management of Data, pp. 313–324 (2014)

Using Domain Ontologies for Text Classification. A Use Case to Classify Computer Science Papers

Janneth Chicaiza[✉][iD] and Ruth Reátegui[iD]

Universidad Técnica Particular de Loja, Loja, Ecuador
{jachicaiza,rmreategui}@utpl.edu.ec
http://www.utpl.edu.ec

Abstract. The web facilitates the creation, publication, and exchange of a wide variety of information. Particularly, the dramatic growth of unstructured web content makes text classification in a basic task to automate. Although well-known classification methods come from natural language processing and the machine learning fields, in this paper, the authors address the classification task as the ability to recognize topics or concepts in a text. To achieve this goal, we use a domain ontology as a driver of this process. The main motivation behind this work is to take advantage of the existing domain ontologies to classify and analyze the scientific production of a certain area of knowledge. Preliminary findings obtained by classifying a subset of Computer Science papers encourage us to remain researching in this area. Also, we will continue to discover a better way to improve results by combining it with other well-known approaches for text classification.

Keywords: Text classification · Domain ontology · Computer Science · Scholarly production · Scopus

1 Introduction

The web facilitates the creation, publication, and exchange of a wide variety of information. Particularly, it is populated with a high volume of unstructured data. In this environment, information overload, lack of structure, and heterogeneity of content make it difficult for people to find valuable content. Here, ontologies and knowledge graphs have a crucial role to perform tasks such as organization, classification and link distributed repositories of data. In this paper, we focus on the application of domain ontologies for text classification.

The dramatic growth of unstructured content on the web makes text classification a suitable operation to automate. But performing classification on a large-scale implies to address a set of challenges such as (1) to design a solution independent of the domain (2) to solve problems related to information meaning and context. To relieve and funnel the efforts required to classify specialized

B. Villazón-Terrazas et al. (Eds.): KGSWC 2020, CCIS 1232, pp. 166–180, 2020.
https://doi.org/10.1007/978-3-030-65384-2_13

corpus, i.e., centered on a specific field of knowledge, in this paper, we explore an approach based on domain ontologies.

Although well-known classification methods come from natural language processing and machine learning fields, in this paper, the authors explore an approach based on ontologies. The main motivation behind this work is to take advantage of the existing domain ontologies to classify and analyze the scholarly production of a specific field of knowledge.

As a use case, we leverage a domain ontology to classify papers in different disciplines of the Computer Science (CS) field. More precisely, for the classification task, we use the Computer Science Ontology (CSO), which is a large-scale ontology created from million of publications, mainly in the field of CS [10]. CSO connects by using hierarchical relationships more than 23K concepts related to CS and other close fields.

Using CSO, we able to classify a subset of papers by taking the advantages provided by a controlled and hierarchical vocabulary. First, the classification is multi-level, i.e., users can explore graphs of topics, and they decide if the classification is made with broader or narrower concepts of a knowledge field. Second, the classification is multi-label, this implies that the content of each document drives in how many concepts or disciplines it is classified. And, third, the classification is weighted, thus we can know to the main and complementary topics of a resource.

Continuing with the paper, in Sect. 2, the main concepts of supporting this proposal are described. Later, in Sect. 3, we describe the conceptual model to classify text based on domain ontologies, and we explain the process applied to a set of papers. Next, preliminary results are presented. Finally, the conclusions and future works appear.

2   Background

2.1   Text Classification

Text classification is the task that automatically assigns to a document a predefined class. Given a set of training records $D = \{X1, \ldots, XN\}$, each record is labeled with a class value from a set of k different discrete values $\{c1 \ldots ck\}$. Depending on their characteristics, the documents can be labeled for one class (single-label) or for more than one class (multi-label) [8]. In a hard version, a particular label is explicitly assigned to the document, but in a soft version, a probability value is assigned to the document [1].

The text classification process consists of document representation, feature selection or feature transformation, application of data mining algorithms and finally an evaluation of the applied data mining algorithm.

According to [12], classification techniques could be divided into statistical and machine learning (ML) approaches. Statistical techniques are purely mathematical processes, whereas, ML follows three principles: (1) supervised learning, where the system is trained and tested on the knowledge about classes before the actual classification process; (2) unsupervised learning when labeled data is not accessible and no training data is provided to the system; and (3) semi-supervised learning employs a small amount of labeled data and a large amount of unlabeled data for training.

Naive Bayes, SVM, KNN, decision trees, and neural networks are some of the most popular machine learning supervised algorithms. On the other hand, K-means clustering and hierarchical clustering are popular unsupervised algorithms. Another point of view to classified text is through the identification of topics in documents, it is called topic modeling. Latent Dirichlet Allocation (LDA) is a topic model that follows unsupervised learning. LDA model represents documents as random mixtures over latent topics, where each topic is characterized by a distribution over words [4].

All the approaches present some disadvantages. Supervised learning is the most expensive and difficult because it requires a human intervention to label the classes, which is not possible in large datasets. Unsupervised is complicated and has performance issues. Semi-supervised learning improves the classification efficiency, and it is suitable for solving the labeling problem while handling more number of instances of an entity [12].

2.2   Domain Ontologies

An ontology is a conceptual representation of the vocabulary of a knowledge domain. The vocabulary provides a set of terms to describe facts in a given domain, while the body of knowledge using that vocabulary is a collection of facts about a domain [5]. An ontology provides formal descriptions for individuals, classes, relations, restrictions, rules, axioms, and events [9], and it can be codified using the Web Ontology Language (OWL), that is a semantic web computational logic-based language.

An ontology can be used: to share a common understanding or consensual knowledge of the structure of information accepted by experts in a domain, to reuse of domain knowledge, to facilitate the analysis of domain knowledge, and to use the same terminology in different software applications [3,9]. In the scholarly domain, ontologies are used to explore the academic landscape, to extract information from scientific articles, to classify publications, to research communities, and to forecast research trends [10].

A domain ontology describes relevant entities (concepts or individuals) in a single domain of interest. A domain ontology can also be the model that represents the terms of a domain as a hierarchy of topics expressed as instances of some concept. In this research, we mean to the second notion, that is, domain ontologies are models that describe domain schemes such as classification schemes, thesauri, and subject headings. When we use an ontology to describe a domain, we will be able to connect their entities using special relationships. For example, transitive relationships allow machines to infer new facts: If $A1$ is broader than $A2$, and A is broader than $A1$, then, A is broader than $A2$.s

Nowadays exist domain ontologies in different areas of knowledge such as music[1], marine domain[2], biomedical research[3], genetic[4], etc. For the Computer Science field, there are some non-ontological and ontological schemes to define the concepts of this domain.

The term Non-Ontological Resources (NORs) is defined by Villazón-Terrazas, Suárez-Figueroa and Gómez-Pérez, as those "knowledge resources whose semantics have not yet been formalized by an ontology... These resources are present in the form of textual corpora, classification scheme, thesauri, lexicons, etc." [13, p. 28].

For the CS domain, there are some NORs such as the ACM Computing Classification System (CCS) and WikiCSSH [7]. CCS is a subject classification system devised by the Association for Computing Machinery (ACM). The full CCS classification tree is available in HTML format. The second scheme, WikiCSSH, it is a hierarchically-organized subject heading vocabulary for the domain of CS. WikiCSSH contains more than 7.4K coarse-grained terms (categories) that are associated with more than 0.75M fine-grained terms (pages) in 20 levels.

Regarding the ontological resources, one novel model is the Computer Science Ontology (CSO) [10]. In September 2018, the first version was released, and the latest version was released on June 08, 2020. To date, seven new versions have been released that include new topics and relationships between them. Currently, the model has more than 23K instances of the *Topic* class.

In this paper, we use CSO to annotate and classify a corpus of research papers. CCS is discarded because it is too small to annotate a corpus. On the other hand, although WikiCSSH has the best coverage of the three models, it is not formalized as an ontological model, hence it is not machine-readable. Instead, CSO is easy to process automatically, and so far, it has been a well-supported project.

2.3 Domain Ontologies-Based Classification

Some studies have considered an ontology-based approach to classifying texts from different domains. For example, [6] propose the enrichment of the CS disciplines defined by the UNESCO nomenclature by using the DBPedia categories. Then, a set of open education resources were labeled with disciplines of this controlled vocabulary. In [2] an ontology was proposed as a classifier. Authors use a general encyclopedic knowledge-based ontology to recognize and classify web news documents from numerous domains. Also, [14] applied a domain ontology algorithm to classify environmental regulatory documents. The classification process was improved by utilizing the semantic features of the text.

Furthermore, [11] present a domain-dependent approach to text classification, contrasting the relevant technical terms into the text. To make the approach

---

[1] http://musicontology.com/.
[2] https://projects.ics.forth.gr/isl/MarineTLO/.
[3] http://obi-ontology.org/.
[4] http://geneontology.org/.

more flexible and capable of handling real-world applications, the authors use a thesaurus for locating text words in an ontology. The domain is the occupational health and security application.

Due to the lack of classified training datasets, necessary for traditional text classification techniques, the above studies preferred to use an ontology-based approach. Ontologies skip the training step and allow change the topics of the categorization without any retraining [2]. With an ontology, classification depends on the entities, their relationships, and the taxonomy of categories represented in the ontology [11]. The domain ontology becomes the classifier.

Similarly to [11], our work aims to classify texts, contrasting the information within the texts with a specific vocabulary from an ontology. As we mentioned, in this study, we use CSO because it is a reliable model that has been used for several tasks such as providing recommendations of editorial products, generating taxonomy of research areas, and classification of research papers. Although in the CSO portal[5], a classifier interface is available, we use the CSO model in the background to process automatically more than 3K papers and to classify according to the taxonomy of the CSO concepts.

3   Methodology

In this section, we introduce the conceptual model for the classification task using a domain ontology, then a specific scenery of application is explained.

3.1   Conceptual Model for Text Classification

In ontologies that describe domain schemes, any subject of the domain is an individual of a general class like *Topic*. In this paper, we intuitively differentiate three types of subjects:

- Field is the root subject of the domain. Some ontologies could have more than one top subject, for instance, computer science, mathematics, engineering, and such as well.
- Discipline is a topic close to the root topic or field.
- Annotation is a specific subject. Generally, an annotation is any subtopic of a knowledge field. The granularity low level of annotation is useful to recognize specific topics in the text to be classified.

The above definitions help us to understand how the classification is made.

Figure 1 shows the process to classify a text corpus related to a specific domain. The flow is simple because the ontology defines the subjects of the domain and lead how they are traversed until reach at a level or subject of interest.

As can be seen in Fig. 1, the process starts choosing a text corpus and at least a domain ontology. To get better results, we recommend using more ontologies,

---

[5] https://cso.kmi.open.ac.uk/classify/.

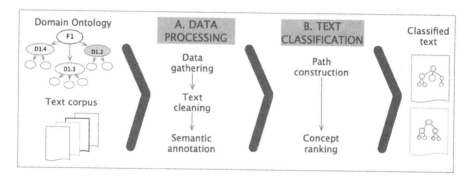

Fig. 1. Conceptual model for text classification

for example, a general or cross-domain ontology and a set of ontologies describing complementary domains. Depending on the specialization level and the multidisciplinary nature of the corpus to be analyzed, using additional ontologies could help us improve the classification process, increasing the accuracy and coverage of the results achieved.

After the sources have been selected, in the data processing stage (A) we collect and clean the unstructured content. When data is ready, ontology is used for the semantic annotation (entity recognition) of the text. To get reliable results, ontology features such as granularity, coverage, and connectivity are crucial. Thus, the ontology ability to recognize concepts depends on the number of entities or topics, and the number of relationships between them.

The next stage is the text classification consists of two tasks: (1) Path construction is made to discover connections between each recognized entity in the text and the target concept (commonly a field or discipline). (2) From the set of paths, we should organize or sort concepts (ranking) according to their relatedness level within the text.

Next, to explain how to perform the two stages of the classification process and the tasks associated with them, a particular case is presented.

3.2 Process Application for Ecuadorian Production in Computer Science

In this section, the authors apply the defined process to classify a subset of Ecuadorian papers indexed by Scopus. Four motivations encourage to the authors to define this scope: (1) Scopus database ease the gathering of data through the Elsevier APIs; (2) the analysis of Ecuadorian scholarly production is a part of a bigger initiative that try to detect publishing patterns, so the goal is to foster its growth and impact; (3) computer science is the area with the highest growth of the Ecuadorian production; and (4) to describe the CS domain exists the ontology CSO, that is a reliable model applied in tasks related to knowledge management in the area.

(A) Data Processing.
- Data Gathering. In early 2020, we collected 3,411 Ecuadorian documents related to the CS field until 2018. The following query was used to call the Scopus Search API[6]:

```
AFFILCOUNTRY(Ecuador) AND SUBJAREA(COMP)
AND PUBYEAR < 2019
```

- Text Cleaning. For the implementation of this use case, we processed 3,305 papers with not empty abstract. Specifically, we used regular expressions to clean the text. Here, we found that the most popular pattern is [∧©. ∗ $IEEE$], indeed 41.8% of the papers have this string.
- Semantic Annotation. To recognize topics in the text, we used the python library cso-classifier[7] based on the CSO model. The CSO classifier takes as input the metadata associated with a paper (in this case, title, abstract, and keywords), and it returns a selection of a set of concepts drawn from the ontology. From the 3,305 papers, we got 38,559 annotations in total, with 4,679 unique entities.

(B) Text Classification.
- Path Construction. To get the paths from each annotation (returned by the cso-classifier) until the CS field, we built a recursive function to traverse the CSO model using the property *broader* which connect a specific topic to a broader one. Figure 2 illustrates the logic of this task: (1) the function receives as input the set of annotations of each paper (2) the function traverses the CSO model until to find the concept "computer science", and (3) the path of each visited topic is returned to the main method which stores results to do the next task.
- Concept Ranking. To compute the ranking for concepts closer to CS, i.e. disciplines, we propose a simple ranking method based on sum weighted reached by each discipline (d_j). To compute this metric ($weighted\_sum(d_j)$), we used the expression (1):

$$weighted\_sum(d_j) = \sum \frac{1}{distance(a_i, d_j)} \qquad (1)$$

where: $distance(a_i, d_j)$ is the shortest path from each annotation (a_i) to a CS discipline (d_j).
Then, based on the value for $weighted\_sum(d_j)$ of each discipline, we compute the ranking for each one.
Figure 3 explains how to compute metrics for a particular paper. Note that a paper, based on its metadata, can be classified in different disciplines and fields. Figure 4 shows the distribution of number of disciplines associated to papers. As can be seen, majority of papers have 5 to 7 disciplines. An exceptional case is a paper with 21 disciplines. Here, this finding demonstrated that in Computer Science, research is multidisciplinary

---

[6] https://dev.elsevier.com/documentation/ScopusSearchAPI.wadl.
[7] https://pypi.org/project/cso-classifier/.

because it is related to a spectrum of several technologies, approaches and application domains.

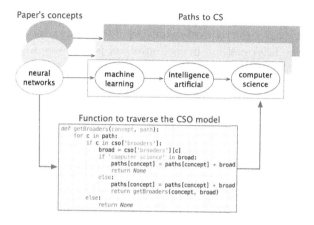

Fig. 2. Traversing the CSO model to get the paths until the CS field

Paper's metadata

eid	title
2-s2.0-36849020013	Using an artificial neural network to improve the transformation of coordinates between classical geodetic reference frames

Weight measureament of each annotation

annotation	discipline	min path	weight
neural networks	artificial intelligence	3	0,3333
radial basis functions	artificial intelligence	9	0,1111
multilayer perceptrons	artificial intelligence	9	0,1111
ann	artificial intelligence	17	0,0588
structural frames	computer vision	6	0,1667
structural frames	statistical model	9	0,1111
...			

Discipline ranking

discipline	sum weigth	rank	field
artificial intelligence	0,6143	1	computer science
computer vision	0,1667	2	
statistical model	0,0588	3	mathematics
...			

Fig. 3. Example of the ranking method

As a result of this process, we obtained a new dataset that defines the annotations, disciplines, and fields of each paper. As future work, we plan to publish the Ecuadorian scholarly production as a knowledge graph (not only publishing metadata but also mining textual content). Thus, some data-driven applications could be developed to foster Ecuadorian research.

3.3   Preliminar Evaluation

To perform a qualitative evaluation of obtained results, we compared LDA words and CSO annotations associated with a subset of papers. First, we identified the twelve most popular disciplines[8], in which, the papers were classified according to CSO. Second, we filtered the papers associated with the top-12 disciplines, thus 2,468 papers were selected to be analyzed. Finally, we processed the papers' abstract using the LDA method in each group of papers (see Fig. 5).

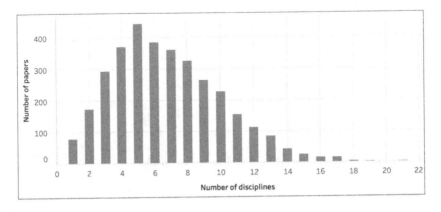

Fig. 4. Distribution of number of disciplines per paper

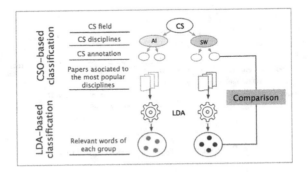

Fig. 5. Logics of the preliminary evaluation

The application of LDA on each group of papers was carried out as described below:

---

[8] The selection of top-12 disciplines was made to ensure enough examples for each group.

(A) Data processing.
- Tokenization. To divide sentences in words or tokens.
- Stop words. Some words were eliminated based on a list of words not relevant to the data.
- Lemmatization. To convert words to lemmas.
- a document term matrix was constructed taking account the occurrences of the words in each document.

(B) LDA
- Disciplines clusterization. Considering the discipline of each paper, 12 groups or clusters of documents were constructed.
- LDA. In each group of documents, that corresponded to the same discipline, LDA model was applied to identified the most relevant words in each group.

In Sect. 4.3, we present the results of the preliminary evaluation.

4   Results

In this section, we present three scenarios which demonstrate the potential of the results provided by the text classification process based on a domain ontology.

4.1   Coverage of Fields and Disciplines

When we analyze research papers, the disciplines associated with each one could be identified by looking for the areas and disciplines of the sources where it is published. But, in computer science, to apply this approach is not enough, because this information is not available for all sources. For instance, in the analyzed dataset, of the 3,305 papers, 2,242 papers have one o more disciplines associated. This number means 1 out of 3 documents has not this information. The main reason is that 3 or 4 papers are published in conference proceedings, and, in Scopus, information for this kind of source is little available. With the method applied, we identify at least one discipline for each paper.

The classification process enables us to discover the most popular fields and disciplines in which the Ecuadorian researchers are working within CS:

- 12 fields: communication, computer science, economics, education, engineering, geology, geometry, linguistics, mathematics, semantics, sociology, and topology. Apart from the field of interest, we discovered other fields in which people work.
- 130 disciplines associated to each field. Apart from the CS disciplines (38), fields with more disciplines are mathematics (28), and semantics (16).

Figure 6 shows the main disciplines and the fields more popular in Ecuadorian papers. To build this visualization, we considered the discipline ranked in position 1 for each paper. Note there are some fields different from CS and these are likely the application areas of the computing.

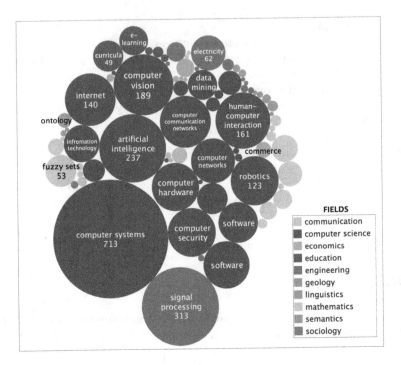

Fig. 6. Fields and disciplines of the classified papers

According to Fig. 6, computer systems, a broad discipline, is the most common. Then, signal processing discipline from the field of mathematics has the second position. The third position is for artificial intelligence that has 237 papers associated with it, i.e., 7% of all papers in CS have this concept as the main discipline of research.

4.2 Research Evolution by Disciplines

Knowing the topics or concepts in which researchers are publishing is valuable information for supporting decision-making. Next goals could be achieved by using this information:

– To analyze the scholarly production from several points of view, that is, considering different levels of granularity of topics.
– To foster research in little-explored topics, but with high potential.
– To identify disciplines evolution over time.

Figure 7 shows the evolution of CS disciplines considering the last four years analyzed (2015–2018). As can be seen here, the production of some disciplines is growing such as computer systems, artificial intelligence, and human-computer interaction, but other disciplines remain static or little studied.

4.3   Topics of the Most Common Disciplines

Figure 8 shows the top words provided by LDA, and the most frequent CSO concepts obtained for the three of the most popular disciplines of CS.

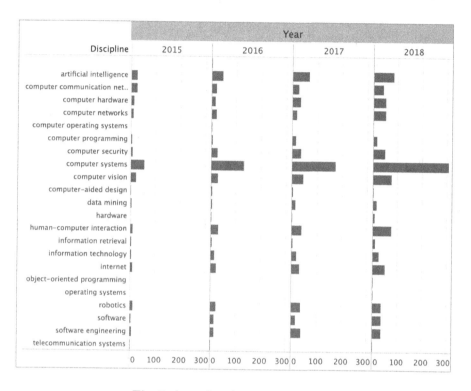

Fig. 7. Annual evolution by discipline

Here, substantial differences are noted in the results provided of each method:

– The main terms identified by each method are heterogeneous. But results can be merged in order to achieve a broader understanding of research. Whereas the CSO terms provide us a more specific point of view of the CS topics, LDA words give us a clue about areas of application or groups of people to whom the research is focused.
– According to LDA, some terms seem to be cross-discipline. For example, "datum" appears in the three disciplines. On the other hand, sets of CSO concepts are disjoint, although, in the CSO model, one concept can connect to several broader concepts.

Discipline	LDA			CSO		
artificial intelligence	model	design	datum	neural networks	machine learning	color images
	time	use	child	classifiers	system design	support vector machine
	patient	language	information	pattern recognition	intelligent systems	svm
	knowledge	therapy	rehabilitation	inference	computer games	knowledge discovery
computer communication networks	network	datum	function	network architecture	wireless communications	sensor networks
	sensor	use	event	wireless sensor networks	network security	internet of things
	vehicle	method	different	communication networks	wireless networks	information security
	channel	node	design	cloud services	wireless telecommunication systems	multimedia contents
computer hardware	use	information	datum	sensors	computer hardware	wsn
	model	different	device	electrical energy	peak power	digital storage
	technique	level	control	ad hoc networks	mobile phones	engineers
	propose	process	technology	computer circuits	field programmable gate arrays	kinect

Fig. 8. Representative topics for the most popular disciplines

5 Conclusion

In this paper, we addressed the classification task as the ability to recognize topics or concepts in a text. To achieve this goal, we propose the use of domain ontologies as a driver of this process. As a use case of our approach, we classify a subset of papers related to Computer Science and indexed by Scopus. We use the Computer Science Ontology because the corpus is specialized in this domain, but the use of additional ontological models is recommended to detect complementary topics and areas of application.

The classification of papers obtained from a scientific database is not a trivial problem. Databases like Scopus use a domain scheme to classify the sources or journals where papers have been published, however, associating these categories to papers is not always a reliable task.

In CS, the most popular source type is conference proceedings (3 out of 5 documents are published here worldwide). In some cases, the categories associated with the proceedings can be very general, this means that the group of documents published there must be analyzed to assign a finer classification. For example, in Ecuador, the most popular conference is Iberian Conference ON Information Systems AND Technologies, in SJR the proceedings are associated with the Computer Networks AND Communications, and Information Systems disciplines. But if we analyze the published papers we find researches that focused on other disciplines or on more specific topics.

When it is not possible to access a set of classified data as input to a supervised text classification algorithm, unsupervised algorithms or methods are the best option. In this work we applied ontologies to classify scientific papers based on their abstracts without the necessity of pre-defined classes, the results were contrasted with LDA topics.

Ontologies provide the opportunity to have a well-defined representation of terms in a certain domain because they allow us to extract useful and high-quality data in a classification task. Nevertheless, in the case of a relevant concept is not defined in the ontology, the term will be lost.

On the other hand, LDA could help to improve the identification of new relevant terms in a text. As an example, in the artificial intelligence area, LDA identified words such as patient, rehabilitation, therapy that do not exist in the CSO ontology. Those words let us infer the existence of artificial intelligence applications in the medical field.

Preliminary findings encourage us to remain researching in this area. Using domain ontologies for the classification task allows us to get a deeper under-standing of scholarly production in a given area. Thus, as future work, we plan (1) to create new ontological models to describe other fields (2) to design more robust and dynamic models for the classification of text, it implies to combine results provide from several methods such as LDA or deep learning-based on, thus we could improve the classification performance.

Acknowledgment. This work has been partially funded by scholarship provided by the "Secretaría Nacional de Educación Superior, Ciencia y Tecnología e Innovación" of Ecuador (SENESCYT).

References

1. Aggarwal, C., Zhai, C.: A survey of text clustering algorithms. In: Aggarwal, C., Zhai, C. (eds.) Mining Text Data, pp. 77–128. Springer, Boston (2012). https://doi.org/10.1007/978-1-4614-3223-4_4
2. Allahyari, M., Kochut, K.J., Janik, M.: Ontology-based text classification into dynamically defined topics. In: 2014 IEEE International Conference on Semantic Computing, pp. 273–278, June 2014. https://doi.org/10.1109/ICSC.2014.51
3. Alsanad, A.A., Chikh, A., Mirza, A.: A domain ontology for software requirements change management in global software development environment. IEEE Access **7**, 49352–49361 (2019). https://doi.org/10.1109/ACCESS.2019.2909839
4. Blei, D.M., Ng, A.Y., Jordan, M.I.: Latent Dirichlet allocation. J. Mach. Learn. Res. **3**(4–5), 993–1022 (2003)
5. Chandrasekaran, B., Josephson, J.R., Benjamins, V.R.: What are ontologies, and why do we need them? IEEE Intell. Syst. Appl. **14**(1), 20–26 (1999). https://doi.org/10.1109/5254.747902
6. Chicaiza, J., Piedra, N., Lopez-Vargas, J., Tovar-Caro, E.: Domain categorization of open educational resources based on linked data. In: Klinov, P., Mouromtsev, D. (eds.) KESW 2014. CCIS, vol. 468, pp. 15–28. Springer, Cham (2014). https://doi.org/10.1007/978-3-319-11716-4_2
7. Han, K., Yang, P., Mishra, S., Diesner, J.: WikiCSSH: extracting computer science subject headings from Wikipedia. In: Proceedings of the first Scientific Knowledge Graphs Workshop (2020). https://www.nlm.nih.gov/mesh/concept
8. Jindal, R., Malhotra, R., Jain, A.: Techniques for text classification: literature review and current trends. Webology **12**(2), 1–28 (2015)

9. Priya, M., Kumar, C.: A survey of state of the art of ontology construction and merging using formal concept analysis. Indian J. Sci. Technol. **8**(24) (2015). https://doi.org/10.17485/ijst/2015/v8i24/82808

10. Salatino, A.A., Thanapalasingam, T., Mannocci, A., Osborne, F., Motta, E.: The computer science ontology: a large-scale taxonomy of research areas. In: Vrandečić, D., et al. (eds.) ISWC 2018. LNCS, vol. 11137, pp. 187–205. Springer, Cham (2018). https://doi.org/10.1007/978-3-030-00668-6_12

11. Sanchez-Pi, N., Martí, L., Bicharra Garcia, A.C.: Improving ontology-based text classification: an occupational health and security application. J. Appl. Logic **17**, 48–58 (2016). https://doi.org/10.1016/j.jal.2015.09.008

12. Thangaraj, M., Sivakami, M.: Text classification techniques: a literature review. Interdisc. J. Inf. Knowl. Manage. **13**, 117–135 (2018). https://doi.org/10.28945/4066

13. Villazón-Terrazas, B., Suárez-Figueroa, M., Gomez-Perez, A.: A pattern-based method for re-engineering non-ontological resources into ontologies. Int. J. Semant. Web Inf. Syst. **6**, 27–63 (2010). https://doi.org/10.4018/jswis.2010100102

14. Zhou, P., El-Gohary, N.: Ontology-based multilabel text classification of construction regulatory documents. J. Comput. Civ. Eng. **30**(4), (2016). https://doi.org/10.1061/(ASCE)CP.1943-5487.0000530

Description of Open Data Sets as Semantic Knowledge Graphs to Contribute to Actions Related to the 2030 Agenda and the Sustainable Development Goals

Jose Eguiguren$^{(\boxtimes)}$ and Nelson Piedra

Universidad Técnica Particular de Loja, Loja, Ecuador
{jeeguiguren,nopiedra}@utpl.edu.ec

Abstract. This work aims to find links between Open Data (OD) and the Sustainable Development Goals (SDG). There is a significant amount of OD published by different organizations from multiple areas of knowledge. However, this data is dispersed in different databases around the world, and it is highly heterogeneous. Consequently, hindering the ability to leverage these vast amounts of information that may contribute to the progress of the SDGs. The Sustainable Development Goals are structured in natural language, limiting the extraction of useful information. This work proposes and describes an architecture that allows the integration between the SDGs and OD through dynamically materializing nodes and edges in the form of a semantic knowledge graph representation built automatically from information stored within repositories of open data sets related to the 2030 agenda and the SDGs domain. The resulting graph represents a collection of interlinked descriptions of named entities and properties that contribute to one another, forming a semantic graph, where each node and edges represents part of the description of the entities, related to it. Doing so may provide better ways to achieve and track the Sustainable Development Goals with already existing information.

Keywords: Sustainable Development Goals · Semantic knowledge graph · Semantic Web · Linked open data · Semantic integration

1 Introduction

To achieve a better and more sustainable future for everyone, the United Nations General Assembly stablished 17 Sustainable Development Goals with 169 targets to work towards. Their objective is to provide a solution to all the global challenges we face by 2030 (Hák, Janoušková and Moldan 2016). Amongst the many efforts that are being done to achieve each goal, capturing data to monitor and measure the SDG targets has become one of the most important [1]. Such

© Springer Nature Switzerland AG 2020
B. Villazón-Terrazas et al. (Eds.): KGSWC 2020, CCIS 1232, pp. 181–194, 2020.
https://doi.org/10.1007/978-3-030-65384-2_14

is the case that may initiatives have been set to foster data collection to aid the SDG. The Global Partnership for Sustainable Development Data was launched in 2015 in order to "strengthen data-driven decision-making" to help accomplish the SDG [2].

Open is the key that allows the access and ability of modifying information so that open resources can benefit individuals or even be integrated and related to provide a better solution for bigger groups [3] (Ahangar 2017). The work by Kassen [4] affirms that the main public value of Open Data is potentially promote the transparency of governments by publishing various resources and also foster the public participation and collaboration. Openness promotes the interexchange of ideas, experiences and knowledge. It also stimulates participants to be actively connected and allows them to create new concepts [5] (King and Baraniuk 2006).

Public access data portals are intended to be used for collecting and sharing data from numerous sources. Publishing data that can be accessed by anyone fosters transparency and collaboration; it can also become easier to manage. These platforms allocate multiple data sets published by different organizations or individuals covering a wide range of knowledge areas. However, there are several problems that may arise when dealing with large amounts of data published in this manner. Some problems regarding multiple barriers that must be overcome due to legal or financial reasons, lack of formation concerning good practices for reusing information, lack of interest, and technological challenges. Another obstacle presented by the nature of Open Data is the high level of diversity found on different data sets. Since standards for structuring data are vaguely used or often completely ignored, data portals end up with heterogeneous sets of data that further complicate its re-use.

Another field where we can observe similar issues presented in public access data portals is the current structure of the Sustainable Developments Goals (SDG). Introduced in 2015, the United Nations defined 17 global goals and 169 targets with a deadline on 2030 where they must be completed [6]. There is currently no easy way to process, connect or query the information present in the SDG. This could be an opportunity to provide means to do so and draw a parallel between the data sets allocated in public access data portals and the SDG. Consequently, this may provide insights that further help in the global race of meeting each goal presented by the United Nations. It is certain that many resources related to the indicators of the SDG exist; nonetheless, they are vaguely dispersed and highly heterogenous. The authors approach to integrate them is to build a layer of Semantic Representation to be able to merge them together. This will be done by using already stablished statistical vocabularies that allow for a robust metadata description and relation to other data sets.

In this paper, authors present a structure of Open Data retrieved from CKAN repositories which are then represented semantically using the vocabularies DCAT and Data cube. The end goal being to link and relate them to the various indicators defined in the SDG. Section 2 describes some principles of semantic knowledge graphs as well as concepts that will be used in this work. It also mentions the success that other authors have had by applying a similar approach to their problems. Then, Sect. 3 defines the approach used in order to achieve said goals as well as some implementations that have been implemented already. Section 4 summarizes the results obtained by implementing the proposed solution. Finally, conclusions and future work are summarized in Sect. 5.

2   Related Work

2.1   Semantic Knowledge Graphs

Tim Berners-Lee and his team in the World Wide Web Consortium (W3C) oversee the process of designing the Semantic Web (SW) that proposes the next step for the architecture of the Web. Its current goal is to provide a knowledge representation of LD as well as increasing the amount of Web resources that are easily interpreted by programs or agents [7] (Smith 2006).

The Semantic Web defines the necessary practices and requirements to achieve a Structured Web. One of these is the use of Linked Data (LD) which is defined by [8] as the "set of best practices to publish and connect structured data on the web". LD is also said to be the next step for Open Data where the information is interconnected, and can be related to other groups of information [9]. LD's principles can be utilized in any field where the main objective is to centralize all information from various sources and stablish relationships that enrich the data that can be found.

Knowledge graphs are related to representation and reasoning of knowledge. Semantic Knowledge Graphs built on a Semantic Web foundation of standards and practices. RDF, the standard used to encode these schemas, has a graph structure. RDF functions as the essential graph framework, semantic vocabularies and ontologies provide a rapidly evolving schema, and standardized/controlled vocabularies, taxonomies and schemas facilitate consistent meaning of data linked across an semantic knowledge graph. LD can serve as an global-wide data platform and helps to provide data for re-use in a more cost-efficient way. Instead of generating data sets per usecase, high-quality data can be extracted from a knowledge graph or a semantic data lake.

Through this open standards-based approach, also internal data and external data can be automatically linked and can be used as a rich data set for any data based task. One of these examples, that satisfy the mentioned criteria, is the SmartLand-LD initiative[1] described in [10] (Suárez 2018). One of its goals is to integrate every component that generates biologic, social, economic and environmental information distributed in different networks. By doing this they seek to provide a semantic structure in which its data will be exploited and linked to the Sustainable Development Goals.

The benefits of LD can be seen very clearly when doing a recollection of information across many different data sources. Such is the case for [11] where LD principles are applied in order to enhance the discoverability of OpenCourseWare (OCW) distributed across many different universities. The solution provided

---

[1] http://smartland.utpl.edu.ec.

includes the semantic integration of the information found in OCW to allow for better filtering options directed to end-users.

3   Proposed Solution

The authors' solution is based around a defined architecture illustrated in Fig. 1. Consisting of 4 main phases that aim to collect, transform, and link open data sources with the SDG.

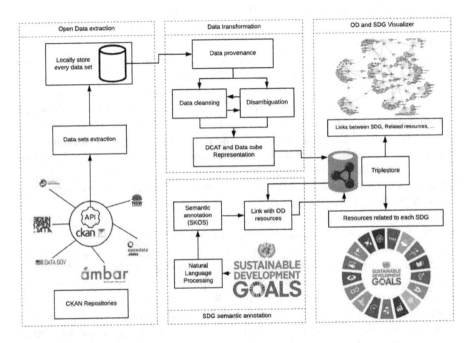

Fig. 1. Architecture defined to build a semantic integration from public access data portals and link them with the SDG

The sheer volume of data may provide information useful to either track, measure or help each goal's progress. Instead of having all those sources of data separated in closed silos, we should integrate them and apply measures that help us gather useful information about them from a different perspective. That being the potential to link said resources to related SDG so that other people in need of such information can find it easily. By using multiple platforms from different countries and organizations we can cover a wide range of subjects that people from around the world can use in their efforts to achieve each goal established by the UN [10,12,13]. Each phase shown in the architecture is described in detail in the following sections.

3.1   Open Data Extraction

The first phase, perhaps the most straightforward one, oversees the extraction and storage of open data sets from various sources. Extraction is relatively simple thanks to CKAN's open platform API. Aside from some few outliers, most repositories used the platform as intended and extraction was just a matter of automation. The following Table 1 summarizes the amount of data sets extracted grouped by source. One data set may have zero or more resources linked to it.

Table 1. Summary of extracted data sets from CKAN platforms

Organization	Datasets	Resources
Ámbar UTPL	558	1238
Europe open data portal	13085	71972
Swiss government	6570	24683
The humanitarian data exchange	11842	48979

3.2   Data Transformation

This stage focuses first on standardizing the data and making sure to keep important details such as their provenance. Each data set is then annotated using the DCAT vocabulary. Each data set is represented by a *Catalog* instance from DCAT's classes. Then it becomes populated with literals based on the data set metadata. Afterwards, tags and groups are added and structured under a concept taxonomy using the SKOS[2] vocabulary. Each one becomes a SKOS concept that gets grouped under the class *ConceptScheme*. Finally, every resource belonging to the data set is added to the *Catalog* using two main classes. *Dataset*, which represents the resource's metadata, and Distribution, which contains data such as its format and URL. An annotated example is illustrated in Fig. 2. Each data set is transformed into an RDF graph representation that can be stored and queried. The following example shows a representation of a single data set.

---

[2] https://www.w3.org/TR/swbp-skos-core-spec/.

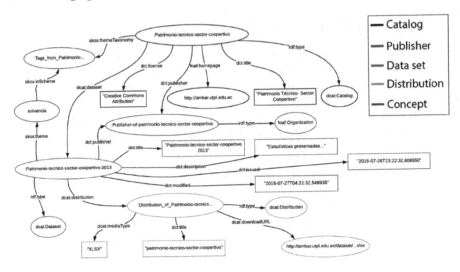

Fig. 2. Ámbar data set represented semantically using the DCAT vocabulary

@prefix rdfs: <http://www.w3.org/2000/01/rdf-schema#> .
@prefix rdf: <http://www.w3.org/1999/02/22-rdf-syntax-ns#> .
@prefix dcat: <http://www.w3.org/ns/dcat#> .
@prefix dct: <http://purl.org/dc/terms/> .
@prefix foaf: <http://xmlns.com/foaf/0.1/> .
@prefix skos: <http://www.w3.org/2004/02/skos/core#> .
@prefix data: <http://opendata.org/resource/> .

#Catalog
data:Cat_logo_de_los_recursos_gastron_micos_mancomunidad_bosque_seco_catalog
     a   dcat:Catalog ;
   rdfs:label   "Catálogo de los recursos gastronómicos mancomunidad Bosque Seco" ;
   dct:identifier   "46452" ;
   dct:license   data:Creative_commons_non_commercial_cualquiera_ ;
   dct:publisher   data:Patricia_chango ;
   dct:title   "Catálogo de los recursos gastronómicos mancomunidad Bosque Seco" ;
   dcat:dataset   da-
ta:Cat_logo_de_los_recursos_gastron_micos_mancomunidad_bosque_seco_038 ;
   dcat:themeTaxonomy da-
ta:Groups_from_cat_logo_de_los_recursos_gastron_micos_mancomunidad_bosque_seco ,
data:Tags_from_cat_logo_de_los_recursos_gastron_micos_mancomunidad_bosque_seco ;
   foaf:homepage   <http://ambar.utpl.edu.ec/>
     .

 # Publisher
data: Patricia_chango a foaf:Agent ;
   foaf:name "Patricia Chango" .
     .

License
data: Creative_commons_non_commercial_cualquiera_
a   dct:LicenseDocument ;
dct:title "Creative Commons Non-Commercial (Cualquiera)"
.

#**Dataset**
data: Cat_logo_de_los_recursos_gastron_micos_mancomunidad_bosque_seco_038
     a   dcat:Dataset ;
   rdfs:label   "Catálogo de los recursos gastronómicos Mancomunidad Bosque Seco" ;
   dct:description   "La presente investigación comprende en la recopilación de los prin-
cipales recursos gastronómicos y turísticos que posee la Mancomunidad Bosque Seco." ;
   dct:issued   "2017-10-25T10:20:45.946195" ;
   dct:title   "Catálogo de los recursos gastronómicos Mancomunidad Bosque Seco" ;
   dcat:distribution da-
ta:dist_Cat_logo_de_los_recursos_gastron_micos_mancomunidad_bosque_seco_038 ;
   dcat:theme   data:Patrimonio , data:Agricultura , data:Gastronom_a , data:Turismo

   .

#**Ditribution**
data:dist_Cat_logo_de_los_recursos_gastron_micos_mancomunidad_bosque_seco_038
   a dcat:Distribution ;
   rdfs:label   "Distribution of: Catálogo de los recursos gastronómicos Mancomunidad Bosque Seco" ;
   dct:title   "Distribution of: Catálogo de los recursos gastronómicos Mancomunidad
Bosque Seco" ;
   dcat:downloadURL "http://ambar.utpl.edu.ec/es/dataset/3acb61b4-053c-43c3-9c08-
e01ca914f1c4/resource/e5879af1-e3c5-4dec-b27d-4ddd22462cf7/download/catalogo-
aprobado2017.pdf" ;
   dcat:mediaType   "PDF"

   .

#**ConceptScheme**
da-
ta: Groups_from_cat_logo_de_los_recursos_gastron_micos_mancomunidad_bosque_seco
     a   skos:ConceptScheme ;
   rdfs:label "Groups from Catálogo de los recursos gastronómicos mancomunidad
Bosque Seco" ;
   dct:title "Groups from Catálogo de los recursos gastronómicos mancomunidad
Bosque Seco" .

data: Tags_from_cat_logo_de_los_recursos_gastron_micos_mancomunidad_bosque_seco
     a   skos:ConceptScheme ;
   rdfs:label "Tags from Catálogo de los recursos gastronómicos mancomunidad Bosque Seco" ;
   dct:title "Tags from Catálogo de los recursos gastronómicos mancomunidad Bosque
Seco" .
#**Concept**
data: Turismo a   skos:Concept ;
   skos:inScheme   da-
ta:Tags_from_cat_logo_de_los_recursos_gastron_micos_mancomunidad_bosque_seco ;
   skos:prefLabel "turismo" , "Turismo" .

3.3   SDG Semantic Annotation

The United Nations provides a public API to access the information about each goal, target, and indicator [1]. Using it allowed a simple extraction of all the information required to apply Natural Language Processing (NLP) and Semantic annotation, as the architecture described. While searching for the best way to apply NLP to the SDGs, we found a tool that gave successful results and enriched our data using Semantic Knowledge Graph approach. FRED is a tool whose purpose is to provide a machine reader for the Semantic Web. [14] states how this tool uses multiple Natural Language Processing (NLP) components and unifies their result into a formal RDF/OWL graph. In this work FRED was used as a mediator in charge of analyzing the content of each goal, target and indicator from the SDG.

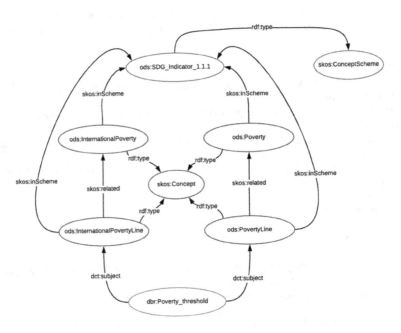

Fig. 3. SKOS representation of the SDG Indicator 1.1.1

The result provided by the tool is a formal representation of the most relevant knowledge of the SDG elements. FRED also has a key advantage that it automatically links the content found to already existing semantic knowledge such as DBpedia[3] resources. The next step is to transform said graphs into an SKOS representation so that we can stablish links with the resources from public data portals. Each class is transformed into a SKOS concept that is then associated to a scheme based on the goal, target or indicator. The relationships

---

[3] https://wiki.dbpedia.org/.

found can be established using the related property of SKOS. If FRED found links to semantic web knowledge, we associate them with the concepts using the DC Terms property *subject*[4].

An annotated example is illustrated in Fig. 3. Similarly, an RDF graph representation is constructed from the SDGs. The following triples describe the Indicator 1.1.1. Finally, the semantic representations of both the SDGs and OD can now be linked. We believe that there are many ways to achieve this and have only scratched the surface of the many possible results. Since the Sustainable Development Goals are now represented in a way that allows complex queries to be executed, there can be several ways to approach it.

Our first approach was to find similar tags and groups that are mentioned in each SDG. This process required two SPARQL queries. The first one queries all existing Catalogs to store their URIs:

```
PREFIX dcat: <http://www.w3.org/ns/dcat#>
select ?catalog where {
    ?catalog a dcat:Catalog .}
```

Afterwards, an automated process executes a SPARQL query for each retrieved URI:

```
PREFIX data: <http://opendata.org/resource/>
PREFIX dcat: <http://www.w3.org/ns/dcat#>
PREFIX skos: <http://www.w3.org/2004/02/skos/core#>
select ?concept ?scheme where {
<URI-from-catalog-instance> dcat:themeTaxonomy ?taxonomy .
    ?concept a skos:Concept ;
        skos:inScheme ?taxonomy ;
        skos:prefLabel ?conceptLabel .
    ?sdgConcept skos:inScheme ?scheme ;
        skos:prefLabel ?sdgLabel .
    FILTER regex(str(?scheme), \"SDG_Goal\")
    filter(?conceptLabel=?sdgLabel)}
```

This query finds similarities between the concepts created from the Sustainable Development Goals and each tag generated from the Open Data sets. Whenever this query returns results, it means that there is a loose relationship between the SDG and the data set. A custom property named *automaticallyAnnotated-Subject* creates a relationship between them. When the process has finished, we can query the amount of links established, visualize them, enrich them, and many other approaches. The results of this experiment are detailed in Sect. 4.

3.4 OD and SDG Visualization

Once the semantic representations of the SDGs and OD have been created, we can also use them to create various visualization tools to provide better

---

[4] http://dublincore.org/specifications/dublin-core/dcmi-terms/2012-06-14/?
v=terms#subject.

insights in those large amounts of data. There can be endless approaches as to what one can present to the user. We are currently focusing on improving the discoverability of Open Data sets, visualizing the knowledge created from the Sustainable Development Goals, and showing the many links created between the data sets and each SDG.

4 Results

The results obtained by implementing the proposed architecture can be divided in two sections. First, the amount of semantic knowledge created from the extracted Open Data sets and the Sustainable Development Goals. Second, the many visualizations that make it easier to understand and use the created knowledge. The former can be summarized in Table 2.

The latter is best shown in our GitHub site that documents the application extensively[5]. This application oversees the implementation of the entire architecture described in Sect. 3. It automates the extraction, transformation, semantic annotation, and visualization of the entire semantic knowledge graph. The following sections describe a couple of cases to exemplify how the results can be useful to others.

Table 2. Summarized results after implementing the proposed architecture.

Summarized results	
Extracted data sets	42,924
Triples generated from data sets using DCAT	2.9 million
Triples generated from the SDGs using SKOS	5,241
Links generated between data sets and the SDGs	6,295

4.1 OD and SDG Relationships

The application provides intuitive search functionality to browse through the entire collection of extracted data sets. Then, individual pages describe the entirety of the data set that covers every detail extracted from the open platforms. These pages also display the relationships between the Open Data sets and the Sustainable Development Goals once they have been created. This allows us to enrich the information from each data set by adding external sources connected by a Semantic Knowledge Graph approach. Similarly, it allows us to show possible connections between the SDGs and the data sets that may help the fulfillment of their targets. The application provides a similar feature which provides searching and filtering tools to discover only data sets that have been linked to SDGs. Thus, making it easier to find data sets that aim towards a particular goal.

---

[5] https://jamesjose7.github.io/sdg-od/.

Fig. 4. Developed application showing the resulting concept taxonomy from the second SDG in a word cloud

4.2   SDG Knowledge Graph

This work aims to transform the current structure of the Sustainable Development Goals into a knowledge graph. The result were several concepts grouped under Concept Schemes. The previous section made use of this graph to establish relationships with data sets. It can also be used by itself to better understand or visualize the information within each goal, target, and indicator. One approach used by the application is to display the various concepts with word cloud graphs. This resulted in a fast and easy way to understand what each goal is about. The created knowledge graph can be used in many more ways by creating SPARQL queries that seek more complex answers.

4.3   Application Features

The resulting application serves two principal purposes. Firstly, the creation of the semantic knowledge graph that represents both the SDGs and the open data sets. Secondly, the visualization of said knowledge in different useful ways. The main features will be briefly mentioned in the following paragraphs, further explanation can be found in the GitHub repository mentioned earlier (see Footnote 5).

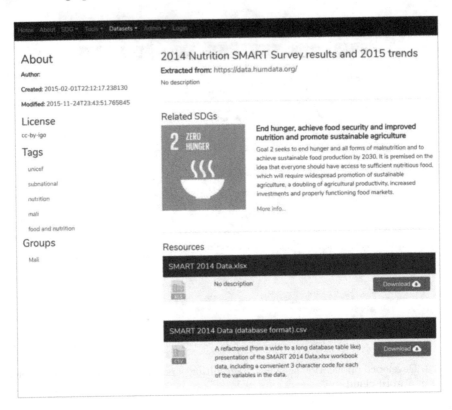

Fig. 5. Resulting application showing information of a data set that has a relationship with the second goal of the SDGs.

Transforming the SDGs into a machine-readable format is a key step in this work. The resulting graph consists of concept taxonomies annotated under the SKOS vocabulary. The application presents this information in three insightful formats. A word cloud per each SDG that displays the most important concepts found, shown in Fig. 4. An interactive graph that shows connections between SDGs that may share the same concepts. Finally, A simpler graph that shows the generated concepts of each SDG separated by goal, targets, and indicators.

Another important feature is the relationships established between the SDGs and the extracted data sets. The first attempt in achieving this was to find datasets that mention concepts from the SDGs. The resulting links, that are explained in Sect. 3.3, can be seen in three different features. A pie graph that serves as a summary of the number of connections established between the SDGs and the extracted data sets grouped by each goal. A table that filters data sets that have relationships to one or more goals. Each row shows the data set's title along with a link to its page and the goal related to it. Finally, each data set has a page that shows its complete information. If a data set has a relationship to one or more goal their information will be displayed as shown in Fig. 5.

5   Conclusions

In this work we have presented how we can leverage the advantages provided by the Semantic Web to allow for a better way to relate and distribute Open Data. The linked data capabilities of semantic knowledge graphs eliminate the dependency on data silos of other data integration approaches, allowing all data to be joined in a global dataspace.

We have proven that a semantic representation of the Sustainable Development Goals can enhance the way we interact with their information by linking them with the extracted Open Data sets. Therefore, improving the interoperability between the SDGs and already existing information. Connecting open data related to the 2030 agenda in a semantic knowledge graph is fundamental to gain a greater understanding of how they relate and apply data to SDGs processes.

The resources described with RDF have a unique, machine-readable identifier (a URI) to each named entity and property throughout the knowledge graph, which enables the graph to connect data the same way regardless of original data set provider, schema, structure variation, technology or any other characteristic. In this way, the URIs at the heart of RDF knowledge graphs are discoverable and searchable, enabling global-wide insight into all data regardless of the apparent differences between the original open data sets.

As it is difficult to clarify the theoretical highlights that are liable for recognizing hostile content, the incorporation of additionally preparing information will push us to get it. For the programmed assessment of an image, we need a message as a diverse methodology. This content is frequently implanted on the image. Subsequently, to catch the inserted content, we can use OCR procedures.

6   Future Work

Future work includes finding more ways in which the Sustainable Development Goals can be related to Open Data. This process involves analyzing the semantic graphs that were produced by implementing the proposed architecture. This work can be expanded by enriching the already created semantic knowledge with information from other sources and enhancing or incrementing the visualization tools to make use of such knowledge.

This work successfully implements a way to dynamically use the information inside the Sustainable Development Goals and find already existing work that can ease the completion of the 2030 agenda by relating them to open data sets. However, other efforts can use the resulting graphs in additional effective ways. Future projects, proposals, or publications can be linked to particular goals to enrich the information related to the SDGs. Then, it could be useful to find various pivotal factors such as available public funding or to what degree are they contributing to solving each sustainability problem. We could also find where most of the work is underway and who are most vulnerable by adding additional data such as geographic coordinates of the origin of the projects and who they target. Thus, the target demographic of this work can range from public organizations aiming to contribute to the Sustainable Development Goals to individuals who seek a more robust set of information related to a particular sustainability problem.

Acknowledgment. The work has been funded and supported by the Universidad Tecnica Particular de Loja (UTPL) and through the SmartLand Initiative (http://SmartLand.utpl.edu.ec).

References

1. Bebbington, J., Unerman, J.: Achieving the united nations sustainable development goals. Account. Audit. Account. J. (2018)
2. Adams, B.: SDG indicators and data: who collects? Who reports? Who benefits. Glob. Policy Watch, 9 (2015)
3. Khan, N.A., Ahangar, H.: Emerging trends in open research data. In: 2017 9th International Conference on Information and Knowledge Technology (IKT), pp. 141–146. IEEE (2017)
4. Kassen, M.: Aslib journal of information management. Management **70**(5), 518–537 (2018)
5. Dholakia, U., King, J., Baraniuk, R.: What makes an open education program sustainable? The case of connexions. Connexions cns. org (2006)
6. Permanent Forum on Indigenous Issues (United Nations) and United Nations. Statistical Division. State of the world's indigenous peoples, vol. 9. United Nations Publications (2009)
7. Alesso, H.P., Smith, C.F.: Thinking on the Web: Berners-Lee, Godel and Turing. Wiley-Interscience, Hoboken (2008)
8. Bizer, C.: The emerging web of linked data. IEEE Intell. Syst. **24**(5), 87–92 (2009)
9. Piedra, N., Chicaiza, J., López, J., Caro, E.T.: A rating system that open-data repositories must satisfy to be considered OER: reusing open data resources in teaching. In: 2017 IEEE Global Engineering Education Conference (EDUCON), pp. 1768–1777. IEEE (2017)
10. Piedra, N., Suárez, J.P.: SmartLand-LD: a linked data approach for integration of heterogeneous datasets to intelligent management of high biodiversity territories. CIMPS 2017. AISC, vol. 688, pp. 207–218. Springer, Cham (2018). https://doi.org/10.1007/978-3-319-69341-5_19
11. Piedra, N., Tovar, E., Colomo-Palacios, R., Lopez-Vargas, J., Chicaiza, J.A.: Consuming and producing linked open data: the case of opencourseware. Program (2014)
12. Eguiguren, J.E., Piedra, N.: Connecting open data and sustainable development goals using a semantic knowledge graph approach (2019)
13. Hák, T., Janoušková, S., Moldan, B.: Sustainable development goals: a need for relevant indicators. Ecol. Indic. **60**, 565–573 (2016)
14. Gangemi, A., et al.: Semantic web machine reading with FRED. Semant. Web **8**(6), 873–893 (2017)

A Machine Learning Method for Recognizing Invasive Content in Memes

Devottam Gaurav[1]([⊠]), Shishir Shandilya[2], Sanju Tiwari[3], and Ayush Goyal[4]

[1] Indian Institute of Technology, Delhi, India
gauravpurusho@gmail.com
[2] Vellore Institute of Technology, Bhopal, India
shishir.sam@gmail.com
[3] Universidad Autonoma de Tamaulipas, Ciudad Victoria, Mexico
tiwarisanju18@ieee.org
[4] Texas A&M University, Kingsville, USA
ayush.goyal@tamuk.edu

Abstract. In the time of web, Memes have become probably the sultriest subject on the web and apparently, the most widely recognized sort of satire seen via web-based networking media stages these days. Memes are visual outlines consolidated along with content which for the most part pass on amusing importance. Individuals use images to communicate via web-based networking media stage by posting them. Be that as it may, in spite of their enormous development, there isn't a lot of consideration towards image wistful investigation. We will likely foresee the supposition covered up in the image by the joined investigation of the visual and literary traits. We propose a multimodal AI structure for estimation investigation of images. According to this, another Memes Sentiment Classification (MSC) strategy is anticipated which characterizes the memes-based pictures for offensive substance in a programmed way. This technique uses AI structure on the Image dataset and Python language model to gain proficiency with the visual and literary element of the image and consolidate them together to make forecasts. To do such a process, a few calculations have been utilized here like Logistic Regression (LR), and so forth. In the wake of looking at all these classifiers, LR outbursts with an accuracy of 72.48% over the PlantVillage dataset. In future degrees, the use of labels related to online networking posts which are treated as the mark of the post while gathering the information.

Keywords: Sentiment detection · Memes Sentiment Classification (MSC) · Supervised learning approach · Multimodal Meme Dataset

1 Introduction

Memes are portrayed by ethologist Richard Dawkins, who is a component of advancement that not at all like normal Darwinian determination is engendered since kinds, is moved from mind to cerebrum. Here, metaphysical thought has

© Springer Nature Switzerland AG 2020
B. Villazón-Terrazas et al. (Eds.): KGSWC 2020, CCIS 1232, pp. 195–213, 2020.
https://doi.org/10.1007/978-3-030-65384-2_15

been radically changed for its present 21st era translation. The Web Image now is generally utilized in online life to communicate with assessments of cyberciti-zens [1]. Some of them are petite broadcasting that moves and starts spreading besides the web-based life stages within few minutes. That broadcasting is sig-nificantly spoken to like pictures, which additionally contain short, fresh, what's more, generally mocking content used to communicate feelings in more detail. These qualities make the images progressively all-encompassing and give sci-entists the driving force to investigate them in extraordinary profundity. Web images incorporate any computerized part which moves values.

Fig. 1. Instances of memes.

The basic form is an expression, for example, the #MeToo development in America [1]. The Internet gives a domain to advanced images to rapidly move from individual to individual, regularly changing in the process as at first imag-ined by Dawkins. In 1982, many emojis were utilized on Carnegie Mellon Univer-sity's virtual release panel so as to signal silliness [2]. As a merger of amusingness, content, furthermore, an image, the emoji got various kinds of images from the

Internet. The images from the Internet may appear in various forms like verses, emojis, recordings. In the Internet's earlier times, pictures with overlaid content started to proliferate by means of Usenet, communication, and memo sheets. In 2000's analysts consider the aforesaid particular pictorial antiques in a multiplied form.

Informal organizations before long rose, permitting these images to become a web sensation. Given the intensity of images to speak to societies and sub-societies, different political on-screen characters progressively use it for conveying the radical information of the changed convictions and texture's activities. The ventures to such an extreme as to guarantee that images have supplanted nuanced political discussion. Images become a straightforward and successful approach to bundle a message for an objective culture. Specifically, images are utilized for legislative issues, amplify reverberation chambers, and assault minority gatherings [3,4]. A few instances of memes utilized for sentiment analysis are here beneath in Fig. 1.

The expanding utilization of Internet images for data tasks has prompted our push to distinguish and describe images that occupy and proliferate inside given world occasions and the discussions that encompass them. Scarcely any examination endeavors have endeavored to catch a thorough dataset of images and afterward record how the images advance, engender, and sway the system. We will likely anticipate the assumption covered up in the image by the joined investigation of visual and printed characteristics. We propose a multimodal Memes Sentiment Classification (MSC) for supposition investigation of images. Our proposed model uses AI structure on the Image dataset and Python language model to gain proficiency with the visual and literary element of the image and consolidate them together to make forecasts.

The paper is composed of details of invasive content which are related to memes in Sect. 2. The earlier research work alongside memes sentiment classification strategies recorded in Sect. 3. Section 4 features the projected effort. The excavating of numerous extracted topographies which gets completed alongside the outcome appears in Sect. 5. Section 6 presents model's optimization process and model's complexities are provided in Sect. 7. Finally, the end is given in Sect. 8.

2   Invasive Content

Hostile substance means to agitate or humiliates individuals by being impolite or annoying. Past work on hostile substance discovery concentrated on despise discourse recognition [5], animosity location [6], trolling [7], and cyberbullying [8]. For the situation of pictures, the hostile substance has been concentrated to recognize bareness [9], explicitly unequivocal substance, objects used to advance viciousness, and racially unseemly substance [10].

Table 1. Examples of memes from Multimodal Meme Dataset

Memes	Category	Caption
M1*	Offensive	2:28 PM THIS IS A WALL INSIDE A NAZI GAS CHAMBER dwebs WHEN A DEMOCRAT MENTIONS GUN CONTROL REMEMBER THIS PICTURE
M2*	NonOffensive	OFFICIAL BERNIE SANDERS DRINKING GAME ! Every time The Bernster mentions a free government program, chug somebody else 's beer!
M3*	Offensive	ALI

*M1, M2, & M3 are respective memes.

Because of the large number of terms and definitions utilized in writing for hostile substance, the SemEval 2019 errand classified hostile content as focused, untargeted hostile content, if directed at that point focused on a gathering or an individual [11]. Motivated by this, we characterize a hostile image as a medium that spreads a thought or feeling which means to harm the social character of the objective individual, network, or lower their glory. An image can be considered as certainly oppressive since it utilizes a non-hostile sentence in the mix with an inciting picture or the reverse way around. The utilization of an inconsequential book regularly darkens the real importance of a slanderous picture or the reverse way around. The dark nature of the image brought about the distinctions in conclusion among the annotators, consequently, we gave various instances of hostile images and non-hostile images. The models are appeared in Table 1[1]. This image follows comparative conduct as the primary model as the thought behind the image is obscure because of cloud content.

By the by, the picture related to the content clears this uncertainty and passes on the thought. To construct a programmed hostile discovery framework, we in this manner must have a decent comprehension of the literary and visual highlights of the image. After that there are two kinds of intrusive substance as invasive text-based content, and invasive images-based memes.

2.1 Invasive Text-Based Content

The model hostile language by building up a Support Vector Machine (SVM) classifier, which takes in highlights physically got from the content and orders if the given content is oppressive or not. [12] have utilized n-gram highlights to arrange if the discourse is harsh or not. There are numerous content-based datasets accessible for animosity recognizable proof, abhor discourse distinguishing proof and Offensive language location (Zampieri, et al.). Among the work referenced, [13] depend on unigrams and examples of the content for identifying despise discourse. These examples are deliberately created physically and

---

[1] https://drive.google.com/drive/folders/1hKLOtpVmF45IoBmJPwojgq6XraLtHmV 6?usp=sharing, Accessed on: May, 20th, 2020, 09:15 AM.

afterward gave to AI models to further grouping. (Zampieri, et al.) manages the order of disdainful tweets in the German language and addresses a portion of the issues in recognizing hostile substance. This examination puts more weight on highlights of single methodology for example content and manual highlight extraction. We take a shot at images that have more than one methodology, for example picture and content and highlight extraction is consequently finished with profound learning strategies.

2.2   Invasive Memes-Based Pictures

Recognizing hostile substance in a picture dependent on skin identification strategies have been proposed for bareness discovery [9]. A few works proposed machine learning frameworks to recognize fitting or in-proper pictures for kids. The examination done by manages hostile pictures also, rebellious logos. They built up a hostile and resistant picture location calculation that recognizes the hostile substance in the picture [10,14]. They have ordered pictures as hostile on the off chance that it has nakedness, explicitly express substance, objects used to advance brutality, or racially wrong content.

3   Related Work

Ongoing advancements in machine learning have made ready to achieve undertakings including multimodal learning. Memes feeling investigation is one such test that requires significant level scene understanding from pictures joined with language displaying of applicable content. Given a picture and a characteristic language message about the picture, the errand is to give a precise grouping about the image, whether it's hostile, interesting, or non-sense. In any case, this assumes a significant job. Researchers had quite recently used various methods consequently, anyway some vision-related techniques are yet to be examined. From the 8 papers that are recorded in Table 2, just 4 source themed papers are represented at this time. Essentially, the Table 2 shows the comparative work did by different conspicuous analysts.

David M. Beskow [15] suggest and assess Meme-Hunter, a multi-modular AI prototypical for characterizing the Internet's pictures by way of images versus non-images, and are compared with uni-modular methodologies. To utilize picture comparability, meme explicit visual eccentric acknowledgment, and aspect identification for discovering and examining the grouped images on Twitter. When image transformation is mapped to a discretionary procedure, the examination affirms Richard Dawkins' idea of image advancement. Jean F. [16] investigates the connection between the suggested semantic significance of picture-based images and the literary substance of conversations in online networking. The conduct of an image is moreover particular as images imitate and change, like qualities in human advancement, during proliferation in web-based life systems. Shardul Suryawanshi [17] conveys that the posting image has become another type of correspondence of the web, due to the multimodal idea of images,

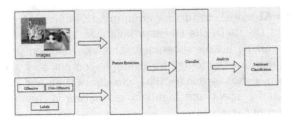

Fig. 2. Design of the suggested effort.

postings of contemptuous images or related occasions like trolling, cyberbullying is expanding step by step.

Despise discourse, hostile substance, and animosity content identification have been broadly investigated in a solitary methodology, for example, content or picture. Devika Verma [18] investigating the relationship of picture-based and printed highlights with an innovative methodology to extract the opinion through the memes.

4   Design of Proposed Work

Scarcely any examination endeavors have endeavored to catch a thorough dataset of images and afterward record how the images advance, engender, and sway the system. We will likely anticipate the assumption covered up in the image by the joined investigation of visual and printed characteristics.

We propose a multimodal Memes Sentiment Classification (MSC) for investigation of images. Our proposed model uses AI structure on the Image dataset and Python language model to gain proficiency with the visual and literary element of the image and consolidate them together to make forecasts Fig. 2.

4.1   Dataset

The structure of our dataset affects our model plan and thusly will be presented before an intensive model depiction. Our dataset comprises of roughly 743 memes, mark, and subtitle triplets with 400 one of a kind picture name sets, procured from1 utilizing a python content that we composed. Marks are short depictions alluding to the picture, for example, the image format, and are the equivalent for indistinguishable pictures. As needs are, each picture mark pair is related to a few (about 160) distinct inscriptions. Prior to the model's preparation along with the inscriptions, the dataset is preprocessed. In the inscription, every letter is in lowercase form, just to coordinate the GloVe group, accentuation characters were appointed with corresponding signs, and obscure signs were brought in the jargon with haphazard term trajectories. A cut was played with the verses shown up in the subtitles: each term that are present in minimal amount in the corpus is assigned a UNK. Inscriptions having UNKs greater than 2 are expelled from the dataset.

Table 2. Summary of the ML/DL based approaches for banana plant disease detection.

Reference	Purposes	Influence	Gaps
[15]	To recommend and assess Meme-Hunter, a multi-modular AI prototypical for characterizing the Internet memes into images versus non-images, and are compared with uni-modular methodologies	To utilize picture comparability, meme explicit ocular oddity acknowledgment, and aspect identification for discovering and examining the gathered images on Twitter. When the images are transformed in a discretionary procedure, that examination affirms Richard Dawkins' idea of image advancement	On the Internet, these images actuate natural predispositions in a culture or society, once in a while supplanting sensible ways to deal with influential contention. Notwithstanding a considerable amount of achievement, their location and advancement are not examined
[16]	To utilize the supposition examination to find full of feeling implications of literary remarks in internet-based life that are underscored by the utilization of meme	It investigates the connection between the suggested semantic significance of picture-based images and the literary substance of conversations in online networking. The conduct of an image is moreover particular as images imitate and change, like qualities in human advancement, during proliferation in web-based life systems	The slant word references required the expansion of slang and unprecedented employment of words. For instance, "prohibited" was not a negative word in the slant word reference, however as far as Facebook gathering participation, prohibiting a part is a negative activity. Moreover, slant investigation of slang phrases was restricted. Expressions such as "Bye, Felicia!" and "negative Nelly" were instances where fundamental upgrades to the supposition word reference were required. This refinement proceeds
[17]	Memes make it much additionally testing since they express cleverness and mockery in a certain manner, due to which the image may not be hostile in the event that we just think about the content of the picture	As the posting image has become another type of correspondence of the web, due to the multimodal idea of images, postings of contemptuous images or related occasions like trolling, cyberbullying is expanding step by step. Despise discourse, hostile substance, and animosity content identification have been broadly investigated in a solitary methodology, for example, content or picture	Very hard to group them as hostile for human annotators just as for AI draws near
[7]	The capacity to become famous online via web-based networking media right away and the renowned images provides an alleyway to explore the utilization examples of the general population and thusly be utilized for examining their notion in the direction of a particular point/occasion	Investigating the relationship of picture-based and printed highlights, which provides a unique methodology to extract the opinion through memes	At first hole examination on the highlights utilized for assumption extraction on images is introduced

(continued)

Table 2. (*continued*)

Reference	Purposes	Influence	Gaps
[19]	An unusual meme compeer's framework is presented in the picture form that may deliver a funny and pertinent subtitle. Besides, the framework can be adapted on a picture as well as a client characterized mark identifying with the image format, giving a handle to the client on image content	The modified beam search is to empower assorted variety in the inscriptions. The model's nature is utilized in knowing the bafflement and social appraisal for the nature of images created and how are they different through the genuine one. The typical produces unique images that can't all in all be separated from genuine ones	Experiment is to catch humor, which shifts across individuals and societies
[20]	Visual memes are significant in light of the fact that they will show feeling, humor, or depict something that words can't. A system is recommended that could be used to arrange web images by certain visual memes and printed highlights	A web meme is a social style that spreads starting with one then onto the next in internet-based life. It is a unit of data that bounces all around with slight alteration. These images have an imperative impact in communicating feelings of clients in informal organizations and fill in as a successful limited time and advertising apparatus	It is an exceptionally troublesome errand to perceive the specific significance and client intension of an image contains wry articulation. Various individuals may decipher a similar picture that has some snide articulations. The equivalent snide picture can be deciphered contrastingly by various individuals. So, it will be exceptionally hard for the framework to distinguish the genuine goal of the picture. It is additionally hard for the framework to comprehend the restrictive sentences

4.2   Information Assortment and Annotation

We built the Multimodal Meme dataset by physically clarifying the information into either the offensive/non-offensive class. The annotations were offered directions to mark if a given image is offensive/non-offensive dependent on the picture and content related to it. The rules about the explanation task are as per the following:

1. The analyst must survey the image in two classes either offensive/non-offensive.
2. Memes can be considered offensive in the event that it plans the accompanying: (a) Homophobic maltreatment.
   (b) Racial maltreatment.
   (c) Non-offensive in any case.
   (d) Most of the images accompanies a picture and subtitle.

The analyst must comprehend that pictures here are going about as setting and assume a significant job in passing on the goal behind it. So, without a doubt, pictures or message alone some of the time may not be significant. The explanation procedure has been done in two stages. In the initial step, a lot

of 50 images have been given to each of the eight annotators. As there was no
ground truth characterized, the larger part of the vote has been considered as
the highest quality level and the Fleiss' kappa [21] has been determined for this
greater part vote. At first, the greatest and least estimation of kappa lied in
the stretch somewhere in the range of 0.2 and 0.3, which indicated a reasonable
understanding between the annotators. After the underlying run, we asked the
annotators for their criticism of the undertaking. The issues that annotators
confronted while marking the information were as per the following:

1. Annotators had an alternate understanding of wry images. Most of mocking
   images had a contention of assessment between the annotators.
2. As the annotators were new to US legislative issues, they were naming the
   images as hostile essentially if their conclusions were harmed.

4.3   Facts Indicators

After the underlying information assortment, the recently made dataset has 743
comments on images.

Table 3. Precipitate statistics of dataset

Data	W*	S*	Ofn*	Nofn*	Total
Train	52	3	190	349	594
Test	50	3	90	96	149
ValDt	50	3	90	96	149

*W-Number of Words, S-Number of
Sentences, Ofn-Number of Offensive
data, Nofn-Number of Non-offensive
data

Table 3 shows a rundown of the dataset utilized for preparing, approving and
assessing our work. Since the quantity of non-offensive memes is higher than that
of offensive ones, we adjusted this by utilizing unique class loads while preparing
our classifier.

4.4   Algorithm 1 (MSC)

Considering the hole recognized in the part of the related work, another new
method is proposed which is subject to the assumption arrangement of the
images. The proposed methodology is named Memes Sentiment Classification
(MSC) procedure which relies upon Supervised Learning (SL) technique. In this
programmed strategy, the images of a picture are arranged. This strategy is
basic in light of the fact that memes are visual delineations joined along with

content which for the most part pass on entertaining importance. Individuals use images to communicate via a web-based networking media stage by posting them. However, regardless of their immense development, there isn't a lot of consideration towards image wistful investigation. Our proposed model uses AI structure on the Image dataset and Python language model to gain proficiency with the visual and literary element of the image and consolidate them together to make forecasts. The proposed Algorithm 1 is given underneath:

Algorithm 1. Memes Sentiment Classification (MSC)

INPUT:
P:Labelled dataset
Lb:Labelled set
OUTPUT: Categorize the facts as offensive/non-offensive.
1: $P \leftarrow Read(P)$ / * $reading\ of\ the\ datasets * /$
2: $TK \leftarrow Label(P, Lb)$
3: $dt_{cm} \leftarrow Combine(TK, Lb)$
4: $dt_{cl} \leftarrow Clean(dt_{cm})$
5: $dt_{tr}, dt_{ts} \leftarrow Splitting(dt_{cl})$
6: $Ftr \leftarrow TF\_Vect(dt_{tr})$
7: $Predt \leftarrow Prediction(dt_{ts})$
8: $Acurcy \leftarrow Acry\_Score(Predt)$

Algorithm 1 Description

The memes dataset $P = p_1, p_2, ..., p_m$, is occupied with a tag set Lb and p_m is the mth particular document which is available in P. i,j,k are the positional requirements where $\forall_{i,j,k} \in 1, 2, ..., m$ and m refers to the length of the dataset P. The categorization of the meme is done into two sets as offensive/non-offensive. The essential reason for doing this is to perceive the sentiments of the required memes. For the offensive one, it is indicated as 1, and for non-offensive one it is meant as 0. Subsequent to arranging it, the images are further pre-processed for cleaning the information. This is accomplished for evacuating the irrelevant features during the cleaning process. Moreover, they are being parted in the proportion of 80:20 which implies 80% represents the training part, and rest is for the test part. The entire information is taken from Multimodal Meme Dataset (see Footnote 1). From the aforementioned illustration, coordinated calculation takes the accompanying phases as given underneath.

4.5   Pre-processing of Information

The portrayals of the meme's substance are finished with the assistance of highlighted vectors for example message is in the class or not. At the point when such vectors are joined for dataset assortment, at that point, they are alluded to as Categorized Datasets. With large amount of meme documents, the ensuing set of data bring about tremendous and inadequate assemblies. To solve the aforementioned concerns, a few strategies are utilized in diminishing the components of trajectories. By utilizing the Tokenization, Stop word expulsion, and Stemming, feature qualities are improved further. Later, the pre-processed features are separated through the utilization of the feature extraction strategy in the following phase.

4.6   Feature Extraction

Feature Extraction deals with a subgroup of extraordinary feature cosmos. The ultimate way to get a reasonable numeral feature subset are done with just evaluating it through legitimate structures while preparing the information. To do such a process, a meme sentiment filter is built. The universal portrayal of meme sentiment filter is in Eq. 1:

$$\phi\left(Gt, \phi\right) = \begin{cases} offensive\ if\ (lb_{ofn} = 1) \\ non-offensive\ if\ (lb_{nofn} = 0) \end{cases} \tag{1}$$

here ϕ refers to the vectored restraints. The function θ is utilized to indicate if the memo Gt is offensive/non-offensive. The reason for the image estimation channel is to expel the superfluous structures through the marked set of data. Therefore, the named set of data are gathered alongside the continuous term ftr_{ij} to shape a TF-IDF (Ftr) as in Eq. 2:

$$Ftr = \sum_{i,j=0}^{m} ftr_{ij} = \sum_{i,j=0}^{m} \left(\left(\frac{N}{Z}\right)_i \times \log\left(\frac{N}{Y}\right)_j \right) \tag{2}$$

here N refers to the term's quantity which is there in the dataset, Z refers to the aggregate sum of footings which is there in the dataset P, $Ftr = ftr_{11}, ftr_{22}, ..., ftr_{ij}$, and Y is the measure of the archive that has happened. In the following stage, the removed features are characterized further.

4.7   Classification

To finish the strategy of a calculation order in a robotized way, an all-around prepared calculation is utilized where it gives a shot to check for designs from the data. This prepared calculation is named a model. Correspondingly, the classifier has been created. The inspiration driving creation of the classifier is to arrange the named data according to their portrayal or gauging the data. The specific arrangement of calculations, $Alg = alg_1, alg_2, ..., alg_m$, are applied on the separated list of capabilities. The arrangement model is indicated underneath in Eq. 3: -

$$\omega\left(Alg\right) = \begin{cases} offensive\ if\ (Pred_{ofn} = lb_{ofn}) \\ non-offensive\ if\ (Pred_{nofn} = lb_{nofn}) \end{cases} \tag{3}$$

where $Pred_{ofn}$ is the anticipated offensive label related with a meme; along these lines, $Pred_{nofn}$ is the projected non-offensive label associated with meme

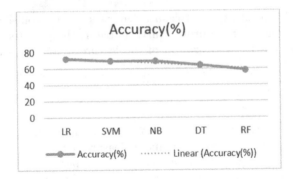

Fig. 3. Performance comparison of diverse classifiers.

and ω is a function which operates on an assumed set of algorithms (Alg). In the wake of anticipating the information, the classifier's accuracy (Acurcy) is assessed to pass judgment on its presentation in a method of right forecasts. This is given underneath in Eq. 4:

$$Acurcy = \left(\frac{Crt_{pdt}}{T_d} \right) \qquad (4)$$

where Crt_{Pdt} is the entire number of forecasts that are done accurately and T_d is the all outnumber of expectations?

5   Experimental Outcome

The investigations are done through the assistance of footsteps specified in Algorithm 1. To complete the examinations as determined afore the operation of Pycharm programming. The information is gathered from the Multimodal Meme Dataset (see Footnote 1). For assessing the trial results, the informational indexes are separated in the proportion of 80:20 which implies 80% of the information is enclosed in the preparation set and the rest data is enclosed in the test set. The preparation of the classifiers is done on the prearranged training set, make expectations with the test set's data and finally, the calculation of accuracy, precision, recall, F-1 Measure and confusion matrix for the particular classifiers are totaled.

Here various classifiers have been taken for assessing the performance of the order model. They are recorded in Fig. 3. The accuracy of LR seems, by all accounts, to be the most elevated among the various classifiers with a precision of 72.48%. The purpose of this is LR doesn't make an earlier presumption over the information, in this way, subtleties of information are not disappeared. Because of this, every single example of the preparation data is contrasted effectively all together with creating the great expectation result. Consequently, the LR classifier performs best in contrast with others regarding precision. While the precision of others is more prominent than or equivalent to 64% aside from RF classifier which groups an exactness of 58.38%. Along these lines, accuracy, recall, and F-1Measure are figured which are recorded in Table 4.

Table 4. Computation of precision, recall, and F-1 measure

Cl*	Pr(%)*	Rc(%)*	F(%)*	Pm*
NB	80.00	70.00	65.00	Nil
SVM	79.00	70.00	66.00	max_iter = 100
DT	68.00	64.00	53.00	max_depth = 5
RF	76.00	58.00	44.00	max_depth = 5
LR	81.00	78.00	67.00	Nil

*Pr-Precision,   Rc-Recall,   F-F-1Measure,   Pm-Parameters, Cl- Classifiers.

From Table 4, while looking at the exactness of the classifiers, it is obvious that LR accomplishes the most noteworthy accuracy of 81.00%; the other three have lesser than or equivalent to 80.00% aside from DT. DT has a lower accuracy of under 80.00%. The particular parameters of classifiers are recorded in Table 4. Be that as it may, for review and F-1 Measure, all classifiers have their worth lesser than 80.00%. Figure 4 delineates the confusion matrix that are arranged in various configurations. The corner to corner divide having dull blue shading delineates about the pictures that are ordered effectively to their separate classes. This right pace of characterization done is named True Positive Rate (TPR) and others are called False Positive Rate (FPR) [22, 23]. The models are additionally decided with the assistance of simply considering one confused class genuine classification and other diverse classes are simply bogus class. Aside from the above mentioned, some of them wrongly arranged and effectively grouped have appeared in Table 5.

Table 5. True Label Vs Predicted Label.

Text	TL*	PrL*
Bernie or Hillary? Be informed, Compare them on the issues that matter. Issue: Real Nigga Hours Smash dat mutha fuckin like Button!!!	Non-offensive	Non-offensive
Who Cares what Trump SandIn 2005 Mike Green He was Democrat Back Then So it's not his fault!!!	Offensive	Offensive

*TL-True Label, PrL-Predicted Label.

Table 5 shows the forecasts of different content classifiers. In the principal model, the genuine mark for the image is non-hostile, whereby the content classifier predicts it accurately. In the subsequent image, the picture in itself can be considered offensive however the content related to it is ambiguously Non-offensive whenever considered alone. The content classifier neglects to recognize the genuine mark.

6   Optimization of the Classification Model

To pass judgment on the exhibition of the calculation, the two significant inquiries emerge here are: (1) Do the measure of information required during the preparation stage are adequate? To respond to such inquiries, the conceivable arrangement is done for checking the dataset's dimension throughout the preparation period. By doing the expansion of the dimension that are related with the preparing information, this turns out to be a lot of complexity towards the learning of the model so that every piece of the preparation information can fit properly. Also, there might be certain piece of the preparation information could possibly fit [24,25]. This is because of the nearness of some clamor in the preparation information. Accordingly, the cross-approval score is decreased all the more adequately.

This happens because of an expansion in the limit of the model for summing up the information. In any case, on account of little preparing set of data, the overfitting and incapably of the model can occur with the test set. Based on the grounds that a definitive point of a calculation is to improve the model to perform. Be that as it may, there are a few disadvantages of the proposed calculation as (1) It experiences summing up the outcome on the test part in a progressively exact manner. These happen in light of the fact that a few measures of clamor are available with the test set of data. Because of that, wherever a slight mistake is done within the preparation portion, this results in a large blunder within the assessment data. (2) The presentation which is related with the suggested calculation diminishes somewhat so that it is suitable with the entire data record. This normally occurs only when there is amount of information is less during preparation interval.

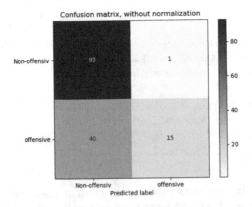

Fig. 4. Confusion matrix.

While illuminating alike disadvantages for the anticipated calculation, a k-fold (k = 1) cross-validation procedure is utilized. This approval procedure is utilized to evaluate the presentation of the characterization calculation among the data record. The quantity of approval chances that are vital for little datasets as compared with the bigger data record and the little dataset entails a little measure of stretch thru the culture stage. In spite of having a few disadvantages of the proposed calculation, there are a few favorable circumstances as (1) It gives away from with respect to the reasonable element of each classifier for identifying the URL as spam, benevolent, malevolent, ruination, and phishing. (2) The precision level which is cultivated with the anticipated calculation are complex with the different calculations. Those are obviously legitimized only after the consequence of the arrangement exactness of LR is 72.48%. To advance the archetypal, some type of punishment is given equally valuable to the choice capacity. The objective for that punishment is to just assistance in cutting off the little subsections of highlights. Here, just littlest one is gotten with the help of subdivisions of highlights. For accomplishing that objective, the punishment is thru an equivalent to 0.1%. Although advancing the information, countless disputes are confronted however few are referenced underneath:

1. Annotators had an alternate understanding of wry images. Most of mocking images had a contention of assessment between the annotators.
2. It is exceptionally hard to locate the important highlights thru the subgroups for NP-hard issues since the classifier's exactness might lessen lackadaisical once unimportant highlights are further involved all through the erudition procedure. Because of those disputes, the way toward removing the significant highlights is summed up by finding the ideal highlights. In any case, ideal highlights could conceivably be exceptional on the grounds that comparable exactness can be accomplished by utilizing two disparate capabilities [26,27].

7   Model's Complexity Computation

Time complexities are one of the most noteworthy models for computing the adequacy of a calculation. To register the intricacy of the proposed calculation, it is expected to discover the quantity of estimation paces that are involved in the calculation. The quantity of count phases may differ through the data record length. Let the data record length is (p), and (q) is the quantity of significant highlights. In the event that the data record length is extremely enormous, at that point a lot of time is taken for calculation and the other way around. To complete such procedure, at first, a named include grid of $(p \times q)$ is made. To figure the time intricacy of this named highlight grid, (p) might be roughly equivalent to (q), i.e., $(p \cong q)$. This tends to $(O(p^2))$ in light of the fact that the size of the dataset is enormous at first.

A few sections may contain loud highlights and others may not. On the off chance that preparation is finished with this marked component grid, at that point calculation stint might be extremely in height, and thus, the exhibition of the suggested calculation may diminish. To diminish the calculation time or increment the exhibition of the anticipated calculation, applicable highlights are chosen. As it were, boisterous highlights are evacuated that might yield consistent phase, that is, $(O(1))$. Next the expulsion of the loud highlights, the set of data encompasses just $(p-1)$ highlights. These capabilities are additionally isolated into littler subsets. This is done to make the preparation procedure simpler. Subsequently, the time multifaceted nature stays a $(O(p\ log\ p))$. From $(p-1)$ digit, (1) is ignored in light of the fact that digit (1) is extremely little. At long last, time multifaceted nature might assess in 3 circumstances: (a) The finest incident motivation happens only after the pertinent highlights thru the record, at that point, it might yield $(O(p\ log\ p))$. (b) The most pessimistic scenario motivation happen once together significant and loud highlights are available within the record, at that point, it may proceed $(O\ (p^2))$. (c) For normal cases, the time intricacy will be $(O(p\ log\ p))$. Space multifaceted nature $(S_P\ (p))$ processes the amount of retention essential for the capacity reason via the calculation anytime. Space intricacy is the summation of all out sum of components and stack space. Stack space is fundamentally the measure of additional room occupied via the calculation in Eq. 5, i.e.,

$$(S_P\ (p)) = \sum_{i,j=0}^{m} \left((p_i \times q_j) + St_{p_i q_j}\right) \tag{5}$$

Here, (St) is the Stack Space. In the meantime, here are just (p) sum of components, so it might yield $(O(p))$. To calculate the stack space, it may gross $(O(log\ p))$. Based on the grounds that partition makes the preparation procedure to prepare the record without any problem. Thus, absolute $(S_P\ (p))$ is $(O(log\ p))$.

8   Conclusions and Future Opportunity

A methodology is proposed for the arrangement of offensive substances in memes which is dependent on pictures and content related to it. For this reason, we enhanced a current memes dataset with offensive/non-offensive names with the assistance of deliberate annotators. This Multimodal Meme dataset was used to prepare and assess a multimodal arrangement framework for identifying hostile images. Results show the improvement in holding hostile substance when both content and picture methodology related to the image was thought of. Despite the fact that as a cure, manual assessment by a head ought to be incorporated before blocking offensive substance. The outcome appeared by the content classifier shows exactness near the multimodal classifier and once in a while better. While the picture classifier has a lesser possibility of recognizing and holding hostile images all alone, the multimodal classifier shows enhancements in holding hostile images. This recommends there are more odds of improving exactness by expanding the heaviness of printed highlights while joining it with visual components of the image. The future bearing of this examination centers around the use of labels related to online networking posts which are treated as the mark of the post while gathering the information.

The future bearing of this exploration centers around the utilization of labels related with internet-based life posts which are treated as the mark of the post while gathering the information. This will assist us in gathering more preparing information. Here, we utilized the Mutimodal Memes dataset, yet to maintain a strategic distance from the predispositions caused due to utilization of the particular space, an assortment of images can be included from various spaces. The methodology of consolidating modalities can be reached out for other sight and sound substance, for example, sound and video. Connecting the picture and content embeddings for speaking to images could be improved upon by combining embeddings.

As it is difficult to clarify the theoretical highlights that are liable for recognizing hostile content, the incorporation of additionally preparing information will push us to get it. For the programmed assessment of an image, we need a message as a diverse methodology. This content is frequently implanted on the image. Subsequently, to catch the inserted content, we can use OCR procedures.

Compliance with Ethical Standards. This assessment was not sponsored by any honor. No creatures were included. Neither any of the appraisals are associated with people or creatures nor performed with the assistance of columnists. Trained assent was secured from every single individual part connected with the assessment.

References

1. He, S., et al.: Ranking online memes in emergency events based on transfer entropy. In: IEEE Joint Intelligence and Security Informatics Conference 2014, pp. 236–239. IEEE (2014)
2. Bai, J., Li, L., Lu, L., Yang, Y., Zeng, D.: Real-time prediction of meme burst. In: 2017 IEEE International Conference on Intelligence and Security Informatics (ISI), pp. 167–169. IEEE (2017)
3. Adamic, L.A., Lento, T.M., Adar, E., Ng, P.C.: nformation evolution in social networks. In: roceedings of the Ninth ACM International Conference on Web Search and Data Mining, pp. 473–482 (2016)
4. Joseph, R.B., Lakshmi, M., Suresh, S., Sunder, R.: Innovative analysis of precision farming techniques with artificial intelligence. In: 2020 2nd International Conference on Innovative Mechanisms for Industry Applications (ICIMIA), pp. 353–358. IEEE (2020)
5. Jose, N., Chakravarthi, B.R., Suryawanshi, S., Sherly, E., McCrae, J.P.: A survey of current datasets for code-switching research. In: 2020 6th International Conference on Advanced Computing and Communication Systems (ICACCS), pp. 136–141. IEEE (2020)
6. Aroyehun, S.T., Gelbukh, A.: Aggression detection in social media: using deep neural networks, data augmentation, and pseudo labeling. In: Proceedings of the First Workshop on Trolling, Aggression and Cyberbullying (TRAC 2018), pp. 90–97 (2018)
7. de la Vega, L.G.M., Ng, V.: Modeling trolling in social media conversations. In: Proceedings of the Eleventh International Conference on Language Resources and Evaluation (LREC 2018) (2018)

8. Arroyo-Fernández, I., Forest, D., Torres-Moreno, J.M., Carrasco-Ruiz, M., Legeleux, T., Joannette, K.: Cyberbullying detection task: the EBSI-LIA-UNAM System (ELU) at COLING'18 TRAC-1. In: Proceedings of the First Workshop on Trolling, Aggression and Cyberbullying (TRAC 2018), pp. 140–149 (2018)

9. Tian, C., Zhang, X., Wei, W., Gao, X.: Color pornographic image detection based on color-saliency preserved mixture deformable part model. Multimed. Tools Appl. **77**(6), 6629–6645 (2018)

10. Gandhi, S., et al.: Image matters: scalable detection of offensive and non-compliant content/logo in product images. arXiv preprint arXiv:1905.02234 (2019)

11. Zampieri, M., Malmasi, S., Nakov, P., Rosenthal, S., Farra, N., Kumar, R.: SemEval-2019 task 6: identifying and categorizing offensive language in social media (OffensEval). arXiv preprint arXiv:1903.08983 (2019)

12. Djuric, N., Zhou, J., Morris, R., Grbovic, M., Radosavljevic, V., Bhamidipati, N.: Hate speech detection with comment embeddings. In: Proceedings of the 24th International Conference on World Wide Web, pp. 29–30 (2015)

13. Watanabe, H., Bouazizi, M., Ohtsuki, T.: Hate speech on Twitter: a pragmatic approach to collect hateful and offensive expressions and perform hate speech detection. IEEE Access **6**, 13825–13835 (2018)

14. Chatrati, S.P., et al.: Smart home health monitoring system for predicting type 2 diabetes and hypertension. J. King Saud Univ. Comput. Inf. Sci. (2020)

15. Beskow, D.M., Kumar, S., Carley, K.M.: The evolution of political memes: detecting and characterizing internet memes with multi-modal deep learning. Inf. Process. Manage. **57**(2), 102–170 (2020)

16. French, J.H.: Image-based memes as sentiment predictors. In: International Conference on Information Society (i-Society). IEEE **2017**, pp. 80–85 (2017)

17. Suryawanshi, S., Chakravarthi, B.R., Arcan, M., Buitelaar, P.: Multimodal meme dataset (multioff) for identifying offensive content in image and text. In: Proceedings of the Second Workshop on Trolling, Aggression and Cyberbullying, pp. 32–41 (2020)

18. Verma, D., et al.: Sentiment extraction from image-based memes using natural language processing and machine learning. In: Fong, S., Dey, N., Joshi, A. (eds.) ICT Analysis and Applications. LNNS, vol. 93, pp. 285–293. Springer, Singapore (2020). https://doi.org/10.1007/978-981-15-0630-7_28

19. Breier, J., Hou, X., Jap, D., Ma, L., Bhasin, S., Liu, Y.: DeepLaser: practical fault attack on deep neural networks. arXiv preprint arXiv:1806.05859 (2018)

20. Smitha, E.S., Sendhilkumar, S., Mahalaksmi, G.S.: Meme classification using textual and visual features. In: Hemanth, D.J., Smys, S. (eds.) Computational Vision and Bio Inspired Computing. LNCVB, vol. 28, pp. 1015–1031. Springer, Cham (2018). https://doi.org/10.1007/978-3-319-71767-8_87

21. Fleiss, J.L., Cohen, J.: The equivalence of weighted kappa and the intraclass correlation coefficient as measures of reliability. Educ. Psychol. Measur. **33**(3), 613–619 (1973)

22. Gaurav, D., Yadav, J.K.P.S., Kaliyar, R.K., Goyal, A.: Detection of false positive situation in review mining. In: Wang, J., Reddy, G.R.M., Prasad, V.K., Reddy, V.S. (eds.) Soft Computing and Signal Processing. AISC, vol. 900, pp. 83–90. Springer, Singapore (2019). https://doi.org/10.1007/978-981-13-3600-3_8

23. Wilson, S.R., Magdy, W., McGillivray, B., Tyson, G.: Analyzing temporal relationships between trending terms on Twitter and urban dictionary activity. arXiv preprint arXiv:2005.07655 (2020)

24. Gaurav, D., Tiwari, S.M., Goyal, A., Gandhi, N., Abraham, A.: Machine intelligence-based algorithms for spam filtering on document labeling. Soft Comput. **24**(13), 9625–9638 (2020)
25. Mishra, S., Sagban, R., Yakoob, A., Gandhi, N.: Swarm intelligence in anomaly detection systems: an overview. Int. J. Comput. Appl. 1–10 (2018)
26. Reyes-Menendez, A., Saura, J.R., Thomas, S.B.: Exploring key indicators of social identity in the# MeToo era: using discourse analysis in UGC. Int. J. Inf. Manage. **54**, 102–129 (2020)
27. Rahul, M., Kohli, N., Agarwal, R., Mishra, S.: Facial expression recognition using geometric features and modified hidden Markov model. Int. J. Grid Util. Comput. **10**(5), 488–496 (2019)

Author Index

Printed in the United States
By Bookmasters